Report Cards

Report Cards

A Cultural History

WADE H. MORRIS

Johns Hopkins University Press
Baltimore

© 2023 Johns Hopkins University Press
All rights reserved. Published 2023
Printed in the United States of America on acid-free paper

2   4   6   8   9   7   5   3   1

Johns Hopkins University Press
2715 North Charles Street
Baltimore, Maryland 21218
www.press.jhu.edu

Library of Congress Cataloging-in-Publication Data

Names: Morris, Wade H. (Wade Hampton), Jr., 1981–author.
Title: Report cards : a cultural history / Wade H. Morris
Description: Baltimore : Johns Hopkins University Press, 2023. |
Includes bibliographical references and index.
Identifiers: LCCN 2022057305 | ISBN 9781421447162 (hardcover) | ISBN 9781421447179 (ebook)
Subjects: LCSH: Report cards—United States—History. | Students—Rating
of—United States—History. | Education—United States—History. |
Education—Social aspects—United States—History. | Education—Parent
participation—United States—History.
Classification: LCC LB3051 .M795 2023 | DDC 371.270973 23/eng/20230—dc25
LC record available at https://lccn.loc.gov/2022057305

A catalog record for this book is available from the British Library.

*Special discounts are available for bulk purchases of this book. For more information,
please contact Special Sales at specialsales@jh.edu.*

To Megan

An army of mentors, friends, and complete strangers mobilized itself to help me research and write this book. Above all, I am indebted to Chara Bohan for her years of guidance in advising me on this project as well as a supportive group of scholars who served as mentors: David Stinson, Christine Woyshner, Allen Fromherz, and Yali Zhao. Two of my role models as an educator read early versions of the manuscript and provided invaluable feedback: Susan Ehtesham-Zadeh and Nick Boke. Several brilliant historians of education provided me with advice in the researching and writing of my dissertation, from which this book was developed, even though they were under no obligation to do so: Joseph Kett, Ronald Butchart, Kim Tolley, and Wayne Urban. I am forever grateful to Greg Britton for believing that a history of the school report card could ever work as a book.

There are literally dozens of archivists and librarians without whom this book would not have been possible. They are chivalric knights in my view, working through the pandemic for the love of academia and the discovery of knowledge: Lina Khalil, a professor at the American University of Beirut, and Reem Haddad of International College for helping me conceive of the idea for this book; Ed Varno, Preston Pierce, and Betty McMahon of the Ontario County Historical Society; Brooke Morse of the Ontario County Records Department; Carla Demeco of the First Congregational Church of Canandaigua; Philip Cunningham and Lisa Moore from the Amistad Research Center in New Orleans; Muriel Jackson of the Middle Georgia Public Library in Macon, Georgia; Jennie Cole of the Filson Historical Society in Lexington, Kentucky; Gayle Martinsen of the Wisconsin Historical Society; William McCarthy of the Congregational Library and Archives in Boston, Massachusetts; Edward Blessing of the Library and Archive at the University of South Carolina; Brittany Kropf of Indiana State Library; Maire Gurevitz, Kathy

Mulder, and Joanna Reese of the Indiana Historical Society; Mickey DeVise of the Cincinnati Museum Center; Dale Sheldon and Sue Sheldon of the Sheldon Family Association; Sarah Coblentz at the University of Kentucky archive; Bill Kemp of the McLean County Historical Society in Bloomington, Illinois; Kelli Burmeister, Amanda Brubaker, and Heidi Bauer of the Colorado Department of Human Services; Mary-Jo Miller at History Nebraska; Katie Ross and Katalyn Lutkin at the Greeley Museum in Greeley, Colorado; Lauren Gray and Megan Burton of the Kansas State Historical Society; Tamar McKee of History Colorado; Rachel Schneider of the Phillips County History Museum in Holyoke, Colorado; Kristen Withrow, who gave me a tour of the Lookout Mountain Youth Service Center; Carolyn Cipperly of the Pioneer Museum in Glenwood Springs, Colorado; Jordan Gortmaker of the Colorado State Archive; Leif Anderson of Stanford University's special collections; Tasha Caswell of the Connecticut Historical Society; Steve Schaffer and Katie Murphy of the Milwaukee County Historical Society; Crystal Hurd at the Charles Sumner School Library and Museum in Washington, DC; Lara Szypszak of the Library of Congress; Gerard D. Pelisson of DeWitt Clinton High School in the Bronx, New York; and, finally, Adam Smith of Minnesota State University.

I am indebted to the "Six Pillars" book club, led by Stan Williams. Our cohort gave me a decade's worth of reflection on great works of literature, history, and fiction, which served as a graduate seminar of sorts for reflection and the open discussion of difficult topics. My parents and parents-in-law—Hampton, Carter, Nancy, and Mike—provided free childcare during the researching and writing of this book, as well as feedback on multiple drafts. I am also grateful to the generations of high schoolers whom I have taught for two decades. They have shown me the necessity of keeping history focused, succinct, and relatable.

Above all, none of this would be possible without my wife, Megan. She helped me brainstorm each chapter and selflessly held down the home front while I drove around the country visiting archives. In the process, she accumulated a lifetime's worth of brownie points.

Report Cards

Civil War, Pandemic, and Report Cards

My study of the history of the report card began the day that the world ground to a halt: Friday, March 13, 2020. I was in a school archive in Beirut, Lebanon. I had arrived the day before to research the lives of classroom teachers during the Lebanese Civil War (1975–1990). As soon as I landed at the airport, though, the Lebanese customs officer said I had three days to get out of the country before the airport shut down due to the coronavirus. Logically, most of my archive and interview appointments canceled, albeit with quintessential Lebanese politeness.

Reem Haddad, the communications director of International College (IC), did not cancel. IC is a prestigious private school in Beirut, founded by American missionaries in the nineteenth century, with a long history of educating the city's westernized elite. Reem and I sat down in her office, brainstorming potential primary source materials that might shed light on what teachers endured during the war years. That is when she showed me seventy-eight report cards from IC's graduating class of 1982. At first glance, the documents were unremarkable, listing each student's attendance, deportment, and academic performance. The context of their creation and distribution, though, was fascinating.

Teachers had calculated the grades on these report cards in June 1982, in the midst of one of the most intense periods of the war. The Israeli army had surrounded the western half of the Lebanese capital just a few days before, resulting in a siege of the neighborhood in which IC was located. Medical supplies, food, and even clean water became scarce. The Israeli air force bombed periodically, while pausing to allow civilians to flee through checkpoints. Needless to say, IC ended school early that year, and graduation ceremonies were canceled.[1]

Before fleeing like many other West Beirutis, a handful of teachers and administrators met on campus between bombings to calculate and record grades on report cards. Then parents, while also waiting for breaks in the bombing, came back to the campus to collect their children's reports, sometimes delaying their flights from the siege to do so. Ultimately, teachers, administrators, and parents risked their lives for this piece of paper called the school report card.

I kept copies of those report cards as I rushed home to the United States and puzzled over what to do next in this new era of the coronavirus. When I returned to a life in quarantine, my three daughters (ages four, six, and eight) were adjusting to virtual schooling. It was a grind. Worksheets, in particular, were the bane of my six-year-old's existence, leading to daily tears. Fancying myself something of an expert on schooling, I suggested to my wife that our anxious daughter ignore the homework assignments. My wife disagreed. She pointed out that the missing work would ultimately appear on our daughter's *report card*.[2]

That is when I decided to change my research topic. The extremity of both a war and a pandemic brought into focus the strange power of this relic of academic bookkeeping. The history of the report card needed to be studied.

The modern report card emerged amid a gradual sea change in the late eighteenth and early nineteenth centuries, a change in not just education but also government, religion, and social hierarchies. Michel Foucault (1926–1984), the notorious French intellectual, is famous for perceiving this slow shift in western societies that gave rise to tools of control like report cards. In the eighteenth century, prior to the new systems of surveillance, the "great spectacle of punishment" such as torture, public execution, and severe beatings of children were ubiquitous. Foucault studied how new prisons, insane asylums, and—to a lesser extent—schools increasingly relied on ranking and record keeping to control populations, replacing physical abuse. By the mid-nineteenth century in the United States and Europe, power "proceeded without force," creating "docile bodies" without the subjects even conscious of the transformation. Under this Foucauldian lens, report cards were a tool through which schools maintained control over their students in classrooms and the parents at home.[3]

Foucault, however, never explicitly mentioned report cards. Instead, he helps historians of education recognize the dynamics of power in something as banal as a school's reporting of a student's grades and conduct. To maintain control over children, schools placed students in hierarchies of "perpetual movement." Pitting the students against each other was essential, as was making sure that parents understood that their child's position was never secure for long. The relentlessness of the competition was the main ingredient in the system of control. The report card became a periodic reminder that children should turn their gaze away from the adults who controlled their lives and inward, with routine self-analysis. Foucauldian analysis also highlights how teachers and administrators, while claiming to act on Lockean principles of progress and reason, were actually motivated by a fear of student uprisings.[4]

The genius of the report card was that it prevented student revolt in two main ways. First, unlike the old system of teachers flogging students, the report card was subtle. Grand statements of control and violence could backfire, as nineteenth-century teachers witnessed in the tradition of "turning out," or student revolts that physically forced teachers out of the classroom. The report card represented a power of "minor procedures" that controlled the social body without the social body even realizing that it was being controlled. The new system of power, while masking its desire for control in the rhetoric of Enlightened liberalism, was no longer concentrated in a single figure like a monarch. Power became diffused in the nineteenth century in thousands of classroom teachers. As Foucault phrased it, power was "capillary." The report card was one of those capillaries.[5]

I am defining report cards as the systematic communication from the school to the home, detailing a student's attendance, academic performance, and/or personal conduct. In some ways, these key aspects of the report card are surprisingly consistent for nearly two centuries: attendance, academics, and behavior. On the other hand, an evolution did in fact occur. By the late nineteenth and early twentieth centuries, the intended audience for the reports of teachers grew: from parents to juvenile courts, parole boards, potential employers, and eventually college admissions officers.

The chapters in this volume flow chronologically, with each centered on an individual impacted by the report card's power: a classroom teacher from western New York in the 1830s; an African American teenager from central Georgia in the 1880s; an upper-class, midwestern mother in the 1890s; a Colorado street kid in the early 1900s; a college-bound son of Jewish immigrants in the Bronx, New York, in the 1930s; finally, a Minnesota farm girl in the 1970s. In the conclusion of each chapter, I reflect on the report card's perpetual presence with references to current pedagogical debates, pop culture, and my own experiences as a parent, all in search of insight into educational systems of control.

This book relies on many of the same sources as other histories of education. The report cards are helpful but only to a point. Published sources like newspaper articles, education journals, and nineteenth-century parenting books provided context for the broader pedagogical debates of the time. Administrative records such as minutes of teacher meetings, disciplinary files, and student data gave context to how the report cards evolved. Diaries and family letters provided insight into how individuals responded to report cards. The archives of universities, the Library of Congress, state historical societies, small-town historical societies, church records, and school districts have all been mined for material.

There is a danger in relying on archives as the curator of source material. For generations, archivists around the world have privileged materials left behind by elites, although many archivists are working to correct this pattern. Relying on sources written by whites who described African Americans is particularly problematic. Here, as elsewhere, the skill of reading against the grain is essential. My goals were always to piece together scraps of source material in an effort to center the narratives of people who, for the most part, have been ignored. In examining the source material, my goal was not to contradict Foucault's insights but to deepen them. I hope that I was able to show how ordinary people attempted to maintain agency in the face of one of the most ubiquitous tools of disciplinary power in education: the report card.[6]

Chapter 1 tells the story of a classroom teacher, George Willson (1795–1859), whose 1835 description of "weekly reports" is the earliest reference that I could find to what is now called the report card in the United States. Willson taught at Canandaigua Academy in western New York. Willson's life embodied the broader economic, political, and religious ideologies that gave rise to the report card. His life also reflected the typical tensions between parents and teachers of the era. The report card was ultimately more than a means of communication between school and home. It was an effort on the part of classroom teachers like Willson to leverage their limited power over parents, whose disinterest and lack of support they saw as an existential threat to the common school movement, which was still in its infancy.

Chapter 2's narrative is centered on an African American student, William Baxter Matthews (1864–1940). Matthews was born enslaved near Macon, Georgia. In 1881, he received a report card from Lewis High School, which had been established by northern missionaries fifteen years earlier. By the 1870s, the report card was no longer an initiative of classroom teachers. Superintendents began decreeing their use, centralizing control over not only parents but also teachers. The school administrators who introduced the report card to Lewis High reflected this nationwide trend. Its use, though, also reflected a shift in schools for freed people, away from the idealism in their founding during

Reconstruction and toward the doctrine of social efficiency associated with the restoration of white supremacy in the South. In this context, the report card is a lens through which to study the tensions between two competing visions of education: a means for social mobility versus a means for social control. Matthews, for one, was an excellent student who dedicated his professional career to achieving dignity and social equality for African Americans. However, he worked within institutions modeled on middle-class white culture. For Matthews, the report card offered Black children in the South a promise; if scores were high enough, they would be given opportunities. In aggregate, that promise failed to alleviate the poverty and oppression of the Jim Crow South.

Chapter 3 examines the life of an upper-class mother from Indianapolis: Martha Nicholson McKay (1842–1934). By the 1880s, the report card had succeeded in co-opting the support of parents like McKay. Late nineteenth-century parents, typically mothers, assumed responsibility for their child's behavior and academic success while at school. In this context, the work of historian Ruth Schwartz Cowan is relevant. Cowan recognized that nineteenth-century technological innovations like the coal-burning stove and textile production, while producing efficiencies in the business world, actually burdened women with more work at home. In this context, the report card became another such innovation, making the lives of school administrators more efficient while burdening mothers with more responsibility to oversee their child's schooling. While McKay was from Indianapolis' elite, evidence from diaries and letters suggests that the phenomenon applied to working-class mothers as well. Mothers, though, were not just passive recipients of the burdens associated with the report card. In the 1880s and 1890s, they mobilized in the form of women's clubs to counteract the increasing demands of being a parent of schoolchildren. These women's clubs allied themselves with schoolteachers against school administrators, becoming advocates for classroom teachers against the increasing demands of bureaucratic school systems. The report card was a microcosm through which to study these shifting alliances.

Chapter 4 traces the experiences of Andrew Monroe [pseud.] (1894–1971), a Colorado adolescent, as he navigated the state's juvenile corrections system. In 1906, Andrew appeared before a judge in Garfield County for truancy and larceny. In sentencing Andrew to reform school, teacher-written school report cards were presented as evidence. In the following six years, reform school teachers submitted report cards to the parole board before which Andrew appeared. The reports documented Andrew's scholastic scores, his behavior, and his whereabouts; Andrew attempted escape three times before finally succeeding on his fourth try, in 1912. Ultimately, Andrew's story reflects the growing power the report card to dictate the literal difference between freedom and incarceration, and the lengths to which children would go to resist that power.

Chapter 5 takes place in the Bronx, New York, and tells the story of Daniel Schorr (1916–2010), the son of Russian-Jewish immigrants. Daniel grew up in poverty in the 1920s and 1930s. His parents recognized that Daniel's future relied on him someday attending college. By the time that Daniel graduated from high school, college admittance demanded high marks on transcripts. This requirement was especially true for students like Daniel, who needed scholarship money. Therefore, the stakes for the information written on periodic report cards once again grew. Report cards foretold futures in elite professions like law and medicine or lives of manual labor. Paradoxically, just as anxiety over report cards mounted in high schools across the country, students like Daniel increasingly satirized the concept of periodic reporting of grades and deportment. Students used yearbooks and school newspapers to make fun of the teachers who issued report cards. They made fun of their parents for placing so much importance on the reports. And they made fun of each other for caring so deeply about grades. In the end, student humor was a reclaiming of agency within the broader system of disciplinary power.

Finally, chapter 6 examines the childhood and adolescence of Kirsten Albrecht (b. 1960), who attended an alternative school that banned the use of report cards. Kirsten grew up on a farm outside of Mankato, Minnesota. The small college town was home to a laboratory school, which—from 1968 to 1977—joined a wave of pedagogical reform known as the alternative school movement. Kirsten thrived in a learning environment that eschewed grades, lacked formal classes, and built a community in which teachers and students pursued their innate curiosity as equals. The general enthusiasm for alternative schools did not last, however. In 1977, Kirsten's school closed due to budget cuts, a casualty of a counterrevolution against alternative schools that gave rise to the accountability movement. By the fall of 1977, Kirsten began receiving report cards at her new traditional school, but she never abandoned her pedagogical idealism. As an adult—while parenting during the peak of the accountability movement that built schooling around test scores—Kirsten transformed her life and career to give her three daughters the type of alternative education that she received, one absent of report cards.

If there is a broader significance to this study of the origins and evolution of the school report card, Foucault might point the way. In this book, I attempt to make the familiar unfamiliar. I hope to create a bit of discomfort in how we communicate the periodic ranking and surveilling of students to parents, highlighting the artificiality of its origins and subtle changes in its evolution. While accepting the Foucauldian framework that the report card is indeed a tool of disciplinary power, my goal is to humanize Foucault's analysis with social history. Yes, lives are shaped by capillaries of disciplinary power like the report card. Yet, humans have agency of sorts to respond in ways of their own making. Ultimately, the lives of ordinary teachers, parents, and students show us that we have the power to reshape student surveillance and record keeping altogether, perhaps into an education system more conducive to joy.

CHAPTER ONE

Rousing the Attention of Parents

In September 1835, George Willson (1795–1859) claimed to have invented the report card. He was not a famous pedagogue or educational theorist, nor was he a renowned school administrator. He was a classroom teacher at an all-boys school called Canandaigua Academy in western New York. He was not a particularly inspiring teacher. One colleague remembered the unusual slowness with which Willson spoke, making him the subject of ridicule among his students.[1]

Willson explained the idea of report cards while attending a lyceum meeting. The members of the lyceum were discussing the primary challenge to local schools: parents. They were concerned about parental disengagement, indifference, and unwillingness to support teachers in disciplinary disputes. As a solution, Willson suggested a new tactic with which he had been experimenting. He had been sending home "weekly reports to parents [about] the punctuality, deportment, and comparative merit of the pupil in his recitations." According to Willson, the weekly reports were effective in "rousing the attention of parents and securing a practical and beneficial interest in the success of their children."[2]

George Willson began his teaching career at the dawn of the common school era, prior to the widespread expansion of publicly funded schools. Pupils attended schools for a few months a year, if at all. Student bodies were rarely "graded," meaning students were not typically divided by age and academic accomplishment. Few schools hired full-time administrators to oversee classroom teachers and even fewer were organized into districts under the leadership of superintendents. Willson and most of his peers were unfamiliar with the practice of written examinations. Instead, Willson evaluated his pupils' understanding of reading and arithmetic with oral recitations. At the end of the school year, teachers like Willson invited community members and local dignitaries to public "expositions" in which students would demonstrate their new knowledge in the form of performances. Prior to the 1830s, there is little evidence that teachers sent home report cards.[3]

By the end of Willson's teaching career in the 1850s, however, schools had grown into institutions much more recognizable to twenty-first-century

Americans. Willson not only played his part in being one of the teachers who conceived of and promoted the use of report cards, but his life also reflects the ideological shift in the general population that gave rise to modern schooling. First, Willson used academic competition in his classroom, comparing and ranking students daily in their performance on oral recitations. Willson's reports then communicated those rankings to parents each week. Second, Willson lived through the height of the religious revivalism of the Second Great Awakening, which gave rise to a new antebellum debate over corporal punishment. As teachers like Willson moved away from physical force as a means of control, the question emerged over how, exactly, schoolmasters would maintain discipline over unruly adolescents. The report card was one educational innovation that could be used to replace physical force, although the debate over corporal punishment continued for the next century and a half. Finally, Willson's politics shaped his creation of the report card. As a Whig, Willson viewed the report card as a means through which he could instill Enlightenment-inspired reason in his pupils, a rationality that was necessary to combat the demagoguery that Whigs associated with Jacksonian Democrats. These two main ideologies—religious fervor and republican virtue—gave birth to modern American schools.[4]

Finally, Willson's life also gives insight into parent–teacher tensions in the antebellum period and the lengths to which teachers innovated to co-opt parental support. References to conflict with parents were ubiquitous in the memoirs of teachers, journal articles written by teachers, and the minutes of teacher association meetings. Willson mentioned report cards as a way to co-opt parents, to persuade them to support schoolmasters in student–teacher disputes. Tracing the origins of what we now call the report card therefore reveals that teachers were the drivers of educational change in the antebellum period–not pedagogues, not educational theorists, nor administrators. The study of Willson is therefore a study in how the ubiquitous tools of disciplinary power, instruments like report cards that shaped the experiences of generations of children, grew out of the innovations of ordinary teachers.[5]

George Willson was not from Ontario County, New York. He was born in 1795 in Stockbridge, Massachusetts. He moved to Canandaigua, which sat at the intersection of Canandaigua Lake and a turnpike that ran east to west, in the early 1820s. Willson was likely following his older brother who became one of Canandaigua's most successful businessmen. As Willson began teaching at the academy, Canandaigua grew to over 5,000 residents. The Erie Canal, which was completed in 1821 and located twenty miles north of Canandaigua, linked western New York to the Hudson River and then to the global port of New York City. By 1860, a year after Willson's death, New York had become the United States' leading producer of beef, wheat, potatoes, lumber, wool, and hops. With the increase in commerce and population, the town's elite educational institution, Canandaigua Academy, also grew, adding a boarding department in the 1830s and renovating the centrally located campus in 1835. Revenue from endowed land, household donations in the form of subscriptions, tuition, and supplemental funds from the New York Board of Regents all paid for the expenses of running the school. According to historian Nancy Beadie, Canandaigua Academy was one of New York's "most highly capitalized academies in the early nineteenth century."[6]

George Willson's personal finances reflected the broader economic growth in western New York. By 1835, Willson was forty years old, much older than

Figure 1.1. Agnes Jeffrey, *Painting of Main Street, Canandaigua,* c. 1835. The building on the right with the small dome was city hall and the meeting place of George Willson's lyceum, where he advocated for the use of weekly reports. Photo used with permission of Ontario County Historical Society, Canandaigua, New York.

the average teacher of the era. He was also much wealthier than the typical teacher. In 1835, teachers in Ontario County earned just $82.75 per year. Willson, meanwhile, amassed thousands of dollars of capital in his lifetime, even purchasing thirty acres of land for $2,050. When he died in 1859, Willson owned stock in the Bank of Geneva and New York Central Railroad, as well as several thousand dollars' worth of bonds lent to a number of other corporations. Willson may have gone into business with his older brother, who transitioned from practicing law and into banking during this period. Regardless of the source of his wealth, Willson was familiar with the process of financial accumulation and his lessons reflected what historian David Hogan described as the increasing "commercialization of the American classroom." At a lyceum meeting in 1833, Willson and his peers announced their official support for the use of "rewards" in school. Willson even created arithmetic word problems relevant to small businesses, like when he asked his students to calculate the relative profits of beer and wine production. Perhaps a newspaper article from 1831 put it best when it said that Willson instilled "honorable rivalry" in his students.[7]

Willson also lived through the height of the religious revivalism of the Second Great Awakening. The phenomenon began in New England around the same time as Willson's birth, moving into western New York with settlers like the Willson family. The Second Great Awakening might best be understood as a democratization of New England Protestantism, shifting focus away from the traditional Calvinist emphasis on sin and toward the emotional euphoria of the conversion experience. Leaders of the movement, like Charles Finney and Lyman Beecher, emphasized the perfectibility of not only individual converts but also society as a whole, all in preparation for the second coming of Christ. The peak of the Second Great Awakening came around 1830 as the number of adherents to Congregationalist, Methodist, and Presbyterian churches increased at a rate of more than twice the population growth. Willson's membership in Canandaigua's First Congregational Church placed him at the center of the Second Great Awakening. Canandaigua was located in what became known as the "burned-over district," a metaphor for the region surrounding Rochester. The nickname captured the passion or heat of intense revivals led by preachers who traversed the turnpikes that connected the various towns.[8]

The movement also transformed the Calvinist view of a child's inherent sinfulness by popularizing the notion that children embodied innocence and God's grace. Influenced by John Locke, the Second Great Awakening emphasized the malleability of children. Corporal punishment, therefore, would only make children more violent. As the historian James P. Jewett wrote, the Lockean influence on the Second Great Awakening led Protestant teachers to believe that "discipline based upon the fear of physical pain is very likely to do [the child] more harm than good." The ideals of Romantic literature seeped into the movement as well, like William Wordsworth's "My Heart Leaps Up," in which the poet, inspired by a rainbow, proclaims "The child is father of the man; / And I could wish my days to be / Bound each to each by natural piety." The religious fervor became intertwined with the temperance movement, and the innocent child, doomed to die young, grew into a trope of temperance novels in this era. The same year that Willson introduced his report card, Na-

Figure 1.2. First Congregational Church, Canandaigua, New York, c. 1900, originally constructed in 1812. Photo used with permission of Ontario County Historical Society.

thaniel Hawthorne published "A Rill from the Town Pump," a short story in which a man drunkenly spends the money meant to feed his children, robbing them of their innocence in the process.[9]

Willson's preacher at First Congregational reinforced the message of the Godlike childhood. In the 1830s, just as Willson was experimenting with report cards, the pastor of First Congregational, Ansel Eddy, referred to children as "capable of restoration to a glory unequalled by man in innocence." Charles Finney, the most prominent leader of the Second Great Awakening, also preached at Willson's church. Willson may have listened to Finney's celebration of "the most delightful piety" of "simple-hearted" children. In place of physical punishment, teachers like Willson were left to find new ways of instilling discipline in their classrooms.[10]

Surviving documentation—from his own writings, from his last will and testament, and even from the minutes of his teacher association—provide windows into Willson's classroom, and the documents reflect someone immersed in the religious fervor of the era and the idealism of the Enlightenment. Willson wrote two teaching instruction manuals, and both texts reflected Eddy's and Finney's influence on Willson's pedagogy. In *The American Class-Reader*, Willson suggests that teachers assign children dozens of readings that would "convey some moral truth." Nine of these passages were Biblical and each emphasized God's grace, not God's judgment: "Forgiveness of Injuries," "The Blind Man Restored to Sight," "The Good Samaritan," and "The Prodigal Son." Willson also read the works of Locke, owning a volume titled *Locke's Essays* as well as a collection of Locke's writings on education. He admired the Swiss pedagogue Johann Heinrich Pestalozzi, who wrote that within each child there is "something, the origin of which, as a gift of God, dates prior to temptation, or to corruption." Even Willson's school took a position against corporal punishment when, in 1833, it hosted the first meeting of the Ontario County Association of Teachers. The association passed a resolution stating that corporal punishment "could be dispensed with."[11]

Republicanism was another ideological transformation that was necessary for the report card's birth. Willson's political persuasion led him to mistrust the uneducated and unruly mob. Education, therefore, was about more than nurturing reason and societal reform. Schools were essential for cultivating discipline in the *demos*, without which democracy might not survive. In *The American Class-Reader*, Willson wrote that a child's bad habits could not be corrected through force or memorization of a text, but through the student's more independent discovery. Teachers should "make [students] *think* and exercise their own taste [emphasis original]." Willson made the same point about independent thought in another book, *A Practical and Theoretical System of Arithmetic,* in which he urged teachers to avoid "laying down naked and arbitrary rules" and instead allow space for a student's "own discovery and investigation." Willson was preparing young men to be participants in republican democracy, which required independent, critical thought.[12]

Cultivating self-governance was the explicit goal of Willson's lyceum, which officially declared its focus on preparing students for "the duties of citizenship." Willson's faith in the ability of reason and reform extended beyond the classroom. For instance, he served as the secretary of the Ontario County Temperance Society and was also involved in western New York's network of abolitionists. As early as 1829, Willson's church desegregated and there is even evidence that Willson participated in the Underground Railroad. Willson's colleague implied as much in his memoirs when he mentioned that "in the

Figure 1.3. Canandaigua Academy, New York, c. 1880. George Willson taught in this school building, which was constructed in 1836, a year after Willson advanced the use of report cards. Photo used with permission of Ontario County Historical Society.

days of the underground railroad and the fugitive slave law" the Willson residence was nicknamed "Timbuctoo [sic] Park," suggesting that escaped enslaved people stayed in Willson's home. Willson's sympathies for abolitionism extended into his lessons. He assigned his students a poem called "The Slave Ship," which depicted enslaved Africans crossing the Atlantic: "And their dim eyes wept, half tear, half blood, / But still they stood upright." Late in his life, in 1854, Willson's opposition to slavery moved him to sign a petition opposing the Kansas–Nebraska Act.[13]

As a Whig, Willson shared in his party's concerns about the populist demagoguery of Andrew Jackson. During Canandaigua's Fourth of July celebrations in 1831, Willson gave a public speech denouncing Democratic support for nullification of federal laws. Willson's bookshelf included the biographies and speeches of the leaders of the Federalist and Whig parties—Alexander Hamilton, John Jay, and Edward Everett—but none of Democrat-Republicans like Thomas Jefferson, James Madison, or Andrew Jackson. Likewise, Willson chose not to include any references to Jackson or other Democrats in *The American Class-Reader*. He did, however, include two speeches from Daniel Webster, a leader of the Whig party at the time. Webster was a vocal supporter of universal education, seeing schools as a "wise and liberal system of police, by which property, and life, and the peace of society are secured." To Webster, schooling could instill the "conservative principle of virtue and knowledge," securing a more stable young republic in the process. Canandaigua's leaders, journalists, and educators shared Webster's instinctive conservatism with regard to the unruly masses, warning that democracy could very easily slide into anarchy. At First Congregational Church, Willson's priest denounced the extremes of the French Revolution from the pulpit, linking Democrats like Thomas Jefferson to the "poison" of Jacobin France. Willson, through his lyceum's subscription to *Common School Assistant*, likely would have read warnings of "a French Revolution, or a New York mob" due to the state's inadequate system of education. Another *Common School Assistant* article feared that inept teachers "sow the seeds of tyranny and anarchy."[14]

In the end, these broad shifts in how Americans viewed children and education were essential for the birth of the report card. Without physical force, classroom teachers like Willson needed new methods for maintaining order. Willson's boss, the principal of Canandaigua Academy, recognized the new predicament of order without force in 1831. The school initiated a series of reforms in which student seating would be arranged in a way that "the teacher's eyes would meet the eyes of every pupil" as well as a system of record keeping that would track "the deportment of the pupil." Willson's innovation a few years later was to take the time to share these records with parents on a regular basis, extending the system of observation into the home while enlisting parental support for control over the pupil. Finally, report cards were fundamentally about instilling self-discipline in children, turning their gaze inward with a weekly barrage of criticism. This discipline, to teachers like Willson, was necessary for a functioning democratic republic.[15]

More than free market principles, more than Lockean-influenced Protestantism, and more than earnest notions of instilling republican virtues, teachers like George Willson were propelled to innovate by an immediate, daily, and tangible challenge: parental indifference on one extreme and parental interference on the other. As common schools expanded, parents inherently mistrusted the teachers to whom they were pressured to entrust their children. Teachers responded by increasingly disparaging the parents for their lack of support, leading to a cyclical breakdown of relationships. These tensions that gave rise to the report card may have been, in fact, more important than the abstract ideologies that defined the zeitgeist of Willson's world.[16]

Complaints of parental apathy fill the memoirs of students from the first half of the nineteenth century. Growing up on a New Hampshire farm in the late 1790s, John Ball struggled to convince his father to allow him to attend a school eight miles away. "My father's education being very limited," Ball wrote in his memoirs, "he did not seem to think any further education than an ability to read, write and cipher in the simple rules to be needful." Ball's experiences appear to be quite typical of the era, as educational opportunities expanded for the children of farmers who lacked formal schooling. In rural New York, William James Stillman remembered that his father "had no opinion of the utility of advanced education for boys in our station [and] was tenacious in his intention to have me in his workshop, where he needed more apprentices." The problem of parental apathy in education transcended region. In 1824, a Columbia, South Carolina, newspaper condemned the general attitude among white South Carolinians "that they value so little the importance of academic education." The newspaper struggled to find ways "to excite the attention of parents and guardians." Two years later, the South Carolina legislature cited parental indifference as a reason for rejecting a plan for government-funded schools. Parents, the legislative report stated, "feel little or no interest" in educating their children.[17]

Teachers noticed parental apathy as well. In 1850s' Wisconsin, there was "an almost unanimous expression" about the "lukewarmness and indifference of parents as exhibited toward the Common Schools." The only solution that Wisconsin's superintendents could find was to insist that parents visit the district schools more often. The problem extended beyond new, state-funded common schools and into more traditional—and elite—academies. In 1812, the trustees of Raleigh Academy in North Carolina circulated their plea in a local newspaper for parental cooperation "in Preserving [the] Morals of Students." William Alcott, a teacher in Connecticut, dedicated an entire chapter of his memoir to parental indifference. Alcott claimed that after decades in the profession he "could not discover that one of them [the parents] entered into the spirit of the thing [their child's education]." Another New England teacher, who began his career in the 1820s, remembered that "parents of the pupils have inherited the idea of education for their children, but knew little or nothing of its nature or importance." Teachers sometimes vented their frustration about parental apathy in front of their students. One school in Florida had to create a rule that explicitly banned teachers from discussing "the faults of their parents or relatives" in front of students. In Massachusetts, a school administrator admonished his audience of teachers for blaming parents for the "the caprice, the waywardness and the stupidity of children."[18]

Perhaps more than indifference and apathy, though, antebellum teachers were frustrated about parents taking the side of students in disciplinary disputes. In 1848, *Massachusetts Teacher*, for example, noted how parents listened to "complaints made by the pupils . . . without rebuke, perhaps with words of sympathy." Two years later, *Common School Journal* published a similar editorial that criticized parents for "blaming the teacher as cruel and brutish," which would inevitably lead to the child becoming "a dunce in the school, a rebel in the discipline, a bad, unruly citizen, a tyrant in his own house, without one delicate trait of moral goodness." Teachers shared this sentiment beyond New England, where the common school movement was less developed. One newspaper in Greenville, South Carolina, wrote that "parents should not be so blinded by [love for children] as to exclude reason and consider their children infallible." The newspaper went on to condemn parents for "listening and giving credence to the tales of their children and encouraging them to tell those tales." Across the continent, San Francisco's *Daily Evening Bulletin* expressed the same critique of parents for defending their children in disciplinary disputes. "By disparaging remarks [parents] help to bring the teacher into contempt," the newspaper reported. "When this natural disobedience compels a resort to punishment, they listen to the exaggerated accounts of this punishment." *Cleveland Daily Herald* defended teachers when the newspaper wrote that the "verbal inculpation and abuse" hurled at the school keep teachers "in a fever of anxiety." The evidence from surviving documentation is irrefutable. During the antebellum period, teachers from across the country felt under parental attack.[19]

The memoirs of pupils, however, describe a degree of teacher violence and intimidation that makes the modern reader wonder whether or not the parents were justified in their concerns. One former New Hampshire student, who attended school from 1804 through 1818, remembered the brutality of his teacher, Mr. Starr, in remarkable details. This "stern commander . . . knocked one lad down with his fist, hurled a stick of wood at another." Families then mobilized and collectively called for Mr. Starr's dismissal. At the same time in South Carolina, J. Marion Sims attended a school led by "Mr. Quigley." Decades later, Sims recounted tales of Mr. Quigley with Dickensian flair. The schoolmaster was a one-eyed Irishman with pock-marked skin left over from a bout with smallpox. Mr. Quigley flogged his pupils "until the youngster vomited or wet his breeches." The great danger of Mr. Quigley, Sims recollected, was that he did not fear parental interference. When a child threatened to tell their parents about Quigley's abuse, "this was of no use," Sims wrote. "Old Cockeye whipped the harder. He was not afraid of any boy's pa." Teachers like Mr. Quigley help explain the actions of some parents who took justice into their own hands, like the father in Newburyport, Massachusetts, who went to the schoolhouse and physically threatened a teacher. The parent was later ordered to pay a $200 fine for "disturbing the school." William Alcott was one of the few teachers who admitted to deserving the anger of parents. As a young teacher, he once tied a child's ankles together with a handkerchief and fastened the child to a nail upside down. Alcott wrote that this incident "merited the indignation against me."[20]

Fundamentally, parents held power to unilaterally fire teachers during the antebellum period. Teachers described their unjust termination at the hands of misguided parents, like when William James Stillman reprimanded a "lazy boy" who just so happened to be the son of a wealthy farmer in rural New York. That mistake ended his tenure at the schoolhouse. Students were aware of this power dynamic as well. Growing up in rural Georgia, A. B. Longstreet recalled a teacher's panic when he was "turned out"—or barricaded out of the schoolhouse—by the pupils. The teacher, according to Longstreet, violently smashed the door in. If the students prevailed in the standoff, the teacher explained, he would be quickly fired by the parents of those same students. A seemingly neutral observer like Hezekiah Prince witnessed the power of parents in a Maine fishing village. While neither an educator nor a parent, Prince still attended a town meeting to discuss whether or not to dismiss a teacher. Prince noted the deep "prejudice" of the parents and that in their rush to judge the teacher, the parents "destroyed the usefulness of the school." One parent in Nebraska even had a young teacher arrested for the assault and battery of their child. A principal of a Massachusetts high school admitted in 1839 that "treatment from parents" was the number one cause of teachers leaving the profession.[21]

George Willson's experiences with parents at Canandaigua Academy seemed to have been typical of the era. Willson slipped in a subtle critique of parents in his second book, *The American Class-Reader* when he quoted an anonymous source who admonished parents for their "ignorance and neglect" in failing to provide a healthy and safe home for children. One of Willson's fellow teachers at Canandaigua Academy emphasized the power of the academy's trustees, men who were Ontario County's most prominent bankers, lawyers, judges, and doctors. The former Canandaigua Academy teacher chronicled in his memoirs how trustees intervened to have teachers fired "for being unpopular" and for being unable to handle the "roguery and tricks" of students. In one incident, Willson himself narrowly avoided a parent-initiated dismissal. Sometime in the 1830s, Willson was tutoring a boy after class in the "mysteries of the Latin tongue, with the view of fitting [the student] for college." Willson apparently grew frustrated with the pupil's "dullness and obstinacy" and decided to lock the boy in the second-floor classroom as extra motivation for the boy to complete his recitations. Willson then proceeded to return home, sit down for tea, and fall asleep. At two o'clock in the morning, Willson awoke and rushed to the academy, only to find the boy sound asleep on the classroom bench. Willson was lucky to survive the incident with his job still intact, especially after dealing with "the lad's stern father."[22]

In addition to his own personal experience with difficult parents, Willson probably read critiques of parenting. For instance, Willson's lyceum subscribed to *Common School Assistant*, which was only published for two years. In nearly every issue, the journal blamed parents for problems at schools. In September 1836, one teacher wrote to the editor to complain about parents who "never visit the school" but will nonetheless "take the children's side and give the teacher all the blame." In January 1837, the journal was critical of parents for not providing their children reading materials at home and a page later, the journal blamed parents for allowing their children to arrive at school hours late or skip entire weeks at a time. In May 1837, *Common School Assistant* held parents responsible for the low pay of teachers. A month later, the journal argued that the denunciation of "the indifference and apathy of parents" must be "heard and felt by every citizen." The pages of *Common School Assistant* gave the impression of a low-grade war between parents and teachers, with teachers on the side of righteousness and progress, while parents represented superstition and selfishness.[23]

In 1836 and 1837, *Common School Assistant* published 581 articles, stories, and letters. Some were just a few sentences long, while other articles stretched several pages. Of those 581 pieces, 126 articles made critical comments about parents of school-age children, or 21.6 percent. That averaged out to be five or six articles each issue that, to one degree or another, placed blame or responsibility for the problems in schools at the feet of parents. Only one issue, the last, which appeared in December 1837, made no critical reference to parents. This disparaging of parents was, most likely, the pedagogical literary world into which Willson was intellectually immersed.[24]

For decades, teachers struggled to find creative solutions to their confrontations with parents. The most common suggestion seems to have been home visits. As early as the 1820s, Hiram Orcutt learned that visiting families in their homes, at least once a year, was the only way to create an "intimate acquaintance" and thus avoid conflict. Not much had changed two decades later in Connecticut, where one author argued that teachers "must visit the parents and explain to them the untold and unspeakable mischiefs of absences and tardiness." Further south in Florida, the tactic seemed so crucial that the state legislature proposed requiring weekly visits to the homes of common school students. Likewise, in 1848, a Massachusetts educator urged teachers to visit parents in their home in order to bridge the "gulf" that typically existed between the two sides. Visiting dozens of homes, though, seemed too high of a cost in terms of time. Some teachers, like T. W. Curtis, thought more creatively and proposed the idea of what would later be termed back-to-school night. Schools should "invite [parents] to meet you [the teacher], on some evening, in the school-room, for the purpose of considering some of the mutual duties," Curtis recommended. The idea was also proposed in *Massachusetts Teacher* in 1848. Even this solution had flaws. Few parents, it seemed, were taking teachers up on the offer to visit the school.[25]

The most effective, most efficient, and longest lasting solution to the war with parents came with the idea to send home a steady stream of written communications in which each student was compared and ranked against their classmates. We now call this means of communication the report card. Willson's 1835 explanation of his "weekly reports" shows that teachers were experimenting with the idea just as common schools spread in the Northeast. In 1840, an anonymous teacher writing in the *Common School Journal* from "Washington City" promoted the use of "weekly reports" as a method of "exercising moral influence" over parents. It is important to note that the author was indeed a classroom teacher, which fit a pattern. The educational innovation was born out of a grassroots experimentation to solve a common problem that transcended region. For the next twenty years, the idea of the report card spread through meetings of teacher associations, passing references in journals, and word of mouth among peers. In 1849 a writer for *Massachusetts Teacher* claimed that this was how the report card spread. The author explained that to solve the issue of parental disengagement, "Some teachers are in the habit of issuing weekly reports, showing the standing and progress of their pupils, for the inspection of their parents." The article added, however, that it was essential that teachers be honest on the merits and shortcomings of their students, so as not to give any false hope to misguided parents.[26]

Several early report cards have survived in the University of Alabama's special collections. The oldest dates from December 10, 1847. The Greene Springs School, located in Havana, Alabama, issued it to a student named W. A. Wynne. Noticeably, it was handwritten. A year later, though, the school employed a printer to create report cards with school letterhead and typeset. During the ten weeks of the fall term of 1847, Wynne was enrolled in Latin, Greek, Algebra, French, Composition, and Prayers. A column next to each subject lists the "number of recitations" that Wynne completed, reflecting an educational system that had not yet employed written assessments. The second column listed the number of days absent; Wynne missed four morning prayers in the ten-week period. The third column quantified Wynne's "average standing," ranking him relative to his classmates in their oral performances. The fourth and final column elaborated a bit, with phrases like "totally good," "tolerably good," and "very bad." At the bottom of the report, the schoolmaster wrote two sentences of explanation. The note is made to a "Dear Sir," presumably the father. The schoolmaster praised young Wynne and described the student's deportment as "gentlemanly." This report card from 1847, just as

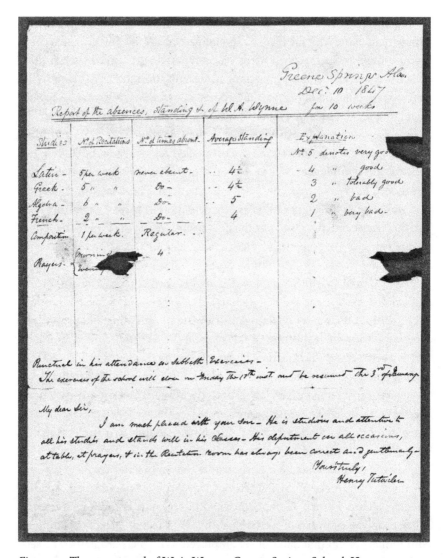

Figure 1.4. The report card of W. A. Wynne, Greene Springs School, Havana, Alabama, 1847. Photo used with permission of the University of Alabama Libraries Special Collections.

Willson's in 1835, reflected the three main categories of information that remain the basis for the twenty-first-century report card: academics, attendance, and behavior.[27]

The idea of sending home periodic and individualized written reports spread in the 1850s. The 1853 meeting of the Massachusetts Teachers' Association, as was typical, lamented the lack of parental support for the state's schools. Also typical for the era, the association's leader, Ariel Parish, could only suggest home visits as the best, albeit inefficient, solution. A year later, *Connecticut Common School Journal* encouraged parents to read weekly reports, the use of which had been growing without being mandated by superintendents. In 1855, a teacher named Almira Seymour promoted her use of report cards in *Massachusetts Teacher*. Then, during the 1858 meeting of the Massachusetts Teachers' Association, the same Ariel Parish who spoke in 1853 but still relied on home visits, discussed the new idea of report cards at length. He suggested, based on the existing experimentation of classroom teachers, that his members use the following categories of evaluation in their weekly reports: "Attendance, Deportment, and Scholarship." The idea then appeared in Illinois' schools. One teacher in the western state claimed that they learned about weekly reports via word of mouth from her predecessor. A year later, in 1860, *Illinois Teacher* reported a survey of principals who praised the practice of writing letters home, and the article recommended using the same categories suggested by Parish two years earlier: attendance, deportment, scholarship.[28]

As the use of the report card spread across the United States, so too did a second innovation that would forever be linked to report cards: written assessments. There is evidence that teachers experimented with written tests throughout the 1830s and 1840s, although prior to 1845 their use was not widespread. In 1845, Boston's schools underwent a testing revolution that set a new standard for schools nationwide. In that year, Horace Mann, the famous superintendent of public schools in Massachusetts, a new position at the time, worked with Boston's school board to mandate the use of end-of-year written exams. He and his allies hoped to rein in the power of schoolmasters. The tests were therefore intended as a way of evaluating the quality of instruction as opposed to the knowledge of individual pupils. Mann also saw written exams as a more private alternative to the method of evaluating children in oral recitations in front of an audience.[29]

After 1845, testing exploded onto the national stage. Like report cards, promotion of testing spread in education journals. *New England Journal of Education*, for instance, argued that "while exhibitions were popular, written examinations were the only accurate way to test what each pupil learned." Throughout the late 1840s and 1850s, newly created school boards in cities like Washington, DC, and Cleveland mandated written assessments. In the 1850s, Horace Mann disciples from New England spread west, gaining control of school boards in cities like Cincinnati and San Francisco. They created committees on "Printed Questions" and policies on "Written Answers for Printed Questions." In 1864, five years after Willson's death, the New York Board of Regents replaced their oral evaluations with written tests. The board of regents tied school funding to the success on these written exams and noticed a 50 percent drop in the pass rate once they removed the principal as the main evaluator of student success.[30]

After the Civil War, as states and local municipalities continued to expand public schools and reorganize the governance of those schools, testing reigned supreme. In 1878, a principal in Chicago announced that he was living through "an age of examinations," including "County Superintendent's examinations, School Board examinations, State examinations, legal examinations, medical examinations, spiritual examinations." Another pedagogue worried that teachers had become "slaves to the examination fiend." The spread of report cards in the same period fed the testing frenzy. It gave teachers increasing amounts of data on which to rank their pupils. And most importantly, testing and report cards consumed the attention of fathers and mothers, creating allies between once sworn enemies: teachers and parents.[31]

George Willson might have felt a certain kinship with Severus Snape. J. K. Rowling's character in her seven-part *Harry Potter* series is a new archetype for the taciturn teacher, as much interested in control as in the well-being of his pupils. Buried in the details of Snape's character are satirical critiques of education, although Rowling's perspective is a uniquely British one.

For instance, Snape and his colleagues rely on standardized tests to sort their students. The tests, the Ordinary Wizarding Levels (the O.W.L.s), are administered by the Wizarding Examinations Authority, and Snape requires nothing less than the highest score, an "Outstanding," as a prerequisite for admittance to his potions class. Snape is also a ubiquitous presence in Hogwarts's halls, doling out house point deductions and detentions in a quantification of behavior meant to keep the young wizards in line. And, of course, Rowling includes report cards, with the likes of both Hermione and Dudley living in fear of low scores being sent home to parents.[32]

J. K. Rowling was onto something when she dreamed up Snape's villainy. Each of her satirical critiques of education is backed by pedagogical scholarship. For example, twenty years after the passage of the No Child Left Behind Act, a law in the United States from 2002–2015 holding schools accountable for how students learned and achieved, the tides seem to be turning against standardized testing. Authors Shani Robinson and Anna Simonton, among others, have now placed the 2009 Atlanta testing scandal within the long history of Georgia's marginalization and scapegoating of its Black population. Sociologist Annette Lareau chronicled the experiences of parents as they navigated school systems, many of them overwhelmed and intimidated by the educational apparatus. Parents without college degrees, Lareau noted, dreaded parent–teacher conferences in which they felt demeaned by educational jargon and pseudo-science. Academics have also noted how school counseling has contributed to the "legacies of oppression," and that educational psychology can be another tool for control.[33]

A case history of George Willson's life shows that the theme of power in education is both circular and evolving. It is circular in that parents and teachers have always been in opposition to one another. If anything, Willson lived through an era in which teachers and parents misunderstood one another to a much larger degree. The antebellum period also witnessed open violence between parents and teachers. Yet power dynamics have also evolved. There are an increasing number of tools at the disposal of teachers to bend parents to their will. The tracking of students into "honors" and "regular" courses leads to parental neurosis and fear, with tangible outcomes that correlate with race, poverty, and future educational attainment. Fear of damaging a student's chances in college admissions has become a contentious aspect of parent–teacher relations, particularly among affluent families. Even the pedagogical assumptions about critical thought, embodied by Bloom's taxonomy, have been reassessed as a manifestation of the desire for "domination, aggression, and the impulse to control."[34]

George Willson was one step in a process that ultimately led to the creation of Professor Snape from J. K. Rowling's imagination. And yet Rowling's Snape—a cold, imposing figure—does not quite reflect the defensiveness and insecurity among nineteenth-century teachers like Willson. Evidence suggests that Willson was *not* an imposing physical presence, that, on the contrary, he was the object of mockery among his students. He did not seem to be socially powerful; yes, he was involved with local organizations, but always in secretarial roles. He was not a leader. He never became a school administrator. An anecdote has survived of Willson apologetically cowering before a more powerful parent. And yet, Willson was a scholar. He was a published author, he was well-read, and by the 1830s he was a middle-aged man in a young person's profession. Willson probably longed for respect. With his system of report cards, he was making a statement to parents: I am a professional; what I do is important; listen to my expertise. Ultimately, Willson offers perspective on just how effective teachers have become at manipulating parents into submission. Perhaps the power of the report card, refined by generations of teachers, are more magical than anything even J. K. Rowling could conceive.

CHAPTER TWO

Unity, Efficiency, and Freed People

In December 1881, William Baxter Matthews (1864–1940) received a report card from Lewis High School. Matthews, who was born enslaved, was fifteen years old at the time and was training to become a teacher in Macon, Georgia. The American Missionary Association (AMA) had established his school fourteen years earlier during Reconstruction and with financial assistance from the Freedmen's Bureau. These report cards were the first ever issued by Lewis High, marking a new era in the school's early history.[1]

During the decades immediately after the Civil War, American schools underwent a national transformation, changes that led to Matthews receiving his report cards. Newly created school boards imposed new hierarchies on a once decentralized system, placing principals in charge of classroom teachers and superintendents in charge of principals. From the top, district administrators began mandating the use of report cards, less as a means of control over children and increasingly as a means of control over the teachers themselves. This was a major shift in the purpose and power of the report card, the first such shift in the report card's centuries-long odyssey.

The new position of "principal" evolved in these decades. Once seen as a lead teacher who was first among equals among the faculty, principals grew into middle managers, modeled on corporate governance structures, with the power to dictate policies to classroom teachers. By the turn of the century, just as enthusiasm for the cult of industrial efficiency was reaching its peak in the United States, teachers criticized principals as being more of "an autocrat, a boss, or a czar" than "a leader in educational ideas." Reigning over principals were superintendents. At a St. Louis conference in 1880, the National Education Association created its first Department of Superintendents, and in the process declared its "belief in authority." A skeptical classroom teacher in Oregon reflected widespread mistrust of the new school hierarchies when she wrote that the new position of superintendent could be the "radiant light" or "the center of darkness." Meanwhile, teachers at schools like Philadelphia's Central High School permanently lost the "entrepreneurial autonomy" that they once enjoyed. Prior to the Civil War teachers tended to be self-governing, making decisions on hiring, curriculum, and discipline in faculty assemblies. By the 1880s, however, district administrators had replaced teacher autonomy with a hierarchical governance structure. The same process occurred in cities like San Francisco, Memphis, and New York, where one reporter criticized public schools as overly bureaucratic and "lifeless."[2]

Report cards played a role in the centralization of this control. As district offices struggled to regulate and review teacher performance in the 1870s and 1880s, principals and superintendents increasingly decreed the use of report cards. They sent inspectors into classrooms to evaluate teacher "proficiency," and they sometimes found classroom teachers as "so unscientific that in judging them by minimum requirement I should regard their standards as very low." Report cards therefore became a means through which administrations could document not just student performance but also the completion of basic exercises on the part of teachers. By 1900, the unity, efficiency, and standardization of practices like the periodic issuing of report cards had led some critics to deem public schools as "regimented, mechanical, and mindless," equal to the atmosphere of an industrial factory.[3]

The themes of increasing social efficiency, standardization, and hierarchy were all present at Macon's Lewis High while William Matthews attended. In 1881, the American Missionary Association sent to Lewis High a new principal with a mandate of creating more alignment with other schools in its network, employing a mix of written assessments, grading, and the sending home of report cards. The principal, a twenty-six-year-old Wisconsin native named Willard Hodge, explained that his goal was to make Lewis High "more advanced" by creating academic "unity and efficiency."[4]

Race complicated the relationship between Matthews and his report cards. By the late 1870s, as white southern elites began to reestablish their political and economic supremacy, northerners had grown exhausted by the egalitarian crusade of Reconstruction. In the 1880s Lewis High became less revolutionary, less political, and, one could argue, more a tool of social control than a means for social advancement. Matthews received his report cards during this transitionary period in which Lewis High moved away from the idealism of its decentralized founding toward a goal of long-term and bureaucratic coexistence with a white-controlled Macon.[5]

For young Matthews, who was born enslaved, education secured his place in the African American middle class. After Lewis High, he attended Atlanta University, became a principal of schools in both Georgia and then Kentucky, led numerous civic organizations, and died a pillar of his community. Mat-

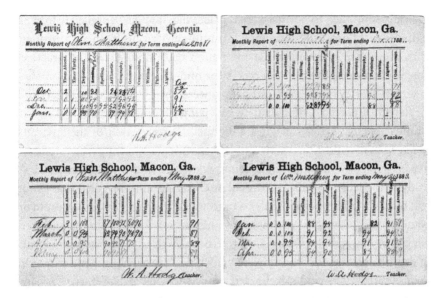

Figure 2.1. William B. Matthews' report cards, Lewis High School, Macon, Georgia, 1881–1883. Photo used with permission of Atlanta University Center Robert W. Woodruff Library.

thews had a knack for schooling, which is evident in the high marks of his report cards. For Matthews' people, however, the promise embodied by high scores on a report card proved hollow, a reality that Matthews never admitted.

William Baxter Matthews was born enslaved in Powersville, Georgia, on July 31, 1864. Powersville was an unincorporated crossroads village about twenty-two miles southwest of Macon. William's parents may have been enslaved by the C. H. Matthews family, who inherited land in Powersville from a Revolutionary War–era land grant. Before the war, the patriarch of the C. H. Matthews clan became the personal secretary to Confederate Vice President Alexander Stephens and later fought in the Army of Northern Virginia. At the time, Powersville was in Houston County, where in 1860 three out of every five enslaved persons worked on large plantations, defined as farms that enslaved at least one hundred people. It is therefore more than likely that Matthews' parents worked on what would have been considered a large system of gang labor associated with cotton production.[6]

William Matthews' mother, Annie Matthews, was born free in Africa. Even though Congress banned the transatlantic slave trade in 1808, native-born

Africans continued to be enslaved in places like middle Georgia. Historians estimate that Europeans kidnapped 1.3 million Africans from 1837 through 1867, even after every major slaving nation had criminalized the practice. One white traveler through Georgia in the mid-nineteenth century estimated that one-quarter of the enslaved people were born in Africa, and therefore illegally transported. Unfortunately, surviving documents do not make clear Annie's specific African origins, although a large portion of the Africans enslaved in the mid-nineteenth century were Yoruba speaking from modern-day Nigeria. She was most likely quite young when she was kidnapped. A study of the ledgers of illegal transatlantic slaving ships revealed that about half of those crossing the middle passage after 1837 were fourteen years old or younger. Annie's origins probably gave her a special status among enslaved people in Powersville, Georgia. Native-born Africans taken to plantations in the mid-nineteenth century were known to "reawaken black Americans to their African past," and slaveholders tended to view native-born Africans with particular mistrust. As some enslavers explained, native-born Africans needed to be "seasoned." One fugitive slave from South Carolina, writing his biography in 1837, remembered that African-born enslaved people felt "indignant" their entire lives and psychologically refused to accept their enslavement.[7]

Matthews did not know the identity of his biological father, which was perhaps because of the context of Matthews' birth. Several weeks before his birth in July 1864, Union cavalry raided the area north of Powersville. In November 1864, when William was just over three months old, William T. Sherman's army bypassed the village of Powersville on its way to Savannah. The Confederate Army harassed Sherman's right flank at the Battle of Griswoldville, which lay thirty-two miles away from the location of Matthews' birth. When Sherman's army was at its closest to the Matthews family, 15,000 Confederate troops were also in the area to defend Macon, making an attempt at escape among enslaved people particularly precarious at that moment. Despite the dangers, between 19,000 and 25,000 enslaved people successfully reached Sherman's army during these months of turmoil.[8]

William's father might have attempted an escape, or he could have been killed trying to escape. It is also possible that William's father was of European ancestry, perhaps an enslaver. William's mother, on the other hand, probably remained enslaved until April 1865 when 13,000 Union cavalry soldiers under General James H. Wilson captured Macon and the surrounding area. If so, the Matthews family would have had a fairly common experience. Many marriages of enslaved people failed to survive the disruption of the Civil War and about 2.75 million people remained enslaved in the South until the Confederate army's final surrender.[9]

It was quite common for formerly enslaved people to assert their new freedom by "coming and going," and Macon was the most obvious destination for an African American family living in Powersville. Macon was founded in 1822 as a trading fort with the Muscogee people along the Ocmulgee River's fall line. By 1860, railroads carried cotton to Macon, which was then transported to Savannah by riverboat. This made Macon a bustling inland port of 8,247 residents before the Civil War. Even during the war, enslaved people migrated to Macon, prompting concern among white Maconites. In September 1864, the local newspaper complained that the enslaved population "demean themselves as if they were free people." In the summer of 1865, the Union army established Macon as one of ninety military posts in Georgia, providing a degree of protection for freed people and increasing the number of refugees. It was also common for freed women like William's mother to find employment in urban centers as domestic workers. However, there were also reports in Macon of white mistresses preferring servants without children, complaining that Black mothers were "annoyances" and that children like William were "pests." By 1867, the Black population of Macon had more than doubled, from 2,851 prior to the war to 5,946.[10]

Despite emancipation, the Matthewses' lives were probably precarious. During Reconstruction in Georgia, there were incidents of Black women being scalped or having their ears cut off and of Black men being clubbed, stabbed, tied to trees, and burned to death. The Union army's outpost in Macon only provided limited protection from the mounting resentment among white Maconites. In May 1865, *Macon-Telegraph* complained about the "great crowd of lazy negroes." In 1866, the same newspaper blamed Macon's Black residents for a deadly outbreak of smallpox. In August 1867, six armed white men attacked a Black church near Macon, shooting eighteen civilians and killing three. In 1868, Macon's largest Black church was burned. There were cases of freed women and children starving to death in Macon. Meanwhile, the Union soldiers stationed in Macon collaborated with white Maconites to subjugate the city's Black population. The city council passed an ordinance ordering that all "idle" freedmen be arrested with the penalties of "ball and chain" or conscription into "public works" projects. Federal troops forced freedmen off the streets and confined them to an open-air jail at the courthouse where white Maconites "desiring hands could get them."[11]

Despite these horrors, freed people like the Matthews family claimed Macon as their new home. In 1865, a northern reporter traveled to the city and interviewed an elderly freed person living in a hut. Having given up the security of working for his former enslaver, the freedman explained to the reporter that in Macon he found "freedom, the opportunities, the protection, and the comradery." Young William grew into consciousness in this fragile balance of limited freedom, where formerly enslaved people established new churches, worked in Macon's reemerging factories and expanding railroads, and became skilled artisans. Some freed people established their own businesses. By 1880, Black Maconites outnumbered white Maconites, and the new Black elites increasingly claimed parental leadership of Lewis High School. Writing in 1881, a school administrator described the professions of the typical parents at his school: shoemakers, carpenters, blacksmiths, a dentist, a saddler, railroad employees, US mail agents, upholsters, tailors, preachers, and even a candymaker.[12]

In July 1865, just three months after the Union army captured Macon, Professor John Ogden arrived. He worked for the Freedmen's Aid Commission which, along with the new Freedmen's Bureau, mobilized resources in the North to establish schools for the recently emancipated. Upon arrival, Ogden wrote to the local newspaper to appease any concerns among white Maconites about educating freed people. Ogden explained that he was not there to "incite animosity or ill feelings" among freed people "towards their former masters." Above all, the new schools were meant to "encourage and enforce . . . habits of industry, honesty, kindness, and forbearance." Ogden's efforts highjacked a grassroots, autonomous educational system already in progress among freed people. Macon's Black preachers were holding classes for about 180 students when Ogden arrived. In September 1865, a staff of eleven American Missionary Association teachers traveled to Macon, closed the self-governing African American schools, and organized children into a collection of "Lincoln Schools." Teachers held these Lincoln Schools in a series of churches, emphasizing the basics of arithmetic, reading, and recitation. Three years later, some of these Lincoln Schools merged into Lewis High School, named for the director of the Freedmen's Bureau in Georgia, who allocated the funds to construct a new school building.[13]

The American Missionary Association (AMA), which created and managed Lewis High, was the largest and most significant of the post–Civil War aid societies. The AMA sent collection agents throughout the North, securing donations from wealthy industrialists and modest farmers. The money paid for all aspects of schooling: teacher salaries and housing, supplies, and facilities. From 1861 through 1890, the AMA represented about one-third of the total of $20 million (nearly $500 million in 2020) spent by aid societies and government agencies in supporting freed people.[14]

In 1870, which was the high watermark for the AMA's involvement with southern education, the association sponsored 157 schools for freed people, employing 110 teachers to serve 6,477 students. However, one should not overstate the AMA's importance. The AMA never employed more than a quarter of the teachers in southern Black schools after the war. There were over fifty other northern support agencies, many of which were more willing to hire Black teachers than the AMA. Consensus has emerged among historians that educational efforts such as the AMA's failed to combat the rising tide of postwar white supremacy. Infamously, President Andrew Johnson overturned William T. Sherman's Field Order Number Fifteen, which promised freed families in and around Savannah forty acres of tillable land. This moment has taken on a symbolism for a broader trend. Freed people needed economic independence from their former enslavers but were instead promised mobility through education.[15]

The typical teacher at Lewis High was northern, female, middle class, and white. As such, the teachers reflected the prejudices and worldviews

Figure 2.2. Lewis High School, Macon, Georgia, 1884. On the far left is the newly constructed library. To the right of the library is the main schoolhouse. Behind the schoolhouse is the American Missionary Association's Congregational Church. Across the road is the teachers' home. *Helping Hand* 3, no. 9 (June 1884): 1.

documented by historians such as Ronald E. Butchart, Jocelyn Jones, and Heather Andrea Williams. For instance, William Matthews' philosophy teacher was Stanley E. Lathrop, who also served as the school's chaplain. At various times, Lathrop described "the Negro" as "fallible, ignorant, childlike," labeled Africa as "savage," and observed that "the extravagance and effervescence of [freed peoples'] religious gatherings is becoming more toned down as intelligence increases." However, Lathrop was also from a renowned abolitionist family. He was a combat veteran of the Civil War, having enlisted in the Union army at the age of seventeen in a fit of idealism. While serving as an administrator at Lewis High, Lathrop wrote that "many black teachers are better than whites." Lathrop mobilized the funds to establish the school's library, open to all of the Black community in Macon, and he argued that his students should be taught to "think for themselves and not merely to learn by rote." To state the obvious, Lathrop's views on race, and perhaps those of his colleagues at Lewis High, were complicated.[16]

The school's mostly white missionary teachers were risking their lives to serve students like Matthews. White Maconites heckled, stalked, refused to house, and threatened to kill Lewis High teachers throughout the 1870s. The school's chapel became the central meeting place of Republican political activism during Reconstruction, holding a celebration for the passage of the Fifteenth Amendment in 1868. Macon's leading politicians denounced the school for attempting to "inaugurate social equality" and identified specific teachers who had the audacity of socializing with Black families. Then, in 1875, the Lewis High faculty desegregated. W. A. L. Campbell became the school's first Black chaplain and teacher, followed by William Scarborough in 1876, who taught classics and literature. Scarborough had attended Lewis High in the 1860s and went on to a career as a professor and president of Wilberforce University in Ohio. He met his future wife while teaching in Macon, a fellow faculty member who was both a divorcée and white.[17]

By the late 1870s and early 1880s, as Lewis High grew under AMA's management, southern whites reestablished their control over state governments. The "Redeemers," or southern white Democrats, also set about slashing state budgets for African American schools. Education was one of the hardest hit line items in state budgets, leading to an increase in illiteracy rates from 1880 to 1900 and a widening gap in per capita expenditures between white and Black schools. Lewis High, as an AMA school independent of the state-run public school system, was indicative of a broader trend in other states. Northern missionaries like the AMA attempted to leverage their control of schoolhouses in negotiating with southern white school boards, which sought control over not only Black education but also the physical schoolhouses. The result, in cities like Atlanta, Montgomery, and Raleigh, was a system of dual control. To one degree or another, missionary societies continued to provide supplemental funding and teachers, while school boards claimed the authority to hire administrators and provide the bulk of funds. Even after Reconstruction, teachers in freed-people schools continued to receive death threats and physical violence. Many of these teachers—a mix of northern and southern, Black and white, male and female—believed in public education but did not trust white southerners to manage Black schools.[18]

In 1872, the Union army withdrew from Georgia. This was also the year that Georgia established its first statewide system of public schools. Macon's public schools came under the leadership of Bibb County's first superintendent: B. M. Zettler. Before fighting in the Confederate army, Zettler served on "vigilance committees" on "scout patrols" that captured enslaved people seeking freedom. While quick to blame the Civil War on "out of control abolitionists," Zettler also praised his "trustworthy negro slave," whose life, he contended, was much better before emancipation.[19]

Negotiations for control of Lewis High lasted from 1872 through 1876. On one side, Zettler demanded the use of Lewis High's building as well as the power to appoint its principal and half of its teachers. On the other side, the AMA sought funding from the school board but balked at handing over control to the former Confederate officer. Just as Zettler and the AMA seemed to reach a deal, the superintendent declared that Lewis High's school year would move to the summer months, ostensibly to make way for white students to use the facilities in the winter. The effect, though, would have also been to drive down attendance among African Americans and drive out northern faculty, who typically fled Macon in the summer heat. The AMA, the school administrators, and the parents of Lewis High's students pulled out of the deal in 1875. Then, mysteriously, Lewis High burned. Allegedly, the first time that arsonists tried to set the school on fire was in July 1875. That attempt failed. However, in December 1876, arsonists successfully destroyed the school buildings, but not the school itself. In the spring of 1876, classes had to move to church basements and enrollment dropped to just seventy students. The years preceding William Matthews' enrollment were characterized by a slow rebuilding of new facilities and an increase in students.[20]

William Matthews did not enroll in Lewis High School until the fall of 1881. Matthews' mother had died thirteen years earlier, and his stepfather, who was a "primitive preacher," assumed parental responsibilities. The reference to his stepfather's preaching offers another window into William's early years, as well as the reasons for his attending Lewis High. W. E. B. Du Bois wrote that enslaved preachers were "the most unique personality developed by the Negro on American soil," because of the difficult balance between meeting the spiritual needs of his followers with the suspicions of the enslavers. In the 1830s, in the wake of the Nat Turner rebellion, who was also a preacher, many southern states passed laws banning public religious ceremonies among enslaved people. Therefore, the work of the enslaved preacher had to be done either in secret or with special permission from the enslaver. Either way, enslaved preachers often commanded prestige and respect from both enslaved people as well as those doing the enslaving. Many, perhaps most, of the plantation preachers were illiterate. They therefore relied on their capacity to memorize Bible passages and their gifts of oratory to mark the most important moments within their communities: funerals, marriages, Christmas, baptisms, and revivals.[21]

William Matthews' "Tentative Biography" explicitly mentions why his stepfather sent him to the boarding department of Lewis High. He wanted his stepson to become literate in order to master a knowledge of the Bible. The stepfather was not alone in this goal. Missionary teachers from across the South noted the emphasis that parents placed on biblical literacy. Many parents attended night school to master reading as adults. Learning to read the Bible was a declaration of independence from white-controlled churches and theology that used the Old Testament to justify enslavement. It meant reversing decades of legally mandated illiteracy. Literacy meant gaining access to the millenarian message of the Bible that inspired Denmark Vesey, Nat Turner, and Frederick Douglass.[22]

William Matthews' report cards demonstrated that he could do much more than just read by the early 1880s. The rural schooling he received before the age of fifteen prepared him well for the academic demands he experienced in Macon. Despite being drawn into the more secular profession of education, Matthews never lost sight of the religious upbringing instilled by his stepfather, recording Bible passages in his notebook even as a principal in his fifties. Matthews also continued to believe in the liberatory power of literacy as an adult. Freedom and autonomy via education was a ubiquitous theme in his speeches before his pupils.[23]

The relationship between missionary teachers and African American parents in the South was complicated, and Lewis High was no exception. For instance,

Figure 2.3. William B. Matthews, 1886, at the age of twenty-two. Photo used with permission of Atlanta University Center Robert W. Woodruff Library.

praise among missionary teachers for Black parents was much more common than criticism. Analyzing documents written by whites in which they describe freed people is fraught, though, especially given the "deference ritual" that enslaved people developed as a means of survival. Also, one has to take into account the intended audience. Schoolteachers and administrators knew that their letters would be published and read by the donor class, whose support the teachers needed in order to fund their schools. Teachers were therefore incentivized to focus on the positive. In any case, there were so many articles that praised the eagerness of freed people to learn, that there was most likely truth behind the rhetoric. For instance, in Alabama, two white AMA teachers with experience in northern common schools said that they had never witnessed anything like the support for education as among freed parents. Parental enthusiasm for education removed a major reason to use report cards. Teachers did not need to win over parental support among freed people; they already had it. Indeed, a teacher in Hillsboro, North Carolina, wrote about how surprised she was to see parents visiting the school on a regular basis. The rhetoric of the teachers of freed people was the opposite of the predominant complaint among common schoolteachers in white-majority schools where parents rarely, if ever, visited.[24]

There were other reasons why report cards did not appear, such as parental illiteracy. In 1860, between 4 percent and 5 percent of enslaved Georgians could read, a product of the laws that criminalized the practice of teaching enslaved people the alphabet. By 1880, around the time that Lewis High School began issuing report cards, literacy rates had jumped to 30 percent among freed people in the South. Also, teachers at freed-people schools, given their missionary zeal, may have been more willing to visit the homes of their pupils. The teachers at Lewis High not only made house calls but also entertained Black families in their homes. Finally, it appears to have taken a number of years before northern teachers created a grading system that recorded periodic assessments. Throughout the 1860s and 1870s, Lewis High held end-of-year performative expositions, the style of assessment that predated written exams and periodic report cards. The first evidence that Lewis High assessed students on a regular basis, and thereby gave teachers something to report home, appeared in 1879. Two years later, Lewis High began issuing report cards that communicated student scores to parents.[25]

The evolution of the relationship between parents and teachers at Lewis High reflected a broader trend within AMA's schools. From the late 1860s to the early 1880s, AMA teachers and administrators became increasingly critical of Black parents. Evidence for the decline of the relationship between teachers and freed parents is not just anecdotal. The increasing tensions between parents and AMA faculty can be quantified through a content analysis of the AMA journal, *American Missionary*. Each year the journal published reports written by classroom teachers, including a few from Lewis High, that provided insights into the perspectives of AMA's teachers. The articles took on a tone of field reports, describing the successes and challenges of individual schools from across the South.[26]

Between 1867 and 1881, the number of references to African American parents in *American Missionary* dropped by half. Part of the decrease in references to African American parents did indeed reflect a change in attitude among the mostly white teachers. The regional director of AMA's schools in Georgia, overseeing Lewis High School, wrote that "the novelty" of education "had worn off" among freed parents and "there was a loss of interest and a decreased attendance" in Georgia's schools. In the late 1860s, typically about half of references to parents in *American Missionary* were explicitly positive, praising parental enthusiasm for education and their resilience in the face of adversity. By the late 1870s and early 1880s, positive references to parents had dropped to below 20 percent. Meanwhile, criticism of African American parents jumped from 12–14 percent in the late 1860s to as high as 55 percent in the late 1870s.[27]

By the time that William B. Matthews received his first report card, tensions between parents and teachers were more visible in missionary schools. The period of mutual admiration was over. Missionary teachers at schools like Lewis High had adopted the same rhetoric of mistrust and judgment that was ubiquitous in antebellum northern schools. The atmosphere was ripe for the emergence of report cards.

In the 1870s, parents at Lewis High became increasingly assertive in their relationship with the school and its teachers. In their assertiveness, they reflected the broader trends throughout segregated schools in the South, as freed parents formed committees, signed petitions, and lobbied white administrators on behalf of their children. In the late 1860s, this assertiveness normally took the form of African American parents calling for AMA teachers to be retained, or reassigned, to their school. For example, in 1867, parents in Charleston asked the AMA to "stop the removal of our esteemed friend," a young missionary schoolmarm. A year later in Swansboro, North Carolina, parents worked to stop the removal of a "beloved" teacher who had "formed a bond of hope among us." In fact, almost all of the parental petitions in the American Missionary Association's archive from the late 1860s were positive in nature, requesting that teachers be retained and praising their hard work.[28]

The petitions grew more critical, though, as time progressed. In 1869, parents at a Maryland school were frustrated with the AMA's decision to shorten the school year. The same year in Augusta, Georgia, parents criticized administrators for the "slow progress" among students. In the 1870s, parents grew bolder. For instance, in 1875, a group of Black parents in New Orleans formed a committee to request that a school administrator be removed. "He was not the man we took him to be," they wrote. The most common critique among parents, however, was about the lack of African American teachers. The request for Black faculty confused AMA administrators, who pushed to replace southern Black teachers with more experienced, more accredited, and typically white northern schoolmarms. As southern white school boards assumed responsibility of African American schools, parents mobilized even further. Black parents formed committees and attended school board meetings to demand more funding for and more control over the education of their children.[29]

The year 1874 was a turning point in the history of parental activism at Lewis High. In the 1860s and 1870s, Lewis High parents were willing to criticize teachers individually and to defend their children in disciplinary disputes, but collective action had not yet taken place. The superintendent of Bibb County schools, B. M. Zettler, provoked the mobilization of parents when he called for the annexation of Lewis High into the public school system. Parental opposition to Zettler initially took the form of a petition to the AMA, requesting that the school remain independent from the county school system. When the AMA ignored the petition and reached an agreement with Zettler, Lewis High parents mobilized further by forming a twelve-person "Board of Responsible Managers," drawn from the ranks of Macon's Black artisans, shopkeepers, and church leaders. This group not only wrote petitions and attended school board meetings but also raised funds so that the AMA would no longer need white-controlled Bibb County's financial support. They doubled their efforts in the wake of Lewis High's burning, writing annual reviews of Lewis High's progress. Like so many other parents across the South, the Board of Responsible Managers requested that the AMA appoint an African American principal and that half of all teachers be Black. The local white newspaper, which typically was indifferent to Macon's Black schools, even ran a story about the newfound assertiveness of Lewis High parents. By 1878, the parents demanded from the AMA a longer school year and more funding. At this point the Board of Responsible Managers had become so confident in its ability to mobilize the community that it threatened the AMA with a boycott of Lewis High.[30]

Three years after the parental mobilization, Willard A. Hodge (1855–1917) introduced the report card to Lewis High School in the fall of 1881. Hodge, a white man, was part of a nationwide trend of school administrators adopting report cards in the late 1870s and early 1880s.

In the immediate aftermath of the Civil War, teachers still felt compelled to explain the relatively new idea of sending home periodic communications to parents, just as they had twenty-five years earlier in George Willson's era. In the 1870s, though, references to school reports began to change. Increasingly, administrators decreed their use. One principal of a Pennsylvania school adopted report cards to make his school as efficient as "a factory" or "an army." In response, teachers began to resist the extra work being imposed upon them. *Maine Journal of Education* complained that filing weekly reports "breaks down the energies of the teachers." In 1874, a Massachusetts teacher suggested time-saving strategies for completing report cards. Printing companies catered their advertisements to busy teachers, claiming that with the help of their product, writing reports would "require but little work, yet show[s] all that needs to be told on such a card." The fact that superintendents, not teachers, began signing their names to report cards represented a symbolic shift in the institutionalization of the practice.[31]

Hodge reflected a broader trend that transcended the racialized context of Macon's Lewis High. The offering of free, publicly funded high schools was still novel in this era, and the South was particularly slow to adopt the idea. By 1890, only 6 percent of the nation's fourteen- to seventeen-year-olds (359,949 students) received some form of secondary education. Meanwhile, primary and secondary schools became increasingly bureaucratic. The new figure of the school superintendent saw himself as equal to the most important businessman, searching for more efficient, cost-saving measures modeled on the United States' thriving industrial sector. Testing, born in Horace Mann's efforts to reform Boston's public schools in the 1840s, became a way to centralize power away from schoolmasters and into newly created district offices. The historian David Labaree tracked this phenomenon in a single school, Philadelphia's Central High School. He wrote that, "as internal governance became more bureaucratic, the power and prestige of the faculty fell precipitously."[32]

Hodge was a twenty-six-year-old at the time and was assuming his first post as a principal. He was born in rural Wisconsin and raised by evangelical Protestants who were active in the temperance movement. After attending Oberlin College, Hodge taught for a few years before the AMA hired him to assume leadership of Lewis High in far-off Macon, Georgia. Hodge claimed religion as his primary motive for entering into education, as he sought to share "the power of Gospel" and to "keep these children safely in the fold of the Good Shepherd." He encouraged his students to skip outdoor recess in favor of prayer vigils, and he instituted an essay contest about the benefits of temperance. Even at the end of his life, after he had returned to Wisconsin and had ended his career in education, Hodge continued to work as a leader in the local temperance movement. Like so many promoters of the report card, Hodge approached his work with missionary zeal.[33]

Multiple factors motivated Hodge to issue his report cards. Perhaps the most immediate and most important cause was the same that prompted George Willson forty-six years earlier: leveraging power over parents. By the time Hodge had arrived, the Board of Responsible Managers had six years of experience with overseeing Lewis High. They had fought off efforts from an ex-Confederate on the county school board and they had survived two alleged cases of arson. The parents had raised money to build a new school and could therefore claim a new degree of ownership of Lewis High. For six years they had requested an African American principal but instead they received young Hodge, righteous not only about spreading the Gospel of Christ but also about spreading the gospel of educational efficiency. Hodge's arrival in Macon was probably not a smooth administrative transition.

Multiple sources point toward Hodge's faith in modern forms of academic bookkeeping as a solution for Lewis High's problems. A history of the school, written in 1942, noted that Hodge's main legacy was that he "undertook a thorough grading of the school," meaning he introduced a new system of dividing students by age and academic attainment. Each fall, Hodge announced to parents that the school year would begin with written exams, so that students could be "properly classified." Hodge also changed Lewis High's closing ceremonies in the spring. Prior to his arrival, the school held a three-day exhibition in which students orally recited their knowledge before the public, interspersed with musical performances. Hodge shortened the closing exercises to a single day, relying on written assessments instead of recitations and emphasizing the distribution of "Certificates of Scholarship." Hodge personally reviewed the schoolwork of each senior before agreeing to their graduation certificate, all in an effort to "raise the standard" of scholarship.[34]

Hodge's reforms caused a revolt. A group of seniors, expecting to graduate in the spring of 1882, learned that Hodge was going to withhold their diplomas until they achieved higher levels of academic accomplishment. The decision prompted a protest in the form of several student withdrawals. Hodge endured another six years as Lewis High's principal, and there is little evidence that parents appreciated his reforms. The school's student journal, *Helping Hand*, did not report on his departure. The closest to a compliment that Hodge received in the journal was when he was described as an "efficient" administrator. In 1888, after Hodge had returned to Wisconsin, he wrote that the main challenge to education was a lack of standardization. Students were "not evenly prepared" with too many "generally deficient in language and grammar." He advocated for a "system of examinations," and the report card was an essential link in this system. It provided a means to communicate the results of examinations to parents of students at Lewis High and thus preempt the surprise and frustration of the seniors who were expecting to graduate in 1882. Hodge also attended an AMA-sponsored conference in the fall of 1881 that reinforced the importance of bureaucratic efficiency in the new era of the Industrial Revolution. The stated goal of the four-day conference, hosted by Fisk University in Nashville, was to "increase their [the schools'] efficiency . . . systematizing and unifying the scheme of education for the colored people." *American Missionary* praised the Nashville conference's success at "unifying the normal and preparatory schools." Just a few weeks after attending this conference, Hodge began issuing report cards at Lewis High.[35]

Willard Hodge signed his name on each of Matthews' report cards, beginning in December 1881 and ending with Matthews' graduation in May 1883. The substance of the report had changed very little since Willson explained his idea in 1835. One column tracked Matthews' attendance and "times tardy." In three years, Matthews missed only one day of school. Just as Willson suggested, another column quantified Matthews' "deportment" on a 100-point scale. From 1881 through 1883, Matthews received scores of 95 and 100 for his behavior. Finally, the report card included between nine and thirteen columns for each academic subject, ranging from reading to arithmetic and from philosophy to chemistry. Once again, Matthews appears to have been a model student. His lowest score came in March 1882 with a 75 in composition. Otherwise, Matthews typically earned marks in the 90s. Young William was good at school. Little wonder that he preserved the report cards for posterity and that he pursued a career in education that lasted over forty years in both Georgia and Kentucky.[36]

After graduating from Lewis High in 1883, Matthews taught in rural Georgia while also taking classes at Atlanta University. One colleague described Matthews as "competent, industrious, energetic, and attentive to his students," adding that he was "an efficient teacher . . . a man noted for attending to his own business." At twenty-seven years old, Matthews became principal of Atlanta's Gates City School, about the same age that Hodge took over Lewis High. During his twenty-one-year tenure at Gates City School, Matthews had his own run-ins with parents. In 1906, one parent accused Matthews of "maltreatment" and a grandfather complained that Matthews "condemned his granddaughter for playing in the street, while allow[ing] other children engaging in the play to go free." It probably helped a great deal that Matthews was a Black man managing a Black school. However, by 1909, Matthews seemed to have had enough of the pressures of managing Black education in the Jim Crow South, and he applied for a position in the Taft administration as minister to Liberia. When that attempt to leave education failed, Matthews accepted a position as an agent for an insurance company. Ultimately, Matthews returned to the world of schooling in 1912 when he became the principal of Colored Central High School in Louisville, Kentucky. He remained in that position until 1934, retiring at the age of seventy.[37]

Matthews was far from a revolutionary. In fact, he was quite the institutionalist, joining and helping to lead a remarkable number of civic institutions during his time in Atlanta and Louisville. For example, he was chair of the "colored branch" of Louisville's YMCA, he led fundraising efforts to renovate the sanctuary of the First Congregational Church in Atlanta, and he served on the board of Atlanta University. In the late 1890s, he led the local chapter of the Colored Knights of Pythia, which supported widows and orphans through charitable donations. Matthews organized the Negro Young People's Christian and Educational Conference in 1902. The conference reflected Matthews' belief that African Americans could gain political and social autonomy, perhaps one day even equality, through education. Besides, Matthews' own life was a testament to education leading to social advancement. Born enslaved, Matthews had excelled at school and had firmly established himself in the Black middle class.[38]

It is important not to oversimplify Matthews' relationship wit schooling, however. As a parent, he seemed to view systems of ₴ healthy skepticism. Matthews' daughter graduated from high sch dictorian but in her first semester at college, she struggled academically. William's wife, Ophelia, wrote about her concerns. William, in response, joked that he knew of the professor who had assigned the low grade, and the professor probably did not "even keep a record of the examination. . . . That exam must have been for gym work." Matthews also encouraged his teachers to do more than teach rote memorization. Matthews wanted his teachers to employ the Socratic method, to understand their pupils' assumptions, and to develop lessons that then cultivated independent thought. Yet, Matthews believed that he understood the avenue for African American success. He had, after all, dined with Alonzo Herndon, one of the United States' first African American millionaires, who had turned a handful of barber shops into a Black-owned insurance empire. Success meant navigating and mastering institutions built by whites. This is probably why, in addition to teaching intellectual independence, he insisted that Black people must learn "regularity, punctuality, silence, industry, neatness, accuracy, and obedience," qualities embodied in school reports.[39]

With the hindsight of history, some might criticize Matthews for his conservatism. To some, Matthews might embody the "white is right" mentality, the deference of southern African Americans in the late nineteenth century ascribed to followers of Booker T. Washington. In the twenty-first century, the work of W. E. B. Du Bois seems more prescient. Matthews, to be fair, would probably reject this assessment as a false binary. Besides, he was personally acquainted with both Washington and Du Bois. Washington telegrammed Matthews in the 1890s, requesting his company while traveling from Atlanta to Talladega. Likewise, several letters of correspondence have survived between Matthews and Du Bois, who were both members of the "Monday Club" in Atlanta.[40]

Ultimately, Matthews had to navigate a dangerous world in the Jim Crow South, and, at moments, he seemed to endorse second-class status for African Americans. For example, in 1920 he participated in a committee, sponsored by the governor of Kentucky, on the state's segregated educational system. The committee made clear that "a desire for education and for better living conditions does not in the least mean a desire for so-called social equality." Growing up in Macon in the wake of the Civil War had made Matthews a

Figure 2.4. William B. Matthews, c. 1905, around the age of forty. Photo used with permission of Atlanta University Center Robert W. Woodruff Library.

pragmatist, willing to compromise on his demands in pursuit of more funding for his students. However, Matthews was probably more sincere when he
helped draft the constitution of the Crispus Atticus Chapter of the Sons of
the American Revolution. The organization called for "social and political
combining of all races in a perfect equality" in order to "realize the plan of the
founders of the American democratic republic."[41]

Michael Render grew up in Atlanta, less than eight miles away from William
Matthews' grave. Render is better known by his stage name, Killer Mike. Born
in 1975, Killer Mike is now one of the most well-respected hip-hop artists of
his generation. Both Matthews and Killer Mike were part of Atlanta's thriving
Black middle class, albeit separated by over a century. Historians have labeled
Atlanta the Black Mecca, dating back to the communities of freed people that
emerged during Reconstruction in and around Atlanta's Freedmen's Bureau
outposts. From those outposts, Black Atlantans built Morehouse and Spelman
Colleges, became millionaires, and produced civil rights icons like Martin Luther King Jr. William Matthews led one of Black Atlanta's oldest schools in its
infancy for over two decades, part of the generation of Atlantans who were
born enslaved in rural Georgia but established homes in a thriving urban area.
Matthews, after all, chose Atlanta, not Powersville, nor Macon, nor Louisville,
as his final resting place. Atlanta mattered to Matthews and his generation of
African American elites.[42]

While Killer Mike and William Matthews shared a fondness for Atlanta,
they disagreed over the nature of industrial education. Killer Mike, for one,
would view the school report card with deep cynicism. In June 2020, six days
after downtown Atlanta burned in the wake of George Floyd protests, Killer
Mike released the song "Walking in the Snow," with the lyrics:

> The way I see it, you're probably freest from the ages one to four.
> Around the age of five you're shipped away for your body to be stored.
> They promise education, but really they give you tests and scores.
> And they predictin' prison population by who scoring the lowest.
> And usually the lowest scores the poorest and they look like me.
> And every day on evening news they feed you fear for free.
> And you so numb you watch the cops choke out a man like me
> And 'til my voice goes from a shriek to whisper, "I can't breathe."

Why did William Matthews and Killer Mike have such opposing views on
formal education? One man, born enslaved, viewed schooling as a means

through which his people could gain their freedom. The other, born into Atlanta's middle class, believes that schooling in America perpetuates the enslavement of his people.[43]

The generations of failed promises that separate Matthews and Killer Mike explain part of the difference. Matthews did not have the decades of data to deconstruct his commitment to formal schooling. Since William Matthews' retirement, schooling has failed African Americans on nearly every metric relative to the outcomes for whites: wealth gap, incarceration rates, health outcomes, and more. By 2020, Killer Mike was stating the obvious, and to argue with Killer Mike's lyrics is to deny the empirical evidence.[44]

There is another explanation: report cards induce pleasure. William Matthews was good at school. His Lewis High report cards told him, each month, that he was special, academically gifted. That might be why he kept those pieces of cardboard for sixty years until his death, the earliest documents in all of William Matthews' papers. Lewis High's academic grades and deportment scores did not just prohibit young William from certain actions. Report cards employed positive reinforcement to modify William's behavior. To see himself at the top of his class rank must have been exhilarating for young William, the beginning of a lifetime of achievement in which he rose to the upper echelons of Black America.[45]

To be fair, as an adult, William Matthews held a sophisticated view of the arbitrariness of grades and grading. He was also in his late sixties when Carter G. Woodson published *The Mis-Education of the Negro*, which made some the same points as Killer Mike but nearly ninety years earlier. Presumably, someone as well connected and well read as William Matthews would be familiar with Woodson's work. And yet, there is little evidence that Matthews renounced, or even publicly criticized, the educational system to which he had dedicated his career. The report card is effective, especially because it induces pleasure at an early age. It creates lifelong converts out of many of us.[46]

CHAPTER THREE

Overworn Mothers and Unfed Minds

Martha Nicholson McKay (1842–1934) was a midwestern mother of three daughters who kept their report cards. Several of these report cards have survived in an Indianapolis archive. They show that McKay's youngest daughter, Helen, struggled in arithmetic for years but excelled in reading and history. All three daughters rarely, if ever, missed school.[1]

In addition to report cards, family letters and diaries reveal McKay's involvement with the education of her children. She read to them each night, chaperoned their trips to the public library each week, and took them to the Indianapolis art museum, all in an effort to ensure each girl's academic success. McKay also took on most of the work in the home: sewing clothes, procuring supplies, cooking, and nursing ill family members. To McKay, all of her efforts paid off when the grades were good. In 1891, when Helen, aged sixteen, brought home a report card with high marks, her mother responded "cheerfully." However, McKay's cheerfulness may have masked an inner frustration with mothering in an age of report cards. At one point, McKay wrote that the life of a mother "is a sad story of overworn bodies and unfed minds."[2]

The historian Ruth Schwartz Cowan helps to make sense of McKay's life. In *More Work for Mother*, Cowan argued that a strange phenomenon occurred during the Industrial Revolution. New technology, designed to reduce labor and promote efficiency, actually led to more household work for mothers like McKay. Report cards were one more example of the "Cowan paradox." In the mid-nineteenth century, teachers invented systems of written reporting in part to reduce the amount of time they spent making home visits. The result, though, was that the labor of mothers increased, particularly because of what some scholars of women's history refer to as "separate spheres." By Martha McKay's adulthood, working-class women were being segregated into unskilled sectors; wealthy women, like McKay, were relegated to the private or domestic sphere, which would have included the oversight of a child's education. Report cards were one aspect of this broader story, pushing responsibility for the behavior of the child back onto the mother.[3]

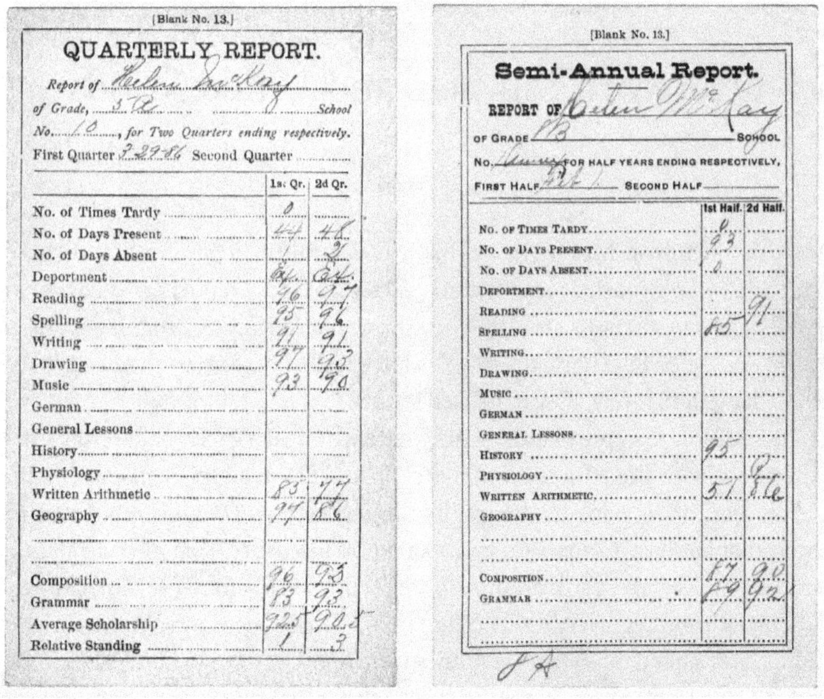

Figure 3.1. Two report cards of Martha McKay's youngest daughter, Helen, 1886 and 1889. Photo used with permission of Indiana Historical Society.

However, mothers were more than passive recipients of increasing educational burdens; they often played an active part in the efforts to improve education. From the 1880s through the early 1900s, middle-class mothers organized literary clubs, initially as a social outlet and for intellectual stimulation. As the 1890s progressed, many of these literary clubs evolved toward civic engagement. Thousands of clubwomen across the country launched campaigns for publicly funded kindergartens, safe playgrounds, and access to public libraries. Defense of teachers was one more issue for clubwomen's new civic engagement. Clubwomen, some of them former teachers, lobbied school boards and state legislatures for higher teacher salaries, better working conditions, and reduced workloads.

The report card was the lynchpin for these developments. Teachers created the report card to strengthen parental support of the teachers' efforts in the 1830s and 1840s. In the 1870s and 1880s, in an era that emphasized industrial efficiency and standardization, school administrators decreed their use. By the 1890s, the report card had successfully held generations of mothers responsible for their children's performance at school. In this era, the report card's power backfired on school administrators. Mothers were now fully involved, not only in their individual child's performance but in the maintenance of the entire educational system. Whereas two generations earlier teachers were seen as the opponents of parents, they now became the allies of mothers. Both teachers and mothers demanded an alleviation from the strain of late nineteenth-century industrial schooling.[4]

Martha McKay's life in the 1880s and 1890s may be illustrative of these developments. For decades, McKay was one of the principal leaders of Indianapolis' club movement. Then, in 1894, after guiding three daughters through Indianapolis' burgeoning public school system, McKay ran for the city's school board. McKay ultimately failed to win an election in which she could not even vote. However, her career as a mother, a clubwoman, and an advocate for school reform embody two broader trends: the increasing workload of mothers as a result of the report card, and the mobilization of clubwomen to defend the interests of teachers.[5]

Martha Nicholson McKay raised her three daughters in a transitionary moment in the history of motherhood in the United States. In the first half of the nineteenth century, literature celebrated the "moral common sense" and the religious piety of mothers. For Martha's mother, who was a Quaker raising her children in rural antebellum Ohio, the ideal was one of self-sacrifice. McKay, on the other hand, was part of a generation of women who extended earlier notions of *private* separate spheres to include the *public* welfare of children. Recognizing that the new industrializing world of their children was radically different from their own upbringing, mothers in the 1880s and 1890s sought new ideas to borrow. Urbanization, in other words, "complicated parental clarity and confidence." Meanwhile, medicine's success in limiting child mortality led to an era in which journals, memoirs, and parenting books increasingly applied science to child-rearing. Yet women like McKay were not passive recipients of expert advice. They were active agents, sometimes adopting medical expertise and sometimes rejecting it, all while demanding that the state and science do more to protect their children.[6]

The effects of this new era of scientific motherhood were paradoxical. On the one hand, upper- and middle-class mothers became increasingly proactive and civically engaged in schools. They viewed themselves as altruistic actors, extending their self-proclaimed maternal love into the public sphere.

On the other hand, mothers received new levels of expert advice, much of it contradictory. For example, medical journals dispensed advice about how mothers should appeal to cheerfulness in their children, while at the same time blaming mothers for the feminization of boyhood. Experts encouraged mothers to recognize the "pricelessness" of childhood, while being warned against smothering their children with too much love and creating neurotic sons and daughters.[7]

At the center of this new discourse on motherhood was G. Stanley Hall (1846–1924). Hall launched the "child study movement" in the 1880s and 1890s, which applied scientifically validated facts to child-rearing practices. Under Charles Darwin's influence, Hall argued that children needed to pass through a series of natural stages, an evolution, before becoming healthy adults. Education should therefore be transformed to help guide children on this journey rather than forcing children to recite facts in cramped schoolhouses. In the late nineteenth century, Hall traveled to every region in the United States to offer public presentations on childhood and these presentations included indictments of US education. These lectures and their accompanying reports in local newspapers exposed Hall to mass audiences, many of them clubwomen. In the process, Hall popularized a counterattack on an educational system embodied by the now decades-old report card, spreading the idea that grading and assessment were inherently unhealthy. Hall wrote in 1904, "Everywhere the mechanical and formal triumphs over content and substance . . . information over education, marks over edification." Paradoxically, Hall came to conclusions like this one by collecting vast amounts of data in his questionnaires.[8]

Middle-class mothers were some of Hall's most ardent supporters. Historians have linked Hall to the creation of the National Congress of Mothers, the predecessor to the Parent Teacher Association, and have shown that Hall's followers fought against the rising tide of homework. Meanwhile, discourse surrounding schools reflected these broader contradictory messages about motherhood. Mothers blamed schools for causing too much stress, while at the same time demanding that public schools take on a larger role in alleviating the challenges of urbanization. The report card, born several decades earlier to grab the attention of uninterested parents, helped cause this new era of increasing parental anxiety.[9]

The historian Ruth Schwartz Cowan captured another dynamic of the late nineteenth century. In *More Work for Mother*, published in 1983, Cowan argued that a series of nineteenth-century technological innovations created labor-saving efficiencies for men, while at the same time creating more labor for tasks normally performed by women. The invention of the nineteenth-century coal stove, for instance, saved labor hours of chopping wood. At the same time, the coal stove created the new challenge of cleaning soot, a task normally assigned to women. Likewise, the industrial production of textiles provided consumers access to cotton clothing, which in turn caused more work for women to mend and wash the new clothes. The sewing machine's invention would have seemingly reduced the time dedicated to mending-clothes but in fact led to a reduction in women using seamstresses as they took on the task of sewing in the home.[10]

Despite being a member of the local elite, Martha McKay reflected these broader trends of scientific motherhood, separate spheres, and Cowan's paradox. Graduating from Ohio Female College in 1861, she had access to much more formal education than most of her peers. While she grew up in a humble, rural Quaker community, as an adult McKay entered Indianapolis' urban, wealthy elite through her marriage. Her husband, Horace, made his fortune as a real estate investor and served for over thirty years on the city council. In 1886, the McKays moved into one of the grand houses in Indianapolis' affluent North Side neighborhood, a 6,200-square-foot mansion furnished with life-size family portraits. They had at least one maid, Ellen, who typically prepared dinner for the family of five. The McKay daughters also participated in debutante balls in the 1880s and 1890s. The very fact that they attended high

Figure 3.2. The McKay family home, Indianapolis, Indiana, c. 1929, originally constructed in 1886. Photo used with permission of Indiana Historical Society.

school reflected their elite status, given that only 6 percent of teenagers in 1890 received any form of secondary education in the United States. To add an additional layer of complexity, Martha McKay was unusually progressive for her era. She grew up in an abolitionist household. Her husband, Horace, shared Martha's political beliefs, and he commanded a battalion of "colored troops" during the war. The McKays hosted a dinner party for Frederick Douglass in 1877, which was the same year that Martha McKay joined the National Women's Suffrage Association. Suffrage would remain her lifelong political passion.[11]

While Martha McKay's life was one of privilege, her letters and journal entries chronicled the burdens of housework and motherhood. She spent her days mending clothes, cooking many of the meals for her family, and procuring supplies at the market. Martha even dedicated weeks to laboring over handmade curtains. Family letters and diaries are full of references to Martha caring for ill children. One daughter, Daisy, had a chronic illness, a heart disease that left her bedridden. Martha had to take on the responsibility for nursing her ill children because her husband tended to be away from home for long periods of time, while her children awoke in the night crying out, "I want Papa!" In 1891, Horace was injured when the horse he was riding panicked over one of Indianapolis' electric streetcars. He could not walk for a period of time, and once again, Martha was given the tasks of both nurse and manager of the household. In addition to caring for the physical well-being of her family, Martha monitored the emotional health of her children. She noted when one daughter was inexplicably "melancholy all day" and when another had to be comforted after night terrors. Then there were the instances when the mother had to act as diplomat among the bickering sisters. As Martha wrote, managing the emotions of her daughters was more difficult than "presiding over the Senate."[12]

Added to the daily litany of cooking, cleaning, and nursing, Martha McKay oversaw her daughters' schooling. She researched the schools available to her children, meeting in 1878 with administrators to compare school curricula. In 1883, Martha prepared her oldest daughter for the entrance exams of Indianapolis High School, a task made more difficult by the fact that her youngest daughter had contracted measles at the same time. It was Martha who had to listen to her daughters complain about the pressures of recitations and written examinations, and it was Martha who had to deny her daughters' pleas to stay home from school. Martha preferred that her children finish their academic lessons either at the public library or in the McKay family parlor, where she could keep a closer eye on their work. She insisted that her daughters write in personal journals each day so as to improve their literary prose and perfect their grammar. She was also one of the few parents who visited Indianapolis High School. Martha supplemented the school curriculum with her own regimen of art, history, and culture. She exposed her daughters to the world of politics by taking them to Indiana's state house; she introduced them to literature by reading Shakespeare and Harriet Beecher Stowe aloud; she fostered an appreciation of art by visiting Indianapolis' art museum periodically. All of this helped the McKay daughters in the classroom. After years of maternally required Shakespeare, young Helen's essay on *Macbeth* earned her top marks in the class; her "enthusiasm could not be questioned," the teacher commented. Martha must have been proud. She decided to keep Helen's essay on *Macbeth* in her personal papers, alongside Helen's report cards.[13]

Despite the focus and energy that Martha McKay dedicated to the education of her children, she still admitted to being personally unfulfilled. In 1883, Martha confessed in her journal, "I have accomplished nothing at all that I hoped to achieve twenty-five years ago." She found housework particularly laborious, lamenting how her formal education failed to prepare her for the mundane tasks of daily life. She was frustrated about not knowing that rosin soap ruined flannels or that newly bought textiles could "come apart easily," and she claimed that she never mastered the art of baking bread. Martha wrote that the "burden" of housework could all too often "fall back and crush [her]." The challenges did not abate as her daughters entered high school. Martha became consumed with the "universal ambition" that "seizes the children" as "they are sent from home to school." Yet Martha consciously stoked those ambitions in her children. In 1890, just as her youngest daughter, Helen, was entering high school, Martha told her in a moment of quiet reflection, "Remember, Helen, you are to be a grand woman."[14]

Teachers, and later administrators, created the report card to make more work for mothers: to make parents, and by extension mothers, responsible for the behavior of the child at school. This goal was explicit. In 1884, one superintendent in Illinois even included an eight-point list of what parents should do to support their children's education. The list included a new concept: the oversight of schoolwork done at home. Popular culture reinforced the message of the report card, celebrating mothers who sacrificed for the sake of their child's education. In 1878, one author referenced her own mother who, despite the family's poverty and "at great self-sacrifice," gave her "what opportunities

Figure 3.3. Martha Nicholson McKay, c. 1880, around the age of thirty-eight. Photo used with permission of Indiana Historical Society.

for instruction she could obtain." Another book praised James Garfield's mother for her "self-denial" and "toil" despite "scanty supply of food," all so that her youngest child, James, could attend school. In 1891, *Ladies Home Journal* published a story about how parents could use report cards to leverage better outcomes for their children. In the story, the boy's grades increased, and he applied himself "like a little Trojan," in order to earn the privilege of purchasing a bicycle. From Milwaukee, Wisconsin, to Macon, Georgia, local newspapers reminded mothers to read their children's weekly report cards and, if the report did not arrive, to call on the school and request it.[15]

The report card was working, at least according to teachers and administrators. Mothers were spending more time keeping track of their children's academic progress and they were more emotionally invested in their child's behavior. In West Virginia, one superintendent explained that the school's system of tracking each student's progress led to the "delight" of parents who "are informed each month of all that concerns the child's school life." A school administrator in Wisconsin wrote about how periodic reports led to a "corresponding interest [being] awakened on the part of the parents." The town newspaper in Monroe City, Missouri, periodically published the list of schoolchildren on the honor roll; the newspaper reminded the parents of children not included on the honor roll to examine report cards to find "what is lacking and perhaps give some valuable aid in raising the standard of the pupil."[16]

By the end of the century, however, some began to resist the report card's tendency to manipulate parents. In 1895, *Kindergarten Magazine* stated its concern for overburdened mothers of schoolchildren. The responsibility of overseeing her child's "plan of education," the journal noted, "make[s] an anxious mother over-anxious." Maternal anxiety did not concern the U.S. Department of Interior, though. The department included report cards in its 1891 summary of the nation's education systems, celebrating the fact that superintendents across the country had already adopted the practice.[17]

Not every family dynamic was like the McKay's. Archival evidence reveals examples of *fathers* taking the initiative in overseeing the education of their children. An 1885 report card from the Charleston Female Seminary prompted one father, Oskar Aichel, to confront the school's administration about his child's low grades. In another example from 1898, a father in California made detailed arrangements for the oversight of his three sons' education. No mention was made of the mother's role in his correspondence about schooling. Indeed, it was the older brother, not the mother, of a young military school cadet who requested monthly reports about his sibling. The boy, fifteen years old at the time, was enrolled in a North Carolina boarding school run by a "Major Bingham." The older brother wrote to the cadet after receiving each report card from Major Bingham, encouraging the sibling to be "diligent" and proclaiming that the academic scores were making the older brother "proud."[18]

The case of Albert J. Nast (1846–1936) is an example of formally educated fathers taking an active interest in the report cards of their children. Nast, the son of German immigrants, was born in Cincinnati and earned a doctorate in theology before having two children. In 1883, his wife was diagnosed with tuberculosis. For the next twelve years, as his wife slowly declined, Nast edited a paper, taught college-level theology, and traveled across the Midwest to preach. He also oversaw the education of his children. In an 1889 letter to his father, Nast's eleven-year-old son dedicated nearly three pages to explaining the grades on his report card. He clarified that his teacher had miscalculated the number of days he was absent. He also elaborated on his rank in each class. It is only in the final paragraph that the son remembered to wish his younger sister a happy birthday. Meanwhile, Nast's letters to his children were short and to the point. He was a busy man, and the report card was an excellent and efficient way to synthesize information. One letter, written in 1899 to his daughter, is especially revealing. She had just finished her first year at college, on her way to later becoming a Johns Hopkins–educated medical doctor. Nast, reflecting on her academic success, admitted, "I am proud of you in every way."[19]

More often than not, however, archival materials showed that mothers were responsible for overseeing their children's education, and the theme of report cards burdening mothers transcended class, race, and region. An 1880 report card pushed Emily Jane Winkler Bealer (1833–1908) to near emotional collapse. Bealer was a widowed mother of four from Atlanta living in poverty. Her diary mirrored many of the themes of nineteenth-century motherhood: self-sacrifice, feelings of guilt, and, of course, Cowan's theme of increasing household work. She struggled to pay rent, had to pawn her watch, and was forced to borrow money from friends in order to pay her taxes. Nearly every diary entry mentioned some misbehavior on the part of her children, including her twelve-year-old son, Pierre, who was particularly "saucy" and "rebellious." It was Pierre who struggled the most at school. In May 1879, he was sent home for disobedience. Two months later, on the same day her landlord evicted her, Bealer met Pierre's teachers to discuss his schoolwork. Then, in June 1880, came the most positive news that Bealer had mentioned in over a year of diary entries: Pierre received his report card, and it was marked "promoted." Bealer's diary referenced report cards explicitly four times from 1879 to 1882. In that same period, she mentioned some form of communication with teachers another three times. Cowan's paradox applied to Bealer's life. Despite the industrial innovations that were transforming society, Bealer barely had time to feed and clothe her children, much less to educate them. Each month, Atlanta's public schools sent Bealer a new time-consuming task in the form of a report card.[20]

Far from any urban centers like Atlanta or Indianapolis, rural Vermont farm wife Henrietta Fletcher (1845–1916) noted the reception of her oldest daughter's report cards each semester in her letters. Like Bealer, her family was far from wealthy. The Fletchers could not pay for a doctor, even when their baby's "eyes rolled into his head." It is unclear how they paid for their teenage daughter to attend normal school in a nearby town, although Fletcher did periodically apologize to her daughter for not being able to send any money to help support her. Although Fletcher's daily life was spent washing clothes, cleaning corn, stitching mittens, pickling vegetables, and selling hay at the market, her other great task was overseeing her children's schooling. She reported in each letter to her children how they were performing, tracking the youngest daughter's "5 headmarks" in spelling and praising her oldest daughter when a report card arrived in the mail. At one point, Fletcher wrote to her daughter that, despite being poor, the "one thing to be proud of" was her children's academic success. However, wrapping her self-worth in the academic performance of her children proved emotionally straining. Not only did Fletcher's oldest daughter express anxiety before examinations, but the mother also wrote of her relief at the end of the school year. The closing of the school term each fall and spring lifted a burden not just for her children but also for their mother.[21]

Effie McLucas (1852–1904) also saved the report cards of her children. McLucas helped manage her family farm near Bennettsville, North Carolina, and like Bealer, had a son who struggled to behave at school. At one point, McLucas' son accumulated 121 demerits in a single year, prompting a special note from the principal. Since her husband traveled several months each year as a tobacco dealer, she faced the challenges of being a single mother. McLucas' letters to her husband chronicled the difficulty of feeding livestock and finding the necessary supplies in nearby stores. When her husband proposed moving to Florida to pursue a new career, Effie had to remind her spouse about the lack of nearby schools in the area of the proposed new farmstead. It was also Effie who found a new route to the Bennettsville schoolhouse when a nearby bridge washed out in a storm, cutting the McLucas children off from their education. In the midst of the social isolation, the single-parenting, and the struggle to keep the farm going, McLucas was summoned to school. Her son had been disrespectful to the teacher and was forced to stay inside during recess. The boy had avoided getting whipped, McLucas reported, but she doubted he would avoid that fate in the upcoming weeks. School was just one more task that left McLucas "worried most of the time."[22]

Georgia Summers (1854–1939) was most likely born enslaved in Arkansas, where in 1888 she gave birth to her daughter, Jeannette. By the 1890s, the Summers family had moved to Louisville, Kentucky, and Jeannette was enrolled in a local elementary school. Even though there is little archival evidence that sheds light on Georgia Summers' life, the evidence does suggest that Georgia cared about report cards. Jeannette's 1898–1899 report is one of the few relics from her childhood that has survived. Interestingly, the eleven-year-old Jeannette signed her own name in the place reserved for the signatures of parents, suggesting that Georgia could not read or write. There are also no surviving letters between Jeannette and Georgia, despite the fact that they lived in different cities for decades. The details of Georgia Summers' life, unfortunately, remain a mystery. It is safe to draw one conclusion, however: working-class African Americans such as Georgia Summers considered report cards important enough to preserve them for generations.[23]

Laura I. Oblinger (1863–1931) was a working-class white woman who discussed the report cards of her children when corresponding with her husband. The Oblingers were tenant farmers who moved between rural Nebraska, Kansas, and Missouri. As such, they never owned the land they farmed, and Laura Oblinger's lack of formal education can be seen in her broken grammar. Education, though, mattered to Oblinger. After she sent her husband the report cards, one letter stated that the grades were "good" and that "it made me feel a little proud." Oblinger's life was difficult, and she was separated for long periods from her husband, who often traveled looking for employment. In her husband's absence, she managed a series of rented farms and negotiated prices of potatoes and corn, all while finding the time to knit clothes for the six daughters and stepdaughters. There were periods when Oblinger fell ill working in the Nebraska cold; in 1887, she was so sick with chills for four days that she could "almost scream." That year, Oblinger broke her hand working on the farm, and, as the years passed, she increasingly relied on the labor of her daughters to manage the harvest. The most consistent theme in

Figure 3.4. Unidentified woman, c. 1890s, most likely Georgia Summers. Georgia's daughter, Jeannette, was a child when this photo was taken, and she saved it in her personal papers. Photo used with permission of Indiana Historical Society.

Oblinger's letters to her husband, however, was the children's schooling. A teacher requested that Oblinger purchase "a reader," which led to the mother overseeing her daughters' spelling homework every night. In 1887, one of the Oblinger daughters received low scores on a report card. According to Laura Oblinger, the grades were unjust, reflecting a deep prejudice on the part of the teacher toward her family. "I will make it lively for those school mams when I get home," Oblinger wrote. The report card had worked its magic, causing such chagrin on the part of mothers that some threatened violence.[24]

In short, interest in report cards was not confined to elite, upper-class white mothers like Martha McKay. It was a phenomenon that transcended class and race. Nor was interest in report cards confined to urban areas. Many mothers who lived in cities, or on farms, and even some who were tenement laborers, built their self-worth around the academic performance reflected on report cards. While not solely focused on women, archival evidence shows that the burden of overseeing a child's education disproportionately fell on mothers.

Martha McKay parented in an era that, paradoxically, recognized the increasing importance of grades for a child's future but also failed to standardize grading scales. Since the start of the common school movement, teachers experimented with a variety of grading categories: letters like "S" for satisfactory or "E" for excellent, numerical point systems, and sometimes brief phrases like "doing well" or "doing poorly." By far the most common grading system in the 1880s and 1890s was the one-hundred-point scale, which McKay's children received on their report cards.[25]

The practice of assigning students their grades was not without its critics, though. In 1888, the Anglo-Irish philosopher Francis Edgeworth published his critique of the 100-point system, examining the many inconsistencies of how teachers assigned grades to pupils. His main concern was that the grades conferred labels onto students that were not only shallow in their evaluations but fundamentally unfair. "There are some pass men [who are as] good as some of the honor men," Edgeworth wrote. "They [the non-honor students] are huddled unknown amongst the ignominious throng, for want, not of talent, or learning, or industry, or judgement, but luck." The concerns about grading continued in the coming decades. In the early twentieth century, two education critics conducted a survey of 142 schools, requesting that the schools grade a common essay on a 100-point scale. The scores that returned varied from 50 to 98.[26]

The task of creating a common, nationwide grading standard proved daunting for the National Education Association (NEA), even in an age of standardization. In 1894, the NEA's famous Committee of Ten published its report that attempted to liberalize a common curriculum for college preparatory secondary schools. Even so, Charles Elliot, president of Harvard and member of the committee, failed to get universities to adopt a common entrance exam, much less adopt common grading scales. In 1900, the NEA created the College Entrance Examination Board in perpetual pursuit of instilling nationwide standards for secondary students applying to universities. Once again, they could not reach an agreement on the best system for grading and had no mechanism to mandate grading standards to school districts. By 1906, the Carnegie Foundation published its "Carnegie Unit," the standard unit of measurement for high school course credits. None of these monumental and unprecedented attempts at nationwide coordination of secondary schools successfully built consensus on which grading scales primary and secondary schools should use: letter grades, percentages, 4-point scales, or narrative descriptions.[27]

Instead, grading scales remained the domain of individual superintendents and their local school districts. For instance, in 1893 Atlanta's new superintendent was criticized for decreeing the city's first standard grading scale. At the same moment, Chicago's superintendent was criticized for not enforcing an existing grading scale. Newton, Massachusetts's superintendent went to the extreme of introducing a weighted point system that calculated grades based on the "efficiency" of different classes. For example, science classes counted as 12 "pupil-recitations," while English counted as 19.2 pupil-recitations. As one superintendent put it in 1898, "If a superintendent does not look after tests and prepare examinations, what will he do?"[28]

The one-hundred-point scale worked well enough for many educators. One teacher in Missouri wrote, "If we, who live in the Middle West, read in a New York magazine that a certain man entered college with an average grade of 95 in his preparatory work, we know pretty well what that means, and so it is the country over." By the time that McKay's grandchildren entered school in the 1910s, however, the A through F letter grade system began to dominate school districts. Progressive era reformers tended to desire fewer, broader categories, giving teachers more flexibility in evaluating students. By the 1930s, a survey of 443 schools calculated that 54 percent used letter categories and just 40 percent used percentages. By the 1940s, about 80 percent of schools had adopted the A through F scale.[29]

As early as the 1880s and 1890s, though, parents and teachers questioned the value of sending home periodic evaluations of children. Some argued that the rankings, markings, and percentages failed to convey specific meaning. An editor of a newspaper in Grand Rapids, Wisconsin, made that point when he wrote that "marking in per cents is a sealed book to parents," more likely to cause confusion than to provide helpful insight. A year later in Michigan, another newspaper argued that "parents do not need to look over their per cent on these cards to know whether they [the children] are learning." An example of the confusion caused by vague report cards occurred in Philadelphia, when a mother read "passable" on her daughter's report. Frantic and holding back tears, the mother called for an immediate meeting with the teacher, who had to explain that in fact the daughter was top in the class and that "report cards mean nothing."[30]

Another common concern for parents was that the report card induced anxiety in their children. In 1894, a parent in Pennsylvania noted how the day that schools issued report cards inevitably "brought frowns" upon the faces of children. In Mississippi, parents were told that report cards were "educational corsets" and that these pieces of paper reflected broader problems with a "dull, inert, and uninteresting" educational system. In Michigan, "report card day" led to "gritting of teeth," "clenching of fists," and "occasionally a child is seen crying as if its heart would break." There were stories that report cards instigated fights between schoolchildren. In 1898, a twelve-year-old girl living in Los Angeles "attacked" a classmate on whom she blamed her low deportment score. In Seattle, there was a story about a report card pushing a child to run away from home. The incident occurred when a child handed her mother a poor report card, explaining that the marks were "not her fault and that she didn't want to go to school." That evening, the child disappeared, allegedly fleeing to Tacoma to be with her aunt and away from the tyranny of report cards.[31]

Paradoxically, some parents complained that report cards instilled a false sense of confidence in their children. A California newspaper published the story of "Little Arna," who brought home perfect scores each term, which only made the girl "selfish and proud," and impervious to the feelings of other children. In Oklahoma, a mother was ecstatic that her child was listed first in her class. However, upon questioning the child, the mother realized that her daughter "understood absolutely nothing of arithmetic." In other words, the report card could not be trusted as a true reflection of knowledge. In 1897, a father living in San Francisco complained to the superintendent that his son "brought home a report card naming him as number one." The problem, the father explained, was that his son was "not number one in many things." Parents seemed to instinctively believe what G. Stanley Hall would outline in his 1904 book, *Adolescence*. Grades as recorded on report cards robbed children of some vague innocence.[32]

Teachers joined parents in voicing their concerns about report cards. They had pedagogical objections, namely that they distracted pupils from their inner curiosity. A group of teachers in Pennsylvania made that point in 1887 during a teacher's association meeting. Ten years later in 1897, some of San Francisco's teachers lobbied the superintendent to end the practice of monthly reports, arguing that report cards were merely "giving medals." Someone describing himself as "an old rural schoolmaster" from New York wrote that report cards created "distrust" between parents and schools and, in the process, turned students into soldiers. "They don't think and only obey," he complained, adding, "uniformity in schools means mediocrity." In 1900, a town in Minnesota witnessed a successful teacher-led anti–report card protest. The superintendent dropped the required use of report cards in his schools, convinced that parents had become too obsessed with the periodic marks of their children. Perhaps the most common complaint among teachers about report cards was the amount of time that they spent calculating grades. Teachers expressed their frustration over the added work of report cards in Paw, Michigan, in Wichita, Kansas, in Atlanta, Georgia, and in Sterling, Illinois. In Red Cloud, Nebraska, teachers voiced their concern that, during their vacations, they were "kept busy making report cards." In Chicago, teachers even resorted to paying older students to fill out their pupils' report cards.[33]

By the 1880s, the time spent creating report cards was one more example of the overworking of teachers. Evidence in newspapers suggests that parents, once the natural enemies of teachers, came to their defense in this period. In 1880, a mother called for an increase in taxes in order to pay higher wages to teachers. She cited the time that teachers spent marking papers and calculating grades at home as justification. In 1898, the *New York Times* published a story about a young teacher dying from "exhaustion." The article, reflecting the nineteenth-century trope of "the weaker sex," told the story of Mary Stoddard. She was a "beautiful girl," twenty years old, and overseeing a classroom of sixty pupils. While working late into the evenings, she was "taken with a high fever and was very nervous," dying of pneumonia a few weeks later. The late nineteenth century witnessed a shift in alliances in the world of schooling. Whereas in the antebellum period teachers and parents regarded each other with mutual mistrust, by the late nineteenth century, mothers had become vocal defenders of overworked and underpaid classroom teachers.[34]

Drawn into the life of schools by the report card, women like McKay mobilized in the 1880s and 1890s. McKay used her connections in the women's clubs of Indianapolis, harnessing the collective influence of the city's elite mothers to counter the increasing demands of schools. The women's club movement was a nationwide social phenomenon in the late nineteenth century. These "self-culture" associations were originally intended to be exclusive, social organizations that focused on cultural discussions. From the 1880s through the 1890s, the clubs turned their gaze outward, engaging with public education and defending the interests of teachers.[35]

The teacher–clubwomen alliance reflected an effort to unite women in the home and women in the classroom. From 1870 to 1900, the ratio of female teachers increased from two-thirds to three-fourths, accounting for 82.1 percent of teachers in US cities. Administrators, meanwhile, were typically men, since the authority that came with the title of principal or superintendent "held the greatest masculine appeal," as one historian noted. Throughout the 1890s, women were paid lower rates than their male counterparts for doing the same work; in 1891, for example, female high school teachers were paid $903 on average, while male teachers made $1,303. Elite clubwomen adopted the cause of the generally more working-class female teachers as their own: lobbying school boards, municipal governments, and even state legislatures for better working conditions and equal pay for female teachers. Clubwomen in Atlanta, Memphis, New York, Chicago, and New Haven all advocated for a reduction of teacher workloads, an increase in teacher pay, and improving the conditions of the mostly female teaching workforce. At the same time, the Philadelphia school board, consisting only of men, held the "dullness" of female teachers responsible for boys dropping out of school. Their solution was to cut the wages of female teachers while increasing the wages of male teachers. Philadelphia's clubwomen then mobilized, presenting to the school board a paper on how "the success for our schools has been due to the women teachers" and that the pupils of female teachers actually scored higher than the pupils of male teachers on exams.[36]

Indianapolis was another example of how a vibrant ecosystem of women's clubs led to an alliance with teachers. Martha McKay, mother of three daughters and collector of report cards, was at the center of her city's club movement and became a vocal advocate for school reform. In 1875, McKay became a founding member of the Indianapolis Woman's Club (IWC). The IWC was comprised of a progressive lot, hosting Elizabeth Cady Stanton, Susan B. Anthony, and later Jacob Riis. Beginning in 1892, McKay's club started to become increasingly assertive in the politics of the city's school board. In April 1893, clubwomen discussed teacher working conditions in schools; in January 1894, they met with municipal leaders about overcrowded classrooms; in March 1894, they created a committee to study upcoming school board elections; in April 1895, they resolved that a woman needed to be placed on the school board because women would be more empathetic to the plight of teachers; in April 1896, they resolved that women should be allowed to vote in school board elections. In 1900, clubwomen signed a petition calling for a raise in teacher salaries.[37]

In the midst of this evolution, the IWC nominated Martha McKay to serve on the Indianapolis School Board. The choice of McKay was obvious. She was the mother of three graduates of Indianapolis High School, the most recent being Helen, who had graduated the year before. Perhaps the other members of

Figure 3.5. Downtown Indianapolis, c. 1895. The Soldiers and Sailors Monument is seen in the distance. Photo used with permission of Indiana Historical Society.

the council were aware of McKay's diligence in overseeing the education of her children, her tendency to keep and value report cards, and her habit of augmenting the school day with visits to museums. McKay was also a published author and a defender of teachers. She had written that "teachers in the public schools" are "America's nobility" and she had advocated for the creation of a Teacher's Reading Circle that would promote "systematic lines of study" among teachers while spreading "Pestalozzian principles." Finally, McKay's sister was a well-respected English teacher at Indianapolis High School. This connection gave McKay insight into problems at the high school: the overcrowded facilities, the ratio of 11 teachers to every 500 students, and the fact that teachers taught six classes each day with four different "preps."[38]

From 1883 to 1893, the Indianapolis population more than doubled, from 70,000 residents to nearly 150,000. Meanwhile, the public school system struggled to adapt. When McKay's oldest daughter entered Indianapolis High, the school enrolled 539 students; by the time her youngest graduated in 1893, there were 1,263 students. Instead of constructing new schools, the school board decided to create morning and afternoon schools. Half of the students attended the high school from 8:30 a.m. to 11:45 a.m. and the other half from 1:00 p.m. to 4:15 p.m. Teachers then coached or sponsored clubs late into the evening. McKay, as a parent of students and a sibling to a teacher, must have understood these structural problems. However, in the summer of 1894, McKay was also a grieving mother. Her daughter, Daisy, had died ten months earlier at the age of twenty-three, succumbing to a long degenerative illness, diagnosed as a "heart disease."[39]

The federated clubwomen of Indianapolis were particularly frustrated with the leader of the Indianapolis School Board, John P. Frenzel. The local newspaper wrote that the school board was "under his domination," implying that Frenzel's allies were guilty of corruption. The article pointed out that Frenzel was also the president of the city's streetcar company and that the school board "does his bidding in everything in which he pleases to dictate." Another publication, the pro-suffrage *Indiana Woman*, described the Indianapolis School Board as holding "private grudges" against female employees in the school system. The newspaper praised McKay for her "gallant fight" and concluded that "we cannot allow our go-ahead women to be treated this way." McKay's club was part of a broader anti-Frenzel coalition, taking the radical step of nominating two women to serve on the school board before women could even vote. The clubwomen even campaigned for their candidates by meeting at polling places to convince male voters to cast their ballots for McKay. Ultimately, though, their efforts failed. McKay earned 574 votes to her competitor's 1,006 votes.[40]

There is little evidence that McKay continued her involvement in Indianapolis' public schools after her electoral defeat. Her interest in schooling began with her saving report cards throughout the 1880s. Her involvement blossomed in the city's clubs, where she published papers on education. It culminated with her running for the school board, which converged her suffragist idealism with her passion for defending the interests of Indianapolis' teachers.

In the early 1980s, about fifty years after Martha McKay's death, the McKay mansion fell into disrepair. The home lay vacant for decades, the windows were boarded, and the ceiling caved in. Then, in 2015, a young family purchased the building. Years of reconstruction followed, including the restoration of original McKay-era decorations like a handcrafted wooden mantel that Martha's daughters had carved as teenagers. By 2021, the new owners of the McKay home had two children, one of them enrolled in a nearby elementary school.[41]

The renovation of the McKay home was part of a broader regentrification of Indianapolis' northern neighborhoods. The policy of school choice was an important element in this gentrification process. Schools with higher test scores, after all, attract higher-income families. One of the new charter schools near the old McKay home is Center for Inquiry Seventy, a kindergarten through eighth-grade school that offers the International Baccalaureate program and promotes a reputation for rigor and "in depth inquiry." To be enrolled in this charter school, parents must sign a sixteen-point agreement in which they promise to abide by school rules, support a positive learning environment, and arrive on time. One of the bullets requires parents to attend "report card conferences." The school delivers report cards four times each year and parents are expected to "listen and discuss with [their children] the daily school activities, assignments, newsletters, weekly folder reports, and report cards."[42]

Center for Inquiry Seventy is not without controversy. Some Indianapolis parents are concerned that schools like this contribute to de facto segregation. For instance, white students comprise 60 percent of Center for Inquiry Seventy's student body but only 20 percent of the overall district population. The median household income in the neighborhood surrounding Center for Inquiry Seventy is $140,278, while in Indianapolis as a whole the median household earns $47,873 annually. This dynamic is not unique to Indianapolis, nor to the twenty-first century. High-income parents demand more

Figure 3.6. Martha McKay, 1900, as depicted by her daughter, Helen. Photo used with permission of Indiana Historical Society.

academically rigorous schools, while at the same time expressing anxiety over the strains those demands cause on their families.[43]

Martha McKay was dedicated to the education of her daughters. At the same time, she complained about the time constraints, drudgery, and burdens that overseeing that education caused. She expressed these concerns as early as the 1880s. On the one hand, McKay was bold enough to publish her critique of this dynamic and eventually ran for public office to do something about it. Yet she never questioned the foundation of the educational system that inflicted these burdens. If anything, she sought to make the educational system more efficient, more comprehensive, and even more all-consuming. The parents at Indianapolis' Center for Inquiry Seventy might recognize these qualities as quite familiar.

Martha McKay was at once a subject of nineteenth-century disciplinary power and a perpetuator of it. The report card was the means through which the process occurred, by far the most effective tool in McKay's era for gaining the participation of both elite and working-class mothers. It is a process that continues today, even in the very neighborhood where McKay raised her children.[44]

CHAPTER FOUR

The Eye of the Juvenile Court

For Andrew Monroe [pseud.] (1894–1971), report cards made the difference between incarceration and freedom. Andrew was a street kid. He grew up in a variety of Colorado towns, and the railroad tracks were his playground. He ran away from school, ran away from his mother, and tended to take things that were not his. In 1906, a judge sent him to the State Industrial School for Boys, partially on the basis of information from school report cards. By April 1910, Andrew had been institutionalized for nearly four years at the Industrial School, and report cards were again keeping him from freedom. His misbehavior at the reform school, as well as his repeated attempts at escape, were all documented on periodic report cards that were submitted to the parole board. Given the information on the report cards, Andrew would most likely have been incarcerated for another six years, or until he turned twenty-one years old. But on April 11, 1910, Andrew did what he had done three times before. He snuck out from the Industrial School, made his way to the tracks near Golden, Colorado, and hopped on a train heading east.[1]

Andrew was born in 1894, several decades after the passing of the first state compulsory schooling laws. In the 1870s, many northeastern states like Massachusetts and Connecticut began requiring children between the ages of eight and fourteen to attend school for at least twelve weeks a year. Despite the western spread of these new state laws, the efforts to compel children to attend school were largely symbolic in the 1880s. One California state legislator labeled his state's mandatory school law "tyrannical legislation." Only a handful of municipalities paid for truant officers, who were ridiculed in the press for harassing "hapless urchin[s]" under the watch of the truant officer's "terrible eye."[2]

By the time that Andrew entered grammar school in the early 1900s, however, public opinion had shifted. Fear of urban crime combined with a new progressive push among "child savers" to ban child labor led state legislators to add stronger provisions for the enforcement of truancy laws. Even rural states such as Missouri, Tennessee, and Colorado passed compulsory education laws, with fewer and fewer exemptions for agricultural work. Requirements

Figure 4.1. Truant boys, appearing before one of Colorado's juvenile courts, around the same time that Andrew Monroe [pseud.] was sentenced as a twelve-year-old, c. 1900–1910. Photo used with permission of History Colorado–Denver, Colorado.

for attendance extended from the age of fourteen to the age of sixteen. As the historian Julia Grant points out, the "nearly insurmountable" task of "corralling the boys off the streets and into schools" was a far more challenging endeavor than reformers had anticipated. The report card—written by teachers and school administrators then submitted to court officers and judges—evolved into the lynchpin of the system that did that corralling.[3]

Andrew Monroe was a native-born white, a child for whom the system of juvenile corrections was the "intended beneficiary." Society gave Andrew second chances, and most boys who submitted their reports to juvenile courts avoided incarceration. Yet Andrew refused to comply with the system as a minor, and he grew into an adult who hurt people both physically and psychologically. Andrew's life ultimately reveals a paradox of Foucauldian disciplinary power. In his resistance to the labels imposed on him by reports, Andrew inadvertently reinforced those labels. He was a delinquent, and the more he fought back, the more authorities documented his delinquency. This cycle was self-fulfilling, which led to tragic long-term consequences for boys like Andrew Monroe. "It isn't any use to try," Monroe explained when he was nineteen years old. "Once you've been in [jail], the world will find it out and remind you of it."[4]

The story of Andrew Monroe is therefore a case history in the rela
between report cards and "bad" students. Since the 1830s, parents had
primary audience of school report cards. The early 1900s witnessed an evolution in the purpose of school reports for students who, like Andrew, were
truant and lacked parental supervision. With rising fears of juvenile crime and
the industrial breakdown of family structure, judges became a new audience
of school reports. More and more children became wards of the state, and the
report card was the means through which control was exerted.[5]

Andrew Monroe was born in 1894 in Greeley, Colorado. His father was an aspiring photographer from New York and his mother was a palm reader from
Illinois. These were not typical jobs for a family living in Greeley. The town
was established in 1870 on the edge of the dry northern grasslands of Colorado and the Cache la Poudre River, all within sight of the Rocky Mountains.
Greeley was originally a utopian temperance settlement in which early
colonists paid $150 to join the Union Colony, which entitled them to about
ten acres near the town.[6]

By the time baby Andrew was born, Greeley had prospered because of the
railroad construction boom. Tracks connected the Great Plains to urban centers like Denver and beyond, to the mines and smelter towns in the Rockies.
Greeley had established itself as the potato capital of Colorado, surviving a
decades-long water-rights legal battle with nearby Fort Collins, periodic
drought, locusts, floods, and a blizzard. In October 1894, a few months after
Andrew's birth, Greeley hosted 6,000 tourists to its first annual Potato Festival. The Greeley elite were part of a broader culture of "booster-capitalism,"
in which western towns competed not only for economic advantage but also
for cultural importance. Likewise, Greeley was home to an electric light company, a bicycle club, and a 700-seat opera house. Education was also the
pride of the town. In 1890, the Colorado legislature awarded Greeley the state
normal college, which built on the town's already well-established high school.
And, as always, report cards were a ubiquitous presence, helping to "stimulate
ambition" in the town's youth. The Monroes, however, were not members of
the Greeley elite. They were part of an aspiring entrepreneurial class, whose
lack of wealth, land, and steady employment made their status precarious.[7]

The family did not last long in Greeley, in part because of the failed photography studio of Daniel Monroe, Andrew's father. The tradition of western
migrants sending home photographic portraits began in the late 1840s during
the California Gold Rush. Photography quickly became a big business, with

the United States producing over three million daguerreotypes per year in the 1850s. Technological innovations in the 1880s further reduced the costs of photography, expanding their mass appeal. "Tintyping" replaced the glass plates of the daguerreotypes with thin sheets of iron, reducing the risk that a photograph would break in the mail. Then dry plates made processing even quicker. Yet Daniel Monroe had stiff competition in Greeley. The M. E. Chase studio cornered the high-end market, charging $2.75 for a cabinet photograph. The C. M. Marsh studio was cheaper. For just a dollar, a Greeley resident could receive sixteen photos.[8]

Palmistry, the profession of Andrew's mother, seemed to be even less of a fit for the devout utopian vision of Greeley. Yet fortune telling was not entirely unusual. In the 1890s, writers such as George Bernard Shaw and Oscar Wilde promoted mystic palm reading in England. The palmist Edward Heron-Allen ignited the fad in the United States, traveling across the continent to promote palm reading as a pseudo-science. There was resistance to the fad. Mark Twain, for one, published two pieces exposing the fraudulence of palm reading. In both 1894 and 1904, he argued that palm readers based their fortunes on conversational clues, the client's manner of speech, and dress. Palm reading, in other words, was associated with con artists and with manipulation. Meanwhile, Ervilla Monroe offered readings for fifty cents. She would also attend parties and public entertainments at reduced prices.[9]

Sometime between Andrew's birth in 1894 and the census of 1900, the Monroes moved to one of the most remote regions in Colorado: Phillips County, in the northeastern corner of the state. Once again, Daniel was pursuing his dream of owning a photography studio. The Monroes settled in a town called Holyoke, a railroad stop just across the Nebraska border and part of a new homesteading effort that began in 1887. Holyoke was the hub of commercial activity for Phillips County's 5,499 residents. It included a post office, two general stores, a blacksmith shop, a creamery, and a grain elevator. Daniel Monroe's photography studio called on potential customers to "come and see my samples."[10]

The Monroes had bad timing. They moved to Holyoke in the wake of both the 1893 financial crisis and the 1894 drought that devastated the high plains. By the time the Monroes arrived, homesteaders were declaring bankruptcy and abandoning their new settlements. Survival depended on new techniques of dry farming, which called for half of a farmer's land to remain fallow for a year to conserve moisture. However, dry farming was an imperfect solution to the crises of the 1890s as it took decades to develop. The Monroes did not have decades. By June 1900, they announced in a local newspaper that they would be leaving. It was during this period of business failures and migration that young Andrew developed his first memories.[11]

Andrew was probably six years old when the Monroes rode the Colorado railway back west, through Denver and into the Rocky Mountains. Their destination was Glenwood Springs, Colorado's first resort town on the western slope. Nearly twenty years earlier, the US army forced the Ute people onto increasingly smaller reservations, which opened the western slope to land speculators, cattle ranchers, and miners. The railroads that snaked their way through the narrow canyons carried iron ore and silver to smelting plants, as well as tourists to Glenwood Springs. In 1881, a Swedish immigrant and homesteader dammed the village's natural warm spring and charged ten cents for baths. By the late 1880s, investors from Denver had constructed Hotel Colorado, a massive Villa de Medici. In 1888, a Romanesque bathhouse was constructed across the Colorado River from the heart of Glenwood Springs. By the time the Monroes arrived, there were 1,350 permanent residences, twenty-one saloons, and over fifty prostitutes. All of these factors made Glenwood Springs an attractive choice for the Monroes. There were tourists in the town with disposable income, unlike the homesteaders of Holyoke. The village held well-established schools for Andrew, whose older brother would soon be entering high school. There was also work for Ervilla. Glenwood Springs was the headquarters of the Barnes traveling circus, which employed fortune tellers. Included in the records of the circus is the name "Candy" Monroe, perhaps Andrew's mother who may have adopted Candy as a stage name.[12]

If Greeley was the site of Andrew's birth, and if Holyoke was the place that Andrew first remembered, Glenwood Springs was where Andrew spent his formative years. The town was also where the Monroe marriage dissolved. By 1902, Daniel Monroe had built a photography studio on the corner of Cooper Avenue and Ninth Street, a block away from the heart of town. At some point, Daniel may have stopped running a legitimate business, instead swindling investors of their money, and engaged in fraud. One business partner confronted Daniel at the railroad depot in July 1902. The two men threw punches. Daniel fled town, abandoning his family and his investors. He made his way to Red Cliff, Colorado, where he once again ran afoul of business partners. Sometime in 1903, Daniel ended up in Nebraska and in the process filed for divorce from Ervilla. Then, for some reason, Daniel returned to Glenwood Springs in October 1903, fifteen months after first leaving. Ervilla did not welcome him home. The estranged couple confronted one another in

Figure 4.2. Glenwood Springs, Colorado, c. 1900. Photo used with permission of History Colorado–Denver, Colorado.

front of their children and Ervilla called for the police. Daniel then spent several weeks in jail, and he was only released so that he could financially support his family. A year later, Daniel had once again abandoned the family and traveled to Yuma, Colorado, where he established a photography tent. By 1906, twelve-year-old Andrew reported that he was unaware of his father's whereabouts or even his father's profession.[13]

Judge Ben B. Lindsey created the juvenile court system before which Andrew Monroe eventually appeared. Lindsey was the judge of Arapahoe County, and his courthouse was in Denver. On a typical Saturday in the early 1900s, about 200 children and adolescents, the vast majority of them boys, would crowd into Judge Lindsey's courtroom. For an entire afternoon, each child on probation would stand and read their reports, written by their classroom teachers. These report cards were essential to Judge Lindsey's new and innovative juvenile court. The county government could not afford to hire probation officers, so Lindsey enlisted teachers to serve as his probation surveillance system. According to Lindsey, most of the teachers' reports were positive. However, a series of negative report cards from teachers, documenting a child's insolence and misbehavior, could, and often did, result in a loss of freedom for the child.[14]

In the early 1900s, the middle-class elite of industrialized urban centers like Denver struggled to manage the perceived threat of the working-class and largely immigrant labor force. In response, municipal and state governments created new institutions like juvenile courts, which were a continuation of the existing trends among middle-class "child-savers." Before the 1890s, children typically appeared in the same criminal courts as adults. But at the end of the century, judicial systems were being reformed in deference to the findings of scientific experts. In 1899, the Illinois legislature created the Cook County Juvenile Court, which claimed to be the first of its kind in the United States. Other cities followed, with the stated goal to "personalize the justice system" around the needs of the minors.[15]

In 1901, Lindsey used a loophole in Colorado's statutes to unilaterally create a juvenile court. In contrast to the Illinois precedent, Judge Lindsey emphasized informality. He refused to call a juvenile a criminal and instead he used the phrase a "juvenile disorderly person." Lindsey told one reporter, "We don't try cases. We hear the boys' stories." The Denver press praised Lindsey as a progressive hero, affectionately calling him "Little Ben" (he stood five feet four inches and weighed less than one hundred pounds). Lindsey believed that, through encouragement and empathy, disorderly juveniles could change their habits and reform themselves without the use of coercive force.[16]

Figure 4.3. Judge Ben B. Lindsey and boys in Juvenile Court, c. 1913. Library of Congress.

A bit of a paradox lay at the heart of Lindsey's court. Claiming to be informal and empathetic, Lindsey even described the process within his juvenile court as "elastic" at one point. When he published a blank sample of report cards in 1905, however, the reports were brief and lacked any space for nuance, indicating that he relied on a formulaic system of teacher reports. In one column, teachers rated the probationer's conduct with one-word answers: *good, fair,* or *poor.* In the next column, Lindsey asked teachers to report on the child's attendance. On the back of the card, teachers could choose from a series of binary characteristics: "Unruly or obedient?" and "Stubborn or yielding?" and "Untruthful or truthful?" These rigid and somewhat simplistic categories provided the evidence for determining whether a child ended up in reform school. As Lindsey wrote, the teachers' reports were "the eye of the juvenile court."[17]

Ben Lindsey was featured in progressive journals like the nationally distributed *Juvenile Record,* where he emphasized that for his system to work, "the report must be made by [the probationer's] teacher and principal . . . detailing school attendance and conduct." Articles about Lindsey appeared for wider audiences in the *New York Times* and the *Atlanta Constitution.* He traveled to locations as distant as California, Massachusetts, and Mississippi. It did not take long for other cities to adopt Lindsey's approach. In 1902, Buffalo's teachers returned report cards to probation officers. By 1905, a Kentucky court was using report cards. Then, in 1908, a judge in Los Angeles adopted the practice. In 1912, New York City was using customized school reports in order to "know the quality of mind of each offender," as one judge explained. In Cleveland, a probation officer wrote, "Much of the success of our work is due to the hearty cooperation given by principals and teachers" who "furnish intelligence" through "report cards which pass weekly between the individual teacher and the probation officer." State laws in Massachusetts (1906), Nebraska (1906), and Idaho (1907) expressly required school authorities to make reports to juvenile court judges.[18]

Often, a teacher's report helped keep a child out of reform school. In Phoenix, Arizona, a boy was arrested for fighting, yet the mother was able to show that the incident was an outlier by presenting as evidence her child's consistent "high deportment" scores on his report cards. In New Brunswick, New Jersey, a teacher intervened with her positive reports to prevent one of her pupils from being incarcerated. Yet each year, report cards also led to incarceration. Report cards in Chicago documented one child's 213 absences in just two years, described another child as "the worst boy in school," reported that one

TEACHER'S REPORT TO JUVENILE COURT.

(Delivered to Child.)

Denver, Colo.............. 190..

School ....

Name in full ....

Age .... Grade ....

Deportment ....Attendance ....

Remarks ....

.... Teacher.

PRINCIPAL'S PETITION

Recommending Action in the Interest of Habitual Truants and Delinquents.

Principal ....

Teacher ....

School ....

Date of Report ....

To be sent to the Juvenile Court.

1. Name of Child ....
2. Address ....
3. Sex: ....
4. Age: (Give date and place of birth, if known.)
   .... Years. ....Months
5. Offense: (Habitual Truancy or Incorrigible Conduct.) ....
6. Date of last Offense: ....

Truant officers will assist Principals in obtaining any information which may be lacking.

Principals will please fill out this blank in full, as the information is essential in order to handle the case successfully. State the facts briefly.

7. Name of Parent: ....
8. Occupation of Parent: ....

9. Nationality of Parent: ....

10. Creed of Parents: (In order that the same may be respected in case commitment to an institution or finding a home is ever necessary.)

Father .... Mother ....

11. Have Parents been indifferent about school attendance of child? ....

12. How often has the child been reported to Truant Officer?   LL

13. Has the child ever been arrested, or taken into court as a delinquent? ....

14. Has the child ever been an inmate of any institution? ....

15. If so, which one? ....

16. Record of attendance at school: ....

17. Grade: ....
    Deportment in school: (Good or bad.) ....

CHARACTERISTICS.

This information is for the benefit of the Court and Probation Officials, to be used in an endeavor to assist the child. Unruly or obedient? .. Stubborn or Yielding? .. Dull or bright? Lazy or energetic? .. Generous or selfish? .. Slovenly or neat? .. Ill-tempered or amiable? .. Untruthful or truthful? .. Best work is in .. Poorest work is in .. Has he ever been suspended? If so, when, and for what cause? ..

HISTORY OF CASE.

No child should be referred to the court until the Teacher and Principal have made very reasonable effort to effect a correction in school.

Remarks ....

And I therefore recommend that this child be referred to the Juvenile Court for proper action by the officials thereof.

....................., *Principal*....

Figure 4.4. A sample of the school report card used in Judge Ben B. Lindsey's court, c. 1905. Ben B. Lindsey, *The Juvenile Court Laws of the State of Colorado* (Denver, CO: Juvenile Improvement Association of Denver, 1905), 70–71.

boy took money from a teacher's purse, and alleged that another boy beat a teacher with a stick. All these children ended up in reform school. In New York, a teacher's report of "delinquency" led police officers to arrive at school "with a bench warrant."[19]

The power of the report card began to concern some progressives. *Juvenile Record* captured a court scene in Detroit where a judge scolded a probationer: "I am mad at you. . . . Your report says, 'Bad, bad, bad.'" As the child was threatened with reform school, the boy's mother burst into tears. Critics of the new system recognized that too much power rested with the discretion of teachers. One probation officer in Chicago indicated that teachers could be unfair and that they held deep prejudices toward particular children. At times, the officer would even "get the boy a transfer to another school." By the 1910s, even Lindsey recognized that teachers had abused their power. In the *Denver Weekly Post*, Lindsey warned teachers against threatening children with statements like, "I will turn you over to the police." By the late 1910s, *Juvenile Record*, which had done so much to promote the use of report cards in courts, began to see the excesses of the system. The journal published a fictional piece that dramatized an immigrant child's experiences. Confused and struggling with the English language, the child was condemned by his teacher for being a "naughty boy." With the report in hand, the judge sent the child to reform school, ignoring the tears of the child's older sister, who pleaded in a futile attempt to keep her family together.[20]

In 1903, Judge Ben B. Lindsey successfully lobbied his home state, Colorado, to legally mandate his juvenile court system. Across Colorado, judges had to adopt the same pattern of juvenile justice. First, minors below the age of sixteen would appear before the judge and, if they were found guilty, the judge would commute their sentences to the State Industrial School. Second, the juveniles would be ordered to attend their local public school during the probationary period. Finally, each probationer would be required to appear periodically before the court with written school reports. Girls were subject to both the standard practice of school reports and extra scrutiny into their sex lives. In 1909, a sixteen-year-old girl was sentenced to the State Industrial School for Girls because of her "unusual fondness for men, both married and single." Five years later in Boulder, a newspaper reported on a thirteen-year-old girl's appearance before the juvenile court that led to "a confession that involved at least fifteen boys and men."[21]

Earl Sutherland's experiences in the Montrose County Juvenile Court offered an example of how Lindsey's system was implemented beyond the confines of Denver. The court was overseen by Judge Horatio Wilson Hanes. In September 1907, Judge Hanes found Earl, a local boy growing up on the western slope, guilty of "petit larceny" and "general delinquency." Earl was "running around the street and over the country in the night . . . associating with immoral and vicious persons" all while "growing up in idleness and crime." Following Lindsey's model established in Denver, Judge Hanes suspended Earl's sentence on the condition that the boy attend school and maintain "good behavior." By April 1908, Earl was back before Hanes' court. He had misbehaved at school and then stopped attending altogether. The report cards labeled Earl a truant and Hanes reinstated the teen's sentence to the State Industrial School. The next day, the county sheriff escorted Earl by rail to Golden, the site of the reform school.[22]

In the early 1900s, the Glenwood Springs newspapers warned of a crime wave. Coal miners drank excessively, fought, and sometimes shot each other. Con artists and hucksters, loitering in the town's many saloons, swindled visitors. Bootlegging was ubiquitous and occasionally banks were robbed. In January 1906, the town council called for a squad of night police to be hired. In March 1906, a boy accidentally shot himself. One of the local newspapers also reported the problem of children "doing all sorts of mischief" along the town's railroad tracks, "crawling through box cars" and "boarding running trains." More than likely, eleven-year-old Andrew Monroe was one of these boys on the tracks.

The Monroe family members were no strangers to the legal system. When Andrew was eight years old, Ervilla Monroe appeared before the county commissioners requesting financial assistance. She was behind on rent, and she had four children who needed to be kept warm in the winter. The commissioners granted her an allowance of $15 per month to help. Later that summer, Andrew's older brother, Willard, destroyed a neighbor's garden. The sheriff was called, and Ervilla promised to keep a closer watch on her boys. A month after his brother's arrest, Andrew and two friends hopped a train and traveled twenty miles south to the town of Rifle. On the outskirts of Rifle, the three boys spent their Saturday watching a shooting competition. As they walked back over a bridge that spanned the Colorado River, the youngest of the group, Willie McKissack, fell into the rushing water. He was never seen again.[23]

Instead of running for help, Andrew convinced his surviving companion to keep Willie's drowning a secret. Andrew believed he and his companion would be blamed for the boy's death, and he maintained his silence the next day when police questioned him about Willie's disappearance. Only after Andrew's companion confessed did the truth emerge. In addition to traumatizing Andrew with guilt, the incident provided a window into the eight-year-old's mistrust of authority. Parents, teachers, and especially the police could not be trusted in the mind of young Andrew.[24]

Trouble continued for the Monroe family. In 1905, Andrew and his brother, Willard, wandered into the surrounding woods. When darkness came, the Monroe boys were unaccounted for, and a search party was mobilized. Andrew and Willard were not found until the next morning. By the spring of 1906, Ervilla Monroe was reduced to selling eggs to help pay the rent. In August 1906, Ervilla "deserted" her children, perhaps leaving them to join the Barnes circus as a fortune teller. Andrew thus began living with a foster family whose patriarch was a barber. Andrew spent his afternoons after school selling fruit at the train station and "doing odd jobs" around the shop. The barber described him as a "bright boy."[25]

Andrew may have been bright, but he also tended to run away from authority. Records mention that he ran away from school, ran away from his mother, and ran away from the barber. Sometime in September 1906, Andrew snuck away once again to the railroad tracks, where he stole a handcar. Twelve-year-old Andrew started to trek down the westward slope but was caught several miles out of town. In short, he not only disobeyed court orders by running away from school, but he also committed larceny by stealing the handcar. The county judge, following the process established by Judge Ben Lindsey, which considered school reports, reinstated Andrew's sentence to the State Industrial School for Boys.[26]

Colorado's State Industrial School for Boys was typical of the era. By 1910, when Monroe was sentenced, nearly every state had some form of government-sponsored reform school. Some attended the schools voluntarily. More typically, the minors incarcerated were guilty of "status offenses" or crimes that only applied to children. These included offenses like incorrigibility, truancy, and behaving in a manner that was "beyond control." Industrial schools employed a mix of military discipline, vocational training, and academics in their efforts to reform children. The State Industrial School of Michigan declared that military drills would teach "immediate obedience to orders" to "correct a boy's habits and make him a useful citizen." In Georgia, the industrial school paroled students once they were deemed "good citizens," both from "a humane standpoint" and "an economic standpoint." Alabama's industrial school would only parole a boy once he had acquired a trade like tailoring or woodworking, where a boy could make an "honest living."[27]

Report cards were the means through which school officials communicated to parole boards or superintendents. Since reforming institutions tended to be large, there was a desire for a standardization of the paroling process. Industrial schools therefore relied on point systems recorded by either parole officers, industrial schoolteachers, or company commanders. The juvenile's report card, in other words, became more important than ever before. At the Lyman School, one of Massachusetts' oldest industrial schools, boys would be free once they obtained 5,000 "credits." Report cards reduced the inmates to single phrases like "doing well," "doubtful," and "doing badly." When boys arrived at the State Industrial School of Nebraska, they were automatically given a number of demerits. Each day, the boy had an opportunity to cancel a few demerits with good behavior or add to his total with misbehavior. Once the total number of demerits dwindled to zero, the boy gained his freedom. In

New York, 924 boys appeared before the parole board in a single year. A juvenile obtained liberty when "the required number of reports" were submitted to the parole board without any blemishes.[28]

Even decentralized reform schools with just a few dozen inmates relied on systematic reporting. That was the case at the Virginia Home and Industrial School for Girls, located in the farming community of Bon Air. Despite there being only thirty girls at the school, the superintendent relied on periodic merit reports in her decision to release a minor. Meanwhile, the reporting system at the State Industrial School in Topeka, Kansas, was the subject of an investigation. The governor's office was concerned with the arbitrariness of the parole process and concluded that too much power lay in the hands of company commanders. They were "decent, well-intentioned" but they were also "$40 men," meaning that the meager monthly salary attracted failed farmers and day laborers, men who were "lacking in mental acuteness." These were the employees filling out the ubiquitous weekly report cards that carried so much power to dictate a child's future.[29]

Andrew was twelve years old when he arrived at Colorado's State Industrial School for Boys on October 2, 1906. He was four feet, eight inches tall and he weighed just eighty pounds. His body was riddled with an unusual number of scars: on both elbows, on his abdomen, on his right shoulder, and on his right knee. Perhaps the scars had been accumulated in years of unregulated mischief-making along Garfield County's railroad tracks, or perhaps at the hands of parental discipline. Legal records pointed out that young Andrew had already "bummed trains all over the country." The skill of train hopping would be put to practical use during his many escapes in the coming years.[30]

By the time Andrew arrived, the State Industrial School had existed for just over twenty-four years. In a typical year, about 850 boys would appear before Colorado's juvenile courts, and of those, about 150 would be sent to the State Industrial School. The average length of stay at the school was seventeen months. Andrew was one of approximately 350 boys enrolled at the time, overseen by thirty-four teachers and officers. The stated goal was to ensure that "pupils are enabled to realize the uplifting influence of discipline and rightly directed industry." The campus was nestled on sixty-four acres among the foothills of the Rocky Mountains, and Lookout Mountain rose 2,000 feet above the school. Golden's railroad depot was less than two miles away, and Denver was another fifteen miles to the east, also accessible by rail.[31]

The boys were divided into six companies, A through F, with each company consisting of between forty and seventy pupils. They wore military-style khaki uniforms and were overseen by "company commanders." Andrew was assigned to Company B, also known as "Mr. Davis' boys." Four years before Andrew's arrival, the school underwent an investigation for excessive use of corporal punishment. The investigatory committee concluded that whippings were being "administered upon too slight provocation." One boy was whipped so hard that he could not sleep on his back, and the investigation recommended that the superintendent resign for his inability to "control his fellow officers." Later, another investigation discovered that a boy was handcuffed to a basement table and fed only bread and water for four days.[32]

In a typical day, company commanders would wake the pupils up at 5:40 a.m. The morning would consist of military drills and industrial schooling. Academic work began after lunch and lasted until 4:30 p.m. Before supper, there was time for recess and sports on the parade ground, which was flanked by barracks, the dining hall, and academic classrooms. At 6:00 p.m., supper

Figure 4.5. Industrial School for Boys, Golden, Colorado, c. 1910. Photo used with permission of Denver Public Library, Western History Collection.

was served, and the evening concluded with a chapel service. Judge Ben B. Lindsey made the trip out from Denver to give a chapel talk, at which Andrew was present. Sports were part of the daily experience at the reform school. The State Industrial School for Boys had an excellent baseball team, going undefeated in 1910 and even playing semiprofessional teams. The school band offered a concert to Golden residents in the spring. Andrew, however, was not listed on the roster of any sports team during his time at the State Industrial School nor in any musical group. Families visited nearly every week, but from 1906 through the end of 1910 there was no record of any family member visiting Andrew.[33]

The main emphasis at the Industrial School was on learning discipline through manual labor. On any given day, boys hauled coal from Golden's train station, herded livestock, raked gravel from the school's parade ground, or dug sewer lines. The boys did not always comply. There were instances of "mutiny," and a number of boys received demerits because they "took part in strikes." Perhaps the most common form of resistance was running away, and there were plenty of opportunities. Boys went to Golden unescorted for doctors' appointments; they were allowed to leave to attend funerals, and the superintendent even sent one boy to "run errands" in Denver. On the other hand, there was a distinction between running away, where the boy was captured within a week, and an escape, where a boy was still unaccounted for by the end of the calendar year. From November 1908 through November 1910, only four pupils had escaped. The typical reward for a boy who had escaped was between $20 and $25. In 1910, nineteen-year-old Sidney Maxwell stole the superintendent's horse to make his getaway. He rode the horse across the Great Plains and into Kansas, before being caught nearly 450 miles away. A few years later, fifteen-year-old Fred Palario fled to Denver. When caught, Fred explained that he only wanted to "play a couple of games of pool and have a pack of cigarettes." Several years later, three boys attempted to break their friend out by driving a stolen car onto campus. One boy was shot in the leg as a result.[34]

To be paroled, boys at the State Industrial School needed to earn twelve "badges." Each badge represented a month's worth of obedience and hard work. At the end of each month, teachers and company commanders gathered to "sort demerits" for their pupils' on report cards and then submitted those report cards to the parole board. Demerits were issued for a range of behaviors: "disobedience," "destruction," "poor working," "scheming," and "theft." Boys with positive report cards would be publicly recognized on an honor roll each month. The list of names included between 20 percent and 25 percent of

Figure 4.6. Classroom at the Industrial School for Boys, Golden, Colorado, c. 1910–1915. Library of Congress.

the total student population. Each year, the student with the best grades and deportment score on his report cards received a "$10 gold piece." Andrew's name never appeared on any honor roll.[35]

More than honors, however, the scores on the report card dictated the amount of time that a pupil spent at the State Industrial School. As an example, the parole board chronicled how one pupil began as "lazy, disobedient and impudent." Six months later, the parole board wrote, "conduct - much improved," followed by "good reports" and "paroled." Almost always, the word "paroled" was only preceded by several months of "good reports." Attempting to escape, on the other hand, not only prevented a boy from gaining a new badge but also resulted in the parole board removing badges and extending the incarceration time by months. Inmate card file number 2279 documents Andrew Monroe's repeated attempts to flee the State Industrial School, reporting his efforts to the parole board. This report card, in essence, added years to Andrew's incarceration.[36]

Andrew first ran away with another boy on October 22, 1907, just over a year into his sentence. He used an exit from the school's hospital ward to flee, although he was quickly caught. Andrew's second attempt came in November 1908. This time he was more successful, making his way to Laramie, Wyoming, over 130 miles to the north. In the process of escaping, Andrew suffered a severe case of frostbite. Winter temperatures in Laramie average between 13 degrees and 32 degrees Fahrenheit, occasionally dipping as low as −4 degrees. Presumably, as the fourteen-year-old Andrew struggled to find shelter in Wyoming, the tissues on his fingers and toes began to freeze. Within forty-eight hours, the ice particles in Andrew's extremities would have caused blistering, swelling, and throbbing pains that probably lasted for weeks. Eventually, the tissue died, turned black, shriveled, and hardened. The result was the amputation of Andrew's pinkie finger, two toes on his right foot, and a toe on his left foot.[37]

Andrew hid in Wyoming a few winter months before being caught. The authorities returned him to the State Industrial School, presumably hobbled by a limp and limited in the amount of labor he could perform with his missing finger and toes. Andrew did not repeat the mistake of escaping in the winter. In May 1909, six months after his reincarceration, Andrew escaped once again while "doing field work." This time, he traveled south, presumably by rail, making it to the New Mexico border before being caught and returned in August 1909. By April 1910 Andrew had probably given up on being paroled through legitimate means. His history of escape and his lack of academic success were all documented on his monthly report cards. Then, on April 11, 1910, Andrew slipped away from the State Industrial School for the final time and hopped on a train bound for St. Louis.[38]

In November 1912, Andrew Monroe was eighteen years old. By then, he had made his way to Des Moines, Iowa, and found work in a tannery that specialized in manufacturing gloves. His salary rose from $6 to $17 a week, and the owners of the factory regarded him as "one of the best factory employees." He was even furthering his education at night school. While in Des Moines, Monroe married the daughter of a businessman, and in early November his wife gave birth to their son.[39]

Then, somehow, authorities at the State Industrial School in Golden discovered his whereabouts. Local business leaders, led by Monroe's employer, mobilized a letter-writing campaign to lobby for his pardon. The press labeled Andrew a real-life "Jean Valjean," comparing him to the self-reforming character in Victor Hugo's well-known novel *Les Misérables*. As a result, the superintendent of the Industrial School and the governor conceded to the public and granted Monroe a full pardon. The superintendent even paid for Monroe's train ticket back to Denver, shaking hands with Andrew in person and telling his former pupil that he was proud of him. Andrew was welcomed back by his mother and younger sister as well. Presumably, he had not seen them for several years. The story seemed to be ending happily.[40]

The positive news did not last long. Rachel, Monroe's wife, discovered his criminal past through newspaper reports and their relationship changed to one increasingly characterized by mistrust. Monroe began to "stay out late at nights and grew abusive." In June 1913, just seven months after receiving his pardon, Monroe assaulted Rachel. Their argument began when Monroe accused his young wife of "neglect of their eight months old child." He admitted to choking her in a fit of anger, and Rachel responded by pressing charges of battery.[41]

By 1915, Monroe had moved back to Denver. He filed a lawsuit against the State Industrial School for Boys, claiming that he was unjustifiably whipped while incarcerated there. He claimed $10,000 in damages. Then, in 1916, Monroe and another man were arrested for stealing a car in Denver and driving it across Colorado and most of Nebraska. They were caught in Lincoln, where Monroe eventually pleaded guilty and was sentenced to one to seven years of hard labor. Monroe's 1917 draft card mentions that he was a "laborer" for the state of Nebraska, incarcerated in the town of Lancaster. The draft card also mentions Monroe's missing finger. Eventually released, Monroe found himself quickly re-arrested, this time back in Des Moines for "receiving and concealing stolen property."[42]

Monroe's name did not appear in the papers after his arrest in 1918. Then, in 1939, the superintendent of the State Industrial School for Boys in Golden received a letter. It was from a woman living in Denver, requesting information about someone she suspected was incarcerated at the school decades before, someone named Sterling Ross Monroe. The secretary for the superintendent made the connection that Sterling Ross Monroe was the alias for Andrew Monroe. The woman writing the letter claimed to be his wife, who he had recently abandoned with their two young children. She had discovered that Monroe "had babies all over the country." She explained that she fell in love with Monroe because "he was polite, well-mannered, handsome" but that she only recently discovered that "he had no heart or principle."[43]

After abandoning his second wife, Monroe made his way to Texas, where he began living with his older brother, Willard. He maintained his alias, Sterling Ross, on his 1942 draft card. By that point he was working in Port Arthur on the Gulf Coast, loading and unloading freight on the docks for the Lummis Company. In 1965, at the age of seventy-one, Monroe retired and moved back to his place of birth: Greeley, Colorado. It is not clear why he chose his birthplace to spend the final years of his life. His home was a modest two-room apartment that is still standing, although it is now abandoned. The apartment rests just a few blocks away from Greeley's Lincoln Park, home to the Potato Festival that was held just two months after Monroe's birth. Monroe died in January 1971, at the age of seventy-seven. The Greeley newspaper's obituary of Monroe only mentioned that he was a member of the Weld County Rock and Mineral Society as well as the Colorado Mining Association.[44]

No family members attended Monroe's funeral in January 1971. Monroe's internment card states that he was a "welfare case," meaning the Weld County government paid for the burial lot at Greeley's Sunset Memorial Garden. There was no money for a tombstone, although the location is still documented. When he died, Monroe's gravesite was surrounded by open farmland, within view of the Rocky Mountains. Today, the view from Monroe's grave is blocked by a Home Depot and Best Buy. The farmland has been replaced by a busy six-lane highway, with cars rushing home to beat the traffic.[45]

Something is similar about Andrew Monroe and Alex DeLarge, the protagonist of Stanley Kubrick's dystopian film, *A Clockwork Orange* (1971). Granted, the comparison is not entirely fair. In the first forty-five minutes of *A Clockwork Orange*, Alex and his gang beat a homeless man to near death, sexually assault a woman, and then murder another person. A judge incarcerated Andrew for merely skipping school and stealing a handcart.[46]

However, the final two-thirds of *A Clockwork Orange* seem to parallel Andrew's life. In the film, the authorities imprison Alex with military precision, documenting everything. Kubrick, with off-beat comedic timing, dedicates two minutes and thirty-three seconds of screen time to the process in which the jailkeeper transfers "prisoner 655-321" to the medical clinic, making the viewer sit through each step of the paperwork. The film made the ubiquitous paperwork in each scene more than just sinister. It was comedically absurd.[47]

Around the same time that Kubrick filmed *A Clockwork Orange*, the State Industrial School for Boys changed its name to the Lookout Mountain Youth Services Center. There are no surviving buildings from Andrew's era on the current campus. The oldest structure still standing at the youth center was built fourteen years after Andrew left. The campus has also been reduced to

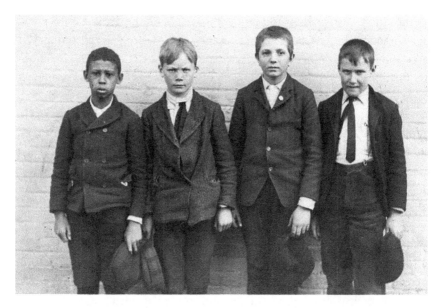

Figure 4.7. Truant boys, c. 1900–1910. Photo used with permission of History Colorado–Denver, Colorado.

twenty-two acres, a third of its original size. It is surrounded by a twenty-foot fence that did not exist in 1910. Perhaps the only recognizable feature on the campus is the parade ground. As it did in 1910, the field serves as a courtyard, flanked by barracks, classrooms, and offices. This parade ground was a central gathering place in the early 1900s, where boys received military training but also where they took breaks for ninety minutes each day before dinner. It was where they played baseball and football, and it might have been where Andrew schemed to escape. Today, boys rarely use the field. Lookout Mountain canceled baseball games out of concern that the bats might be used as weapons.[48]

Since the 1970s, the Lookout Mountain Youth Services Center has become less of a vocational school and more of a prison. *Colorado Sun* labeled Lookout Mountain "Colorado's most troubled youth corrections center." In May 2019, a riot erupted, injuring eleven staff members and sending two to the hospital. From April to June of that year, four minors escaped using bedsheets to climb down windows and over the twenty-foot fence. All of the escapees were "considered violent offenders." In the spring of 2021, another inmate attempted to escape with the help of a friend outside the fence who fired a .380 handgun at the facility's guards. Meanwhile, a crime wave in the early 2020s caused a 141 percent increase in the number of boys imprisoned in the state for murder and manslaughter.[49]

In the end, nothing about the Lookout Mountain Youth Services Center is humorous, Kubrick's brand of dark satirical humor or otherwise. Compared to the very real tragedy of each of Lookout Mountain's teenage inmates, Kubrick's depiction of Alex DeLarge does indeed seem romanticized. Likewise, one should not glamorize Andrew's resistance to all forms of control, surveillance, and documentation. Andrew was probably traumatized as a child by the abandonment of both his parents. His trauma led him to hurt people as he abused and left his own family. He died alone and in poverty. And the tragedy of Andrew Monroe's life continues to be played out in the lives of adolescents each day at Lookout Mountain, and to increasingly violent consequences. It is all tragedy, and no degree of surveillance and documentation seems to stop it.[50]

CHAPTER FIVE

Mobility, Anxiety, and Merit

Daniel Schorr (1916–2010) was the son of Russian-Jewish immigrants. In 1922, when Daniel was five years old and growing up in the East Bronx, his father died of a kidney infection. His father's dying wish was for his two sons, Daniel and his younger brother, to attend college. For a family without money in the 1920s and 1930s, going to college meant winning a rare scholarship. Competition for financial aid was fierce, and colleges increasingly examined high school grades when discerning between applicants. As the school report card approached its hundredth birthday, it became even more important for students like Daniel, as it foretold whether they would enjoy a stable middle-class career or a life of financial instability and physical labor. Increasingly, the report card determined a student's destiny.[1]

Across the United States, children expressed anxiety about report cards in the 1920s and 1930s. The diaries of teenagers describe receiving report cards with anticipation, a periodic ritual that was ingrained into the education system. In letters to family and friends, students listed their grades and compared themselves with classmates. They hated report cards, and they were obsessed with them at the same time. Meanwhile, student newspapers and yearbooks used humor to cope with the stress of having one's future dictated by slips of paper. The report card, the teachers who issued them, and the parents who received them all became the butt of jokes in student publications. Students made fun of the arbitrary nature of grades, the absurdity of their own anxiety about these grades, and the sadistic cruelty of the teachers who issued them. They also made fun of each other. Students cracked jokes about classmates who seemed to care too much about the marks on a report card as well as the students who cared too little, revealing the neurosis caused by the constant surveilling, recording, and ranking of adolescents.

Daniel Schorr was a product of this contradictory climate surrounding grades. He was a good student, and his academic success did indeed secure him a place at the tuitionless City College of New York, which opened opportunities that ultimately led to Schorr becoming one of the nation's leading TV journalists. Yet young Daniel was also an outsider. He described his childhood as one of being "poor, fat, Jewish, and fatherless." He preferred the role of observer to that of student leader or activist. As such, he saw the report card for what it was: a sometimes-cruel attempt at control that also carried the power to make or break a child's future. By both excelling within the system of report cards and criticizing them, Schorr reflected the cognitive dissonance that observant students still live with today.[2]

Daniel's parents were Tillie and Gedaliah Tchornemoretz. The Tchorne-moretzes came from a village called Telechan (sometimes spelled Telekhan) in what is now Belarus. The village included between 300 and 350 Jewish families; the nearest large shtetl (or Jewish town) was Pinsk and lay fifty kilometers to the south. Telechan was surrounded by swampland and forests, which was one source of employment for Jewish laborers. "Forrest merchants" hired Yiddish-speaking Jews as *plotniks* to harvest and haul lumber to the Oginski Canal, which connected the Black Sea to the Baltic Sea. In 1895, when Daniel's parents were still children, a glass factory opened in Telechan and employed several hundred Jewish workers. The workers labored between twelve and fifteen hours a day, yet some still could not afford necessities like shoes. The early lives of Daniel's parents involved subsisting on kasha and barley soup, enduring the long hours at the factory, and fighting back against the "oppression of the landlords."[3]

Daniel's parents also lived in fear of violence in the form of pogroms. The first wave of pogroms erupted in 1881 after the assassination of Tsar Alexander II. Shtetls across the Pale of Settlement, which was the large swath of land within the Russian empire on which Jews were allowed to reside, were targeted for attack. One eyewitness described how ordinary gentiles who lived among Jews suddenly turned into their murderers. "Clerks, saloon and hotel waiters, artisans, drivers, flunkeys, and day laborers" formed "raging mob[s]" that "demolished houses and stores of the Jews," all while the police stood by or even took part. Gentile peasants would typically arrive from the countryside later in the evening, sparking another round of destruction. Daniel's parents would have witnessed the wave of pogroms that lasted between 1904 and 1906. In total, 650 Jewish communities were attacked in less than three years, resulting in about 3,000 murders. Meanwhile, Tsar Nicholas II publicly blamed the Jews for the violence.[4]

Daniel's parents were part of a new, young generation of Russian Jews, who were increasingly secular and open to revolutionary ideas. To defend against pogroms, Jewish factory workers formed Bunds, or political clubs affiliated with Marxist ideology. A Bund was active in nearby Pinsk as well as in the much smaller Telechan. Labor disputes between Telechan's Bund and the owners of the glass factory culminated with a Cossack attack on the village's Jews. Parents, torn between the need to defend their families and the need to stem the cycles of violence that were spinning out of control, felt helpless as they watched their children "swept up in revolutionary movements." The timing of Tillie and Gedaliah's emigration was fortuitous. Just three months after their arrival in New York, the Great War erupted, which ultimately led to new waves of violence in Telechan, this time at the hands of the German army.[5]

It is likely that Daniel's father, Gedaliah, attended one of Telechan's four traditional religious elementary schools, known as heders. These schools, which were sometimes transliterated as "cheder," typically had a single male teacher who conducted lessons in his home. The teacher emphasized memorization of sacred texts. Instead of testing children at the school, parents would ask their children to recite their weekly lessons at the Shabbat on Friday evening. In other words, there were neither test scores to record nor any need to send home report cards. Chaim Weizmann, future president of Israel, remembered beginning his education at a heder at the age of four. He wrote about the "squalid, one-room school" in which a goat would take shelter with the children during cold weather. His teacher was known throughout the shtetl for his "pedagogical incompetence." The inspector of another heder was appalled by the conditions: twenty boys were crammed into a small room, leaving them "shattered physically and spiritually."[6]

Even though many Jewish intellectuals at the turn of the century looked down on heders as backward, most Jewish communities mistrusted the educational alternative: state-sponsored Russian schools. By 1900, heders enrolled 370,000 students while only 60,000 Jewish students attended Russian schools. Ultimately, heders served several purposes for Jewish families living in villages like Telechan. First, they prevented the "cultural slippage" that resulted from the pressures of Russian nationalism, industrialization, and Marxist radicalism. Second, they served as a form of day care for boys, at least until the age of thirteen, allowing parents to find work. Finally, heders succeeded in creating relatively high literacy rates among Jewish males, much higher than the general Russian population. This was essential. In the absence of land ownership, scholarship and learnedness became a source of prestige, in what the historian Saul Stampfer has called a "knowledge-based status system."[7]

The twenty-four-year-old Gedaliah may have decided to flee Telechan with his young wife to avoid conscription into the Tsar's army. If so, his situation would have been typical, albeit dangerous. The Tchornemoretzes would have had to cross the German border illegally, make their way to Berlin, en route to the port of Hamburg. From there, Tillie and Gedaliah most likely would have boarded a ship to London, crossed England by rail, and then boarded a second and final ship in Liverpool for the passage across the Atlantic. Along the way, Tillie and Gedaliah might have read Yiddish leaflets, which were printed by profiteering steamship companies, promising freedom and riches in the United States. The couple was taking part in an historic exodus. Between 1881 and 1914, one-fifth of Russia's Jewish population fled the empire, with 80 percent settling in the United States. In 1880, about 80,000 Jews lived in New York City. By the time that the Tchornemoretzes arrived, the number had increased to 1.4 million. The year that they traveled, 1914, was also the peak year for the migration. In the nine months before the outbreak of war in September 1914, 138,000 Jewish immigrants arrived in the United States.[8]

At some point in the journey to the United States, the Tchornemoretzes changed their last name to Schorr, which made Daniel's later career in television more tenable. Jewish associations established aid societies that went to Ellis Island to help translate Yiddish, and they also helped find housing and jobs for Jewish immigrants like the Schorrs. As one historian wrote, the first task of the migrant was to "hunt for signs of Jewishness" in storefront windows, butcher shops, and bakeries. This hunt would have led the Schorrs to the Lower East Side of Manhattan, where over 300,000 Jewish immigrants crammed into an area of just two square miles. In the 1880s, German-American Jews had already established themselves in the garment industry centered in the Lower East Side, and they were quick to employ their coreligionists in the subsequent decades to work in factories. Housing for the new arrivals usually consisted of cramming four or five people into a single-room tenement.[9]

Gedaliah had no stated artisanal skills when he arrived. He worked as a waiter but later tried to become a real estate agent, although it is not clear that he had any success. Daniel's mother, Tillie, worked in the garment industry. By the time of Daniel's first memories, the family was no longer living in the Lower East Side, which by the 1920s included just 25 percent of New York's Jewish population. In fact, 200,000 Jewish families like the Schorrs left the Lower East Side between 1916, the year of Daniel's birth, and 1925. One motive for the exodus was the overcrowding of schools. In the early 1900s, the city had to turn away between 50,000 and 60,000 Jewish children who were trying to enroll in public schools. Sixty children would crowd into a single classroom, sitting three to each chair. The Schorrs, however, seemed to have instinctively understood what so many other Russian-Jewish families realized: education was the means through which their children were to advance in the United States. When Gedaliah Schorr died in 1922, at the age of thirty-two, he was prescient in his understanding of the increasing importance of college. Gedaliah's dying wish was that his sons earn college degrees. In making that wish, Gedaliah was part of a national trend.[10]

Educational historians such as Roger L. Geiger, Charles Dorn, and Ezekiel Kimball have observed that by 1900 working-class Americans viewed college as a way to "buttress their social position" and that the "culture of aspiration" in the early twentieth century created new demands for college degrees.[11] The historian David F. Labaree wrote that, during the first three decades of the twentieth century, "working class consumers increasingly turned attention toward college as the new zone of educational advantage." Statistics that track the increasing demand for high school and college degrees support these general assertions. High school enrollment doubled every decade between 1890 and 1940, from 11 percent of teenagers enrolled in high school in 1870 to 71 percent in 1940. With each year of increasing numbers of high school graduates, colleges increased their enrollments as well. In 1870, just 1.7 percent of the US population between the ages of eighteen and twenty-one were attending college. By 1930, the number had risen to 12 percent.[12]

Gedaliah Schorr died at the beginning of a new "selective admissions" era for colleges. At the turn of the century, just as working- and middle-class Americans recognized college as a means for social mobility, administrators liberalized subject requirements for entrance. In particular, the requirement to learn Greek was a major barrier for most working-class students in the nineteenth century. In the 1890s, a group of college professors and administrators, known as the Committee of Ten, along with the National Education Association, helped standardize high school curricula by loosening college requirements to bring them more in line with secondary school course offerings. The result was an influx of demand for college spots that forced deans to become more selective in their admissions. Writing in 1925, just three years after the death of Gedaliah Schorr, one analyst of the changing dynamics of US colleges stated, "Hitherto, speaking generally, any high school graduate could easily enter college . . . formerly, the colleges competed for the students; now, students compete for the colleges."[13]

High school grades became a deciding factor in who was admitted. Prior to 1910, passing a high school course was all that really mattered, not the individual scores or rank that might be displayed on a report card. In 1913, the federal government recommended that college admissions examine "relative rank in the high school class" as a means of discerning between applicants. At the same time, Harvard and Yale adopted an admissions system that examined not just completion of high school courses but grades within those courses. In 1918, Columbia followed suit. This was also the era that gave birth to the use of nationwide standardized tests in college admissions, as described by many scholars of educational history. The standardized test movement grew out of the work of French psychologist Alfred Binet, who inspired his American counterparts to design the IQ test for the US Army during the First World War. Like the IQ test, a group of Harvard and Princeton administrators sought to design a test that could evaluate natural intellectual talent, not just knowledge. Thus was born the Scholastic Aptitude Test, or SAT, which was first administered in 1926 to mostly Ivy League scholarship applicants.[14]

Yet journalists and academics at the time recognized that even more emphasis was placed on high school grades, not SAT scores. In 1931, one writer warned his readers that "admission on the basis of high school certificates . . . predominates in America at the time." He came to that conclusion after surveying the admissions policies of 287 colleges, with 40 percent requiring that applicants submit their class rank. In 1933, the year that Daniel Schorr graduated from high school, the Associated Press found that out of the 517 colleges they surveyed, 63 percent placed high school grades as the most important prerequisite for admittance.[15]

Students took notice of these tidal shifts in college admissions. Across the nation, the greater emphasis on college degrees as a means of social mobility, combined with the importance of high school grades in securing a spot in those colleges, caused noticeable anxieties. A high school teacher in New Jersey wrote that "an increased emphasis upon the general school record" for high schoolers applying to college had changed the atmosphere of learning in secondary schools. Teachers, the author explained, were "too much concerned with the aim of preparing pupils to meet college entrance requirements." Students from locations as far away as North Dakota, Utah, and Texas wrote publicly about their anxiety over grades on report cards. They wished, as one Florida adolescent wrote, their "folks could sign [report cards] with their eyes shut." In Cleveland, a senior stated that her one memory from high school would always be her "nervousness the day before report cards came out."[16]

In the privacy of their diaries, teenagers marked the periodic release of report cards with both obsession and stress. Near Oakland, California, one teenage girl's diary chronicled her social life, describing a variety of boys who were "despicable creatures" and others who were "awfully cute." She did not mention her classroom experiences at all, except when teachers issued report cards. Each semester she dutifully listed grades, writing that with one report card she "thought [she] was going to cry." Two thousand miles away in Illinois, another teenage girl used her diary to track her daily activities in the Glee Club, her study of Cicero, and her attendance at the local theater. It was only when her report card was issued that her attention turned toward her goal of someday attending college. In Arkansas, one boy's diary focused on his attempt to "convince Anne to break her date" and his favorite radio shows. His only reference to school came at the end of the year when he listed the grades on his report card, admitting that he could have tried harder in the two classes in which he earned Cs. One girl, attending high school in Washington, DC, wrote about her aspirations to become a professional writer. That meant attending college, and the grades on her report cards were "good ones," although she took issue with one teacher who gave her a "G," and she promised herself to work hard to achieve all "Es" next time.[17]

The emphasis on, and often stress over, report cards can be found in nearly every type of primary source that documented the life of high school students. In segregated Black schools in Nashville and Washington, DC, reports were a source of "dread" and caused "weeping and moaning and gnashing of teeth." In segregated white schools in Port Arthur, Texas, and Greensboro, North Carolina, students wrote that receiving report cards was the worst part of attending high school. A working-class kid in Los Angeles, attending the Manuel Arts High School, kept all of his monthly report cards, despite mediocre grades and few prospects for attending college. The daughter of a Tennessee insurance salesman documented the two main sources of her anxiety: her weight and her report cards. In Bloomington, Illinois, one high schooler made it clear in her letters to a friend that she had no intention of attending college. She nearly failed the tenth grade. However, each semester she wrote to her former classmate to compare report cards, saying to her more studious friend, "I wish I had your grades." City kids in New York and Connecticut documented the periodic tensions that emerged with report card distribution. Farm kids in Chickasaw, Oklahoma, in Dublin, Georgia, and in Peshatin, Washington, were as equally tense as their urban counterparts.[18]

The fact that young Daniel grew up in poverty in the East Bronx made his ultimate success even more remarkable. By the mid-1920s, when the Schorr family moved to the Bronx, 585,000 Jews lived in the borough, accounting for half of the population. The wealthier Jews, typically of German descent, resided in the West Bronx along Grand Concourse. Working-class Jewish families, typically of Eastern European descent, lived in the East Bronx along Fox Street. In an interview later in his life, Schorr emphasized that his community was "poor but respectable," reinforcing the notion of another East Bronx resident who wrote that the community gave Jews a "sense of security." The East Bronx also had a reputation for political radicalism and, indeed, Schorr remembered that many of his friends "called themselves communists," with Stalinists and Trotskyites debating one another in their free time. Schorr added, "I never became part of the movement, I just reported on them. I was always detached." Schorr probably witnessed political radicalism beyond esoteric debates. In December 1930, when Schorr was fourteen, the Great Depression led to the collapse of a predominantly Jewish bank called the Bank of the United States. Four hundred thousand Jewish depositors, many of them from the Bronx, lost their life savings. In the subsequent years, East Bronx residents were routinely evicted from their apartments, leading to protests and sometimes street violence. Schorr later wrote that, "Poverty can be a great spur, at least it was for me."[19]

During this period, Daniel's mother worked as a seamstress in the garment industry, riding New York City's rails six days a week to factories in Manhattan. Schorr, meanwhile, helped the family by selling *Bronx Home News* on the street. By the early 1930s, just as Schorr entered high school, 232,000 New Yorkers had lost their jobs and one million received subsidized relief from the state. This number included the Schorr family, who were part of the 12 percent of the Jewish population in the city on public assistance, which amounted to $25 per month for the Schorrs. At one point, a social worker investigated Tillie Schorr for neglecting her sons while she was away at work. Daniel, his mother, and his younger brother all lived in their apartment at various times with three uncles and an aunt. Daniel's maternal grandmother also arrived from Russia, and Daniel remembered that she tended to leave her dentures in the bathroom.[20]

The family was too poor to pay for a reception after Daniel's bar mitzvah, and a grammar schoolteacher, noticing the shabby clothes that the Schorr brothers wore, "gently inquired" about their circumstances and bought Daniel's younger brother a new pair of trousers. At one point, Daniel started to engage in a minor crime to earn money. His offense was to illegally sell sunglasses at the Botanical Gardens, which landed him in jail. Years later, Schorr

Figure 5.1. The staff of the *Clintonian* yearbook at DeWitt Clinton High School. Daniel Schorr, seated in the first row and third from right, was editor of the yearbook. A special thanks to Gerard Pelisson for locating and scanning this photograph in the DeWitt Clinton High School archives.

still remembered his mother crying when he appeared before a judge, who let him go with a warning. For the Schorr family, the 1920s and the 1930s were characterized by "more fear than hope," as one historian of the Bronx wrote about the Jewish American experience during the Great Depression.[21]

Daniel had a complicated relationship with his Jewish identity. He loathed the fact that his family spoke Yiddish at home, calling it a "ghetto jargon." Yiddish was associated with poverty, and public school teachers denigrated the language in favor of English. Schorr admitted as an adult that he "resented his mother's accent" and that he deliberately avoided bringing his friends to his apartment out of embarrassment, while also envying friends whose parents were born in the United States. Daniel quarreled with his uncles, who accused him of abandoning his Jewish roots in favor of American consumerism. However, Daniel was rarely exposed to the outside world of gentiles, with the exception of public school. He did not remember having any non-Jewish friends. His mother also maintained the mistrust born from experiencing Russian pogroms. She would tell Daniel, "Every time I see a cross, I see the blood of many Jews."[22]

Schorr's mother probably viewed public schools as a threat to her sons' identities, part of a process in which her culture might be lost to the next generation. Indeed, the superintendent of New York City's public schools explicitly stated that the goal of schooling was "Americanization," an effort that he hoped would lead to "absolute forgetfulness of all obligations or connections with other countries." Yet Tillie made great personal sacrifices to ensure that her sons attended public school. During Daniel's early years, teachers sent home reports stating that he routinely talked out of turn and requested that

Figure 5.2. Scene from Bathgate Avenue, East Bronx, New York, near the Schorr apartment, 1936. Photo used with permission of New York Public Library.

Tillie attend meetings at school. Each meeting cost the Schorr family a half day of wages.[23]

As Daniel progressed through the education system, New York's public schools adjusted to the wave of second-generation Jewish Americans. In 1920, 26 percent of public school teachers were Jewish. By 1930, that number had risen to 44 percent, and by 1940, 56 percent of teachers were Jewish. Jewish teachers organized themselves with groups like the Bronx Jewish Teacher Committee and, eventually, Daniel's high school offered Hebrew as an accredited course. By the time Daniel graduated from high school, 80 percent of the students in the Bronx were Jewish.[24]

Historians and sociologists of Judaism have noted the remarkable academic success of Jewish families in the early twentieth century. Some ascribe that success to the "scholastic theory," which argues that text-centered Talmudic studies in Eastern Europe laid the foundation for academic thriving in the United States. For centuries, Eastern European Jews had viewed "learning as the best trade, providing status and financial security," as one historian explained. Other historians counter the scholastic theory with the fact that economic success typically facilitated academic success. Daniel Schorr was therefore an exception. Growing up in poverty, his goal from the age of five was to use education as a means of social mobility. Daniel and/or his mother saved each certificate of academic accomplishment, from grammar school through high school. Included in these papers was also Daniel's selection to the honor society, Arista, which represented years of accumulated success on Daniel's monthly report cards.[25]

Perhaps some of Tillie's anxiety about the Americanization of her sons was alleviated by Daniel's commitment to Hebrew school. Each afternoon, after public school, Daniel would journey to the Bronx Jewish Center to learn Hebrew and study Jewish history. Years later, Schorr was quick to emphasize the secular nature of Hebrew school. From an early age, Daniel was "skeptical about miracles." Despite his disdain for Yiddish and his religious skepticism, Daniel revered Hebrew as representative of an ancient culture. At one point the Jewish Education Association rewarded Daniel with a gold watch for his commitment to studying Hebrew. When Daniel was ten years old, his Hebrew school invited him to leave New York City for the first time and travel to Philadelphia. The students visited Independence Hall for the 150th anniversary of the Declaration of Independence, thus synthesizing Daniel's two identities. All this pleased Daniel's mother. She saved Daniel's monthly report

Figure 5.3. One of Daniel Schorr's report cards from Hebrew school. Daniel's mother received these report cards each month to track his "conduct and work." Library of Congress.

cards from Hebrew school, which tracked her oldest son's "excellence in conduct and work."[26]

Both memoirs of Jewish students and Yiddish newspapers from the era document the high stakes for academic success among children like Daniel. Irving Howe, a socialist writer, attended the same high school as Daniel. In his history of Jewish Americans, he described the criticism that Jewish parents "push[ed]" their children too much. One critic from the time wrote, "Why sacrifice them [the children] at the altar of ambition? Doctors will tell you about students with shattered nerves, brain fever." Bella Abzug, who later became a congresswoman, also grew up in the Bronx and remembered her mother stating, in no uncertain terms, that if she wanted to attend college, her grades needed to be strong enough to win a scholarship. In 1922, the same year that Gedaliah Schorr died, the Yiddish paper in New York, *Forward*, admonished immigrant parents for beating their children over their performance at school. Three years later, in 1925, the same paper once again criticized immigrant mothers for being too obsessed with marks on report cards. The paper wrote, "Many of them [immigrant mothers]—possibly most of them—insist that the children do well in school, see that the report cards are regularly brought home for proper inspection, and scold [their children] if the marks are not satisfactory."[27]

To some Jewish parents, report cards became a symbol of their quest for a better life for their children through education. One mother wrote, "My happiest moment was when my son, five-and-a-half years old, brought his first report card home with all 85–95. I was sure that my little son was going to become a great doctor or lawyer someday." In another story, a family did not really know that their truant son had reformed himself until he returned from school with "good report cards each month." The report card was a barometer for the moral well-being of the entire family. Another boy destroyed his report cards, not because of low scores, but because he was ashamed that his immigrant parents could not read or write, and therefore were unable to sign each monthly report. The incident motivated the boy's mother to attend night school and overcome her illiteracy, all so that she could read her son's reports. Another Jewish student described in a newspaper article, Rosie, cried in shame when she received a C on her report card. The moral of the story was that Rosie channeled her shame into action. The article concluded, "When Rosie opened her eyes the next morning, she felt quite happy again. She was silly to worry about that old report card because she could change it."[28]

Forward recognized the unhealthy focus on report cards and satirized the cultural phenomenon. The newspaper, half of which was written in English and the other half in Yiddish, had a readership of 300,000, mostly in New York City. In 1925, the newspaper declared that report cards were "the meanest invention" because of the wrath they brought down upon Jewish children. In another parody, a father berated his son for low scores on a report card, declaring, "you should be ashamed of yourself." The boy replied, "Aw gee whiz, dad, it ain't my fault. I don't make out the cards." In 1927, the report card was a subject of a cartoon in *Forward*. A working-class father, holding the school report, asks his wife, "Did you ever see such a terrible report card?" The wife responded by asking her husband how many A's he received in his Ukrainian *cheder*.[29]

Daniel Schorr grew up in this report card culture, in which the scores on the reports became a measurement for the relative success of the family's decision to leave Eastern Europe. And Daniel appears to have embraced report

EAST - SIDELIGHTS

Mr. Schmuelson: Did you ever see such a terrible report card? Not a single "A"!
Mrs. Schmuelson: *Nu, nu* it's not so terrible. Between you and me, how many "A's" did you get in *cheder* in Berditchev ?

Figure 5.4. Cartoon, "East-Sidelights," from *Forward*, 1927. *Forward* (New York, NY), January 16, 1927, 4.

card culture with drive and intensity. While in high school, Daniel wrote an essay in which he adapted the biblical story of the prodigal son. Daniel's version was set in the Bronx, with a Jewish American family gathered for the Friday Shabbat. The oldest son returned unexpectedly, after years of spending time in the "pool-room" with "evil comrades." The son, Paul, then refocused his energies on school, and for "two years, he strove and studied, gaining the highest marks." Daniel added that the fictional Paul "worked and labored until finally, he graduated summa cum laude." This essay was one of the few pieces of adolescent writing that Schorr saved until his death, and it captures Daniel's self-conception. Fatherless, poor, and Jewish, Daniel knew that he had to compete to survive. In 1978, an interviewer asked Schorr how he became such a tough journalist. Schorr explained that where he came from, "nothing is ever handed to you," that "everything you get, you have to work twice as hard as anybody else." He added, "growing up on the fringe, a person doesn't make it on manners, wealth, easy club membership, or anything like that." He was "always the outsider, always the Jewish immigrant's son."[30]

Despite the new emphasis in the 1920s and 1930s on high school grades for college admissions, students who came from families with money and connections did not need to concern themselves with low marks. Philip Hardy was literally the worst student at his preparatory boarding school in Pennsylvania, the Hill School. The letters home between Philip and his father chronicle Philip's struggle to pass nearly every class, his forty-five demerits that placed him on "final probation," and the fact that he only obtained nine out of the fifteen credits required for admittance to Yale. In his senior year, Philip scored a 64 in English, a 50 in Latin, a 51 in French, a 64 in Geometry, and a 54 in Trigonometry. Yet Philip's father still arranged for his son to retake Yale's entrance exams, ultimately leading to Philip's enrollment in the university for the fall of 1922. Philip's father happened to be a Yale alumnus and the owner of Nebraska's largest furniture company.[31]

Edward Weschler's high school grades were nearly as bad as Philip's. He ended his senior year with a D– in English, a D– in History, and a D+ in Mechanical Drawing. The highest grade in his high school career was a B in Physical Education. The Weschlers, though, were one of Milwaukee's most prominent families, achieving their fortune in the malting business. Edward's mother was determined that her child enroll in the University of Notre Dame. The university's registrar, examining Edward's report cards, explained to Mrs. Weschler that "applicants are selected on the basis of rank in their class." This fact spelled misfortune for Edward's chances, but Mrs. Weschler persisted. She wrote to the university chaplain, asking him to lobby the registrar on behalf of Edward. The chaplain confirmed that the registrar believed that Edward's grades were too low for admittance. Mrs. Weschler then wrote to the

Dean of the College of Commerce, who agreed to admit Edward despite his D average, on condition that Edward "have good student tutors."[32]

For a student who wanted to enroll in college but lacked familial wealth and connections, the only option was to find a scholarship. The 1920s and 1930s were decades in which local, community-funded scholarships expanded. The primary criterion for nearly all these scholarships was excellent high school grades. In 1922, Minnesota's chapter of the Knights of Columbus began to award scholarships to Catholic University based on academic merit. In 1929, Thomas Edison's company awarded the "Edison Scholarship" to the academically gifted. Alumni clubs in major cities, like New York's Yale Club, raised money so that boys who "led [their] class in scholarship" could attend college. In rural Moscow, Idaho, a local mining magnate established a scholarship for the town's graduate with the highest "scholastic ability." Valedictorians in towns across the country, from Las Vegas, Nevada, to Brownsville, Texas, were awarded annual scholarships, all based on their high school grades. Even local chapters of the United Daughters of the Confederacy raised money for white students with excellent academic records to attend college.[33]

The diaries of recipients of financial aid reveal the importance that students placed on report cards. Virginia Spottswood, for instance, was the daughter of an African Methodist Episcopal preacher. Virginia moved every few years— from Boston, to Buffalo, to Washington, DC—as her father was assigned to different parishes. Her diary entries chronicle scores on each report card and even each test, all while Virginia was still young enough to play with dolls during her free time. Virginia also noted her academic blemishes, like when she missed one word on a spelling test or when her art teacher threatened her with a C for forgetting her pencil. As Virginia grew, so did her interest in boys, one of whom had "such dreamy eyes" that she "dreamed about kissing him." Despite the new distraction of boys, Virginia found time to describe each report card in detail, keeping nearly every report, from grammar through high school. Her diligence and focus on grades paid off. She became the first recipient of the Phi Delta Kappa scholarship, an African American sorority, and one of the only scholarships at the time dedicated to Black women. In their letter to Virginia congratulating her on her award, the sorority was quick to point out that it based its decision on Virginia's high school grades.[34]

Harry Blackmun, the future Supreme Court justice, needed assistance to pay for college. He was the son of a grocer in St. Paul, Minnesota. Like Virginia, Harry saved nearly all his report cards, which documented an upward trajectory in his grades. As an eight-year-old, he was reprimanded for being "deficient in writing." Years later, Harry finished his freshman year with three Bs, but by his senior year he did not score below a 94 in any class. Like Virginia, Harry kept a diary that chronicled the receipt of each report card. His main breaks from studying came when he worked in his father's grocery store in a working-class neighborhood of St. Paul. Also, like Virginia, Harry dwelled on his mistakes, like when he was eliminated from the spelling bee in the second round. In the spring of Harry's senior year, he applied for and won a scholarship to Harvard, paid for by the Harvard Club of Minnesota. There would have been no other way for a working-class kid from Mechanic Arts High School to attend the Ivy League.[35]

Poor Jewish kids from the Bronx had unique challenges in winning financial aid. By the time Daniel Schorr entered high school in the early 1930s, many of the elite colleges had created a quota system to reduce the number of Jewish students. Harvard instituted its quota after decades of dramatic increases in the number of Jewish students: 9.8 percent in 1909, 15.1 percent in 1914, and 21.5 percent by 1922. Meanwhile at Yale, whose board chairman described Jews as "an alien and unwashed element," the peak of Jewish enrollment reached 13 percent in the early 1920s. Harvard made the first and most public attempt to reduce the number of Jews, setting a fixed quota. The president of Harvard, however, was met with a public relations backlash and learned that, as one historian put it, "discrimination required the cloak of ambiguity." New York University and Columbia University followed suit and successfully cut their number of Jewish students in half by 1930. At the same time, Yale and Princeton recognized that selecting students purely on the basis of academic rank forfeited their power over the composition of entering classes. In response, both universities created admissions policies that, for full-paying students, deemphasized academics in favor of letters of recommendation and extracurricular activities.[36]

These actions, taken in the wake of the dying wish of Daniel's father, limited the options of the Schorr family. Daniel did not remember even having a choice about which college to attend. The City College of New York was his only option because it did not discriminate against Jews, and it did not charge tuition. Founded in 1847 as a free college, the city's lawmakers reaffirmed its tuitionless policy in 1926. City College's only criterion for admittance was academic rank, making it one of the most academically competitive institutions of higher learning. The fact that City College also catered to the sons of Jewish immigrants also made it more competitive. To be admitted in the 1920s, a student had to be in the top 40 percent of his graduating class. By 1933, as the Great Depression limited the job prospects of New York's high school graduates, the cutoff for admittance became the top 20 percent. The combination of intellectual rigor and nondiscriminatory admissions gave City College the nickname, "The Proletarian Harvard," producing a radical student body quick to protest fascism and the college's own administration. By the time Daniel enrolled in 1934, nearly 90 percent of the student body was Jewish. Gedaliah Schorr would have been proud of his firstborn son. Most of City College's Russian-Jewish graduates became lawyers, teachers, and doctors, securing a place in the US middle class.[37]

Jacob Arlow, who was a few years older than Daniel, considered applying to City College. Arlow was from Brooklyn, which rivaled the Bronx as the center of Jewish culture in the city. Daniel and Jacob were children of working-class Russian-Jewish immigrants; Jacob's father found work making women's hats. Like Daniel, young Jacob worked hard at school and earned high enough marks to be elected into Arista, the high school honors society to which Daniel belonged. Like Daniel, Jacob also participated in Hebrew school, winning accolades from the Jewish Education Association. His father was active in the Order of the Birth Sholom, which made Jacob eligible for their scholarship of $400 per year to help pay tuition. The first criteria listed on the scholarship application was "school record," and Jacob had those records. He saved all his report cards. When Jacob attempted to gain admittance to Columbia, however, he met resistance. After an interview with an administrator, Jacob was deferred, instead enrolling in New York University. The experience left Jacob with a competitive edge, much like Daniel's. Upon Jacob's death, friends and family noted that "he had a keen sense of inferiority as a child of immigrants, considering himself a guest who had to work hard to show he deserved this country's hospitality."[38]

As the son of Jewish immigrants, Daniel had to compete to survive, and he did indeed thrive in the realm of gaining good marks on periodic report cards. Out of thousands of students, Daniel was one of the forty-two selected to represent DeWitt Clinton High School in the Arista honors society, a reflection of his academic prowess. Yet Daniel still held an outsider's view of the American educational system, especially its focus on ranking children. For Daniel, student publications were the outlet for voicing his dissent: *Clinton News* and the DeWitt Clinton High School yearbook. He served as an editor of both, and he left a written record of his subtle criticism. Humor, for Daniel and his fellow student authors, was their means of protesting an educational system embodied by report cards, and once again, Daniel's experiences offer insight into a nationwide pattern of how some children coped with the pressures of surveillance, reporting, and ranking.[39]

By the time Daniel enrolled, DeWitt Clinton High School was one of the largest schools in the United States. A year before Daniel arrived, Clinton High opened a new campus on twenty-one acres in the north side of the Bronx, equipped with an auditorium, science labs, a printing shop, and capacity to educate over 5,100 students. By the time Daniel graduated, Clinton High enrolled about 12,000 students, which necessitated the opening of five "annexes" due to overcrowding. Despite increasing enrollment, the school was a national

Figure 5.5. Central High School student cartoon, 1926. "Advisory" was the school's term for quarterly report cards. *Central Bulletin* (Washington, DC), October 27, 1926, 1.

symbol of efficient education. Diplomats and dignitaries toured the campus. Babe Ruth and Lou Gehrig came to promote the hometown Yankees, receiving a ten-minute standing ovation in the auditorium. The school produced a litany of artists, Nobel laureates, and celebrities, including the writer James Baldwin, the physicist Robert Hofstadter, and the actor Burt Lancaster.[40]

The newspaper articles and yearbooks that Daniel wrote and edited have survived in DeWitt Clinton High School's archive. They reveal that Daniel was indeed skeptical of the supposed academic meritocracy of an American high school. In his junior year, he criticized the Board of Education's unwillingness to hire new teachers and thus alleviate the overcrowding. In another article, Daniel—inspired by Sinclair Lewis—railed against the hypocrisy of local leaders. Daniel joked about voter fraud in the student government elections. He mocked overly restrictive rules in the school cafeteria. He even mocked individual teachers for their dullness and lack of clarity in the classroom. And, like thousands of students across the United States, he made fun of report cards. In the 1930 *Clintonian* yearbook, Daniel and his coauthors mocked a teacher, Mr. Anthony, for the unusual severity of his grading. For a satirical gift, the editors of the yearbook gave

Figure 5.6. DeWitt Clinton High School, seen from Mosholu Parkway, Bronx, New York, c. 1945. Photo used courtesy of Bronx County Historical Society Collection, Bronx, New York.

Mr. Anthony "one hundred permanent report cards so that he may write his autobiography."[41]

For high schoolers across the United States, humor embodied the power to build community through laughter. If report cards represented extreme individualization, then humor embodied community. If report cards pitted students against one another by ranking them, then student jokes about report cards might therefore be seen as an attempt to reestablish community by tearing down hierarchies. For example, students in Cleveland announced the distribution of end-of-semester report cards with the headline, "Misery Loves Company." In Indianapolis, one senior offered her "everlasting smile" to help the freshmen cope "on report card day." The male students at Dunbar High School in Washington, DC, bonded over the fact that "so many boys received D's on their reports" because they were all "too broad minded." Students were sharing their common experiences of alienation, breaking down barriers of isolation with jokes.[42]

Student publications made jokes at the expense of Marie in Montana, Mary Anne in North Carolina, and Charles in Ohio, all for their efforts to get good grades on school reports. In another example, a poem appeared beneath a student's picture. Presumably, this female student was at the top of her class academically: "There's Fanny Bogomolny, modest and kind, / Possesses what we call a very sound mind, / For her, the report card had ne'er a terror, / I doubt whether she e'er committed an error." In New York, a school newspaper made a joke at Bella's expense, pointing out that she tended to fret over bad test scores, only to receive a "99" on her report card. The ridicule that some students faced for their high marks was, in part, an attempt by the student body to reestablish an egalitarian subculture, free from the hierarchy imposed by grades.[43]

Students also mocked teachers. In one publication from 1922, a student brought a box of candy for his teacher, on whom he had a crush. The Valentine's Day gift was ruined when the student received his report card in return. "The old hen!" the student exclaimed about his former love interest. In 1927, students sarcastically thanked teachers for preventing their names from appearing on the honor roll and for allowing them to spend more time in study hall. In 1928, students depicted teachers distributing report cards as "wolves gloat[ing] over their prey." In 1932, high schoolers begged teachers to "have pity" on report card day, as if teachers were medieval courts of justice, dispensing judgment without due process.[44]

Student humor, while helping teenagers feel better about low grades, did not lead to a revolt or even serious demands for reform. Instead, most jokes implied a degree of passivity on the part of students who received report cards, such as when students reminded their classmates to "wear a coat of armor home" on report card day. Students joked about being "too scared" to look at their report cards, about avoiding their families altogether instead of sharing information on school reports, and about it taking them "four days to figure out a method of approach to the parents and break the sad news." For students at Wayzata High School in Minnesota, life "passed smoothly" until "we received our report cards . . . which resulted in a gnawing and gnashing of teeth." Report cards even prompted jokes about death, perhaps the ultimate sign of submission. At South High School in Columbus, students wrote: "Report cards. Oh, death, where is thy sting?" At John Hay School in Cleveland, students warned their classmates: "don't commit suicide until you see your own report card with your own eyes," just in case grades might be higher than originally thought. Even Daniel Schorr, who was one of the top students at his high school, joked about his low grades. "This morning, pausing to contemplate my marks," Daniel wrote a few weeks before he graduated, "I decided that it would be advantageous to obtain a few zeros. They will raise my average considerably."[45]

Instead of just voicing their anxiety, which served to perpetuate an unhealthy self-analysis, some students played the fool to power. In creating jokes at the expense of adults, they showed the arbitrary nature of a report card. In one joke, a father in California scolded his son when he said, "I'm not at all pleased with this report." The son responded, "I knew you wouldn't be, but the teacher wouldn't change it." In Michigan, a student waxed poetically that "It isn't getting the card so much / it's taking it home to Dad!" The poem culminates with a line that satirizes the hypocrisy of the system: "But I guess [Dad's] marks weren't all in blue / When he was just a freshie too!" In Minnesota, a student used a yearbook entry to unveil years of cheating. A classmate filled "her own report cards with A's," while at the same time allowing her friends to cheat off her tests. In other words, the grades on reports had been a lie all along. The joke was on teachers and parents.[46]

A few student publications satirized report cards in ways that transcended logic and the ability of written word to convey. The target of their satire was adult reverence for the report card, a reverence that bordered on religious obedience. In Alabama, a student used a spoof of the Lord's Prayer, praying to teachers to "forgive us for making zeroes, as we forgive ourselves for failing; lead us not into copying, but deliver us from stealing; and give us answers to all questions before we begin." In Montana, a student coopted Jesus' Beatitudes to mock report cards. "Blessed are the poor in grades, for theirs is the card of flunks," the student wrote. "Blessed are the meek and suppliant students, for they shall inherit the E's of the teachers." The humor was an attack on the hypocrisy of authority figures, who claimed a morality based on Christian humanism while reducing children to mere numbers on a card. Likewise, in 1933, Daniel Schorr joked about the irony of receiving demerits on his "character cards" for questioning the character of school authorities. Schorr could see that something was hilarious about the hypocrisy of it all.[47]

Daniel may have been irreverent and unjustifiably self-deprecating about his academic success, but he was also driven. In 1933, he did indeed win a scholarship to City College, fulfilling his father's dying wish. While enrolled at City College, Daniel pursued his passion for journalism, writing for the college newspaper, on his way to a long career as a renowned television reporter.[48]

Despite being separated by two generations, comedian Sarah Silverman (b. 1970) and journalist Daniel Schorr share a few similarities. Like Schorr, Silverman's family roots are in Eastern Europe. Her Jewish grandmother, for instance, was born in Vilna, a city about 300 kilometers north of Telechan. New York, as with the Schorr family, became the gateway through which Silverman's ancestors entered the United States.[49]

Silverman and Schorr also shared a biting sense of humor. Granted, as a TV journalist, Schorr's on-air persona was stern, direct, and professional. Even so, colleagues and family remembered Schorr as quite witty, quick to employ puns, and with a playfulness and whimsy once the cameras turned off. In private, Daniel was particularly fond of laughing at the insecurities and arrogance of those in power, a humor that reflected his outsider's perspective to the end of his life. Silverman, meanwhile, began her long career as a stand-up comic just as Schorr's journalistic career was entering its final stages. In 1993, Silverman's brand of mockery led her to join the cast of *Saturday Night Live* and in 2007 won her a sketch comedy show on Comedy Central.[50]

Schorr and Silverman were outsiders, and they maintained an outsider's perspective on US education, while also working within the system to achieve success. Schorr understood the importance of gaining admission to City College, that his father's dying wish depended on him maintaining high grades on monthly report cards. He also recognized the system for what it was. It was not a meritocracy. The odds were stacked against poor Jewish kids like him, forcing young Daniel to redouble his efforts and narrow his focus on academic success. Schorr's relationship with grades was a mix of commitment and cynicism.

Silverman had more academic opportunities than Schorr. As the second and third generation in her family to be admitted to college, Silverman excelled at school in New Hampshire, earning a 3.8 GPA on her report card despite missing three months of high school due to a debilitating depression. Yet she too maintained an outsider's view, using comedy to voice her insights as one of the few Jewish kids in her hometown. Silverman could see that ranking children based on grades was bizarre. There was something cruel, and at the same time ridiculous, about the whole system. In 2007, during an episode of her sitcom, *The Sarah Silverman Program*, Silverman made an interesting point about the nature of academic scores, the stigma of low grades, and authority. In one skit, Silverman's character is pulled over by a police officer. The officer, speaking through Silverman's car window, asks the driver, "Ma'am, do you know why I am standing here?" Silverman pauses, looks confused, and replies, "Because you earned all Cs in high school?" Ten years later, in a different TV program, Silverman worked as a substitute teacher for a day in a Brooklyn public school. She ditches her lesson plan and instead teaches her students how to cheat and how to graffiti the bathroom walls. Through it all, Silverman plays the fool, the simpleton who satirizes the powerful.[51]

Theory of humor helps to make sense of Silverman's satire of formal education. In *Rebelais and His World* (1968), Mikhail Bakhtin examined the phenomena of medieval carnivals. According to Bakhtin, carnivals turned marketplaces into comic pageants where fools and clowns blurred the lines between spectator and participant. Poets performed comedic oral compositions that mocked systems of rank and sacred ritual. The spectators "lived in" the performances for several days, suspending "hierarchical rank, privileges, norms, and prohibitions." Peasants therefore escaped their fear of feudalism, religion, and death, at least temporarily. Carnivals served as a relief from the burdens of hierarchy, creating an alternate reality. It was a means through which the powerless transcended their oppression and celebrated community.[52]

Ultimately, though, Schorr's school newspaper or Silverman's stand-up comedy could not really create a communal celebration like Bakhtin's carnival. Instead, they may have served to reinforce a sense of docility. Contemporary comedy masks the alienation of schools, without really altering realities. Perhaps Schorr's teenage jokes about report cards and Silverman's sketch comedy merely breed detached skepticism, even leading to a passive obedience within the existing power structure. In the end, there is little evidence that any series of jokes have been able to combat the rising power of school reports.[53]

CHAPTER SIX

The Pursuit of Educational Dignity

Kirsten Albrecht (b. 1960) was a Minnesota farm girl who did not receive report cards from fifth through tenth grade. She attended the Wilson Campus School, a laboratory school for what was then called Mankato State College (later renamed Minnesota State University, Mankato). Beginning in 1968, the Wilson Campus School eliminated grades, class schedules, and—by extension—report cards, in a radical reimagining of formal schooling that was sweeping parts of the country at the time. Kirsten began attending Wilson five years after this transformation and remained until its dissolution in 1977. Instead of periodically sending home summaries of conduct, attendance, and academic standing, Wilson used "goal sheets." The goal sheets embodied Wilson's radicalism: students created their own classes, attendance was not mandatory, and teachers were redefined as peers who guided students on their learning journey.

Kirsten's enrollment in the Wilson Campus School was serendipitous, as she came of age during a nationwide movement to reform public schools. The phenomenon was sometimes known as "the open school movement" and at other times "the alternative school movement." Both terms captured the reality that during the late 1960s and early 1970s, thousands of schools experimented with different ways of organizing learning communities and evaluating children. The fact that Mankato State College was located ten miles from the Albrecht farm added to the serendipity. It also happened that, in 1968, a radical pedagogue named Don Glines became the director of Mankato State's Wilson Campus School. Glines immediately abolished report cards.

Kirsten thrived in a school environment that gave children the autonomy to pursue their innate curiosity. She loved Wilson so much that after the school closed in 1977, she struggled to transition to a life in traditional public schools. Later, in the 1990s, Kirsten became the mother of three school-aged daughters in a new pedagogical era that was antithetical to the alternative school movement: the movement to hold students and schools more accountable through testing. Wilson had given Kirsten a deep sense of educational right and wrong, and as the 1990s progressed, she became increasingly disillusioned with public schools. As a result, Kirsten took a radical step to avoid the testing movement: she changed careers and moved to a different city in order to provide her daughters with a similar type of alternative education to that which she enjoyed at Wilson: student-centered, noncompetitive learning, and with no report cards.

Kirsten's life reflects the lengths to which Americans must go to escape the reach of report cards. Few children grow up on remote farms that are a short drive from a college's free, ungraded laboratory school. Even fewer are willing to relocate their lives, as Kirsten did in the 1990s, to an ideal school setting. Ultimately, the fact that Kirsten had to rearrange her life for her children to attend a school without traditional report cards shows that the alternative school movement failed to transform mainstream public schooling. However, Kirsten's story demonstrates that the pursuit of educational dignity without the need for report cards is, in fact, possible.

The alternative school movement of the 1960s and 1970s was not a new phenomenon. It represented the resurgence of a multigenerational debate that can be traced back to Jean-Jacques Rousseau of the European Enlightenment, Johann Heinrich Pestalozzi of the early nineteenth century, and John Dewey of the Progressive Era. By the 1950s, the debate reemerged with the fears of the Cold War. Anxieties arose over the perceived success of the Soviet Union's

Figure 6.1. Kirsten Albrecht (*left*) around the age of fifteen, and her older sister, Liz Albrecht, c. 1975. Kirsten Albrecht Riehle private collection.

educational discipline; even President Eisenhower blamed John Dewey for instilling an unrestrained permissiveness that had taken root in American schools. At nearly the same time, the calls of the civil rights movement for equality created a binary contrast between progressives and traditionalists. Amid President Johnson's war on poverty, the 1960s witnessed a deemphasis in some schools on academic competition in favor of making education a tool for social mobility.[1]

One can therefore understand the skepticism of more experienced pedagogues who, by the 1970s, dismissed the alternative school movement as "old wine in new skins." Yet even these skeptics acknowledged that a new movement was developing that merged Dewey's student-interest-driven classroom practices with even more radical experiments in democratic school administration. The growth of alternative schools was impressively rapid: in 1970, only 100 schools identified themselves as alternative; by 1975, approximately 5,000 schools did so; at its peak in the late 1970s, more than 10,000 alternative schools were in existence, educating an estimated three million students out of a total of roughly forty million school-aged children in the United States. Some of the self-proclaimed alternative schools catered their freedom-inspired education to the interests of college-bound, middle- and upper-class families. Other schools, sometimes referred to as "street academies," held more revolutionary goals. These schools were inspired by the likes of Jonathan Kozol, Ivan Illich, and Paulo Freire and served the most marginalized populations. The two key defining characteristics of the movement, however, were Dewey's principles of building school around student interests and the elimination of grades.[2]

The concept of alternative schooling began in the 1960s as a literary movement. A. S. Neill, a British schoolmaster, inspired many of his American counterparts when he published *Summerhill* in 1960. In the book, Neill described both the theory and the practice of his boarding school in the English countryside, which emphasized freedom, creativity, and radical democratic governance. In 1966, Neill told one interviewer, "Freedom is the answer, letting people be natural and live their own lives without being indoctrinated and disciplined and all of the rest of it." Later in the interview, Neill revealed his messianic vision for transforming public education: "I'd like to abolish [ordinary schools] but I don't think I'll manage it. I'd like to make every school like Summerhill where everybody would be free to learn if they want to learn and play when they want to play and make their own rules about living." As the 1960s progressed, Neill's book became a hit, with the sale of 200,000 copies per year by the end of the decade. At the height of the alternative school movement in the mid 1970s, *Summerhill* was required reading in approximately 600 university courses, which inspired pedagogues in the United States to reframe education as a search "for ecstasy as well as knowledge."[3]

For many of the literary leaders of the alternative school movement, report cards embodied the dehumanizing aspects of industrial schooling. Harvard University's Roland Barth, for instance, criticized schools for being built upon the fear and distrust between teachers and the children, who "expect a test to be sprung on them without warning" and who "recoil on report card day." For John C. Holt, whose 1964 book advocated a radical "unschooling" of American youth, report cards became an allegory for a child's tears, forcing pupils to self-consciously think about their rank in the world as opposed to thinking about the wonders of the world. City College's Charles Silberman wrote about the cruel irony of a report card that tracked whether or not a child "sits still" or "follows direction," all while also displaying "intellectual curiosity." Jonathan Kozol was perhaps the movement's most radical leader. While working as a young classroom teacher in a poor Boston school, he found the district-mandated report card infuriating. It asked him to check a box about whether his students were "respectful of diversity," while at the same time the district created de facto segregated schools. In another incident, Kozol sent a child home with a critical report card that pushed the child's mother to an emotional breakdown. Kozol recognized that the report card was the final blow for a mother struggling to survive, and he concluded that he wanted no part in public schooling. Instead, he opted for a life of activism in alternative schools.[4]

The revolutionary zeitgeist of the 1960s fueled a zealotry for the alternative school movement. Some teachers encouraged their students to emulate the sit-ins and boycotts of the civil rights movement in order to pressure administrators to change their draconian rules. For some, the heart of the movement was the assumption that adults could not be trusted, that tradition was inherently oppressive, and that children were bored with the curricula. The proselytizing culminated in 1969, when several hundred like-minded education reformers met in San Francisco to proclaim a "surging movement" in all fifty states that many hoped would not just serve as a niche alternative but would also transform the mainstream of traditional schools.[5]

Gradually, the movement resulted in tangible, grassroots efforts across the country. The Ford, Carnegie, and Rockefeller Foundations funded a variety of alternative schools, and public school districts organized and paid for many as well. In 1971, New York City's public school district funded ten Harlem schools in an experimental program. Within a few years, the program had grown to twenty-eight schools, with 200 teachers and 5,000 students. Seattle's school board offered thirty alternative schools for over 3,000 students. By the mid-1970s, 60 percent of Long Island's schools offered alternative programs without grades or report cards. In 1978, Dallas created five alternative schools for approximately 1,500 students. Teachers joined the movement for the same reasons that inspired the literary leaders: disillusionment with the status quo. In Idaho, one teacher appeared before the school board to advocate for the creation of a non-graded alternative option. She said that she was tired of seeing her poorest children beaten by their parents every time they brought home low marks on a report card.[6]

A common theme of the alternative schools was the celebration of the innate curiosity of the students. At an alternative school in Oregon, for instance, students enjoyed an entire semester studying ethnic cooking. The first 300 students who participated in a pilot program in Los Angeles built domes, produced puppet shows, and directed silent movies. In Chicago, students incorporated indigenous cosmology to free themselves "from fear, from anxiety, from pain, and from want." The leader of California's Harbor Arena Alternative School, which was housed in a converted doctor's office, explained that "students do exactly what they want to do when they want to do it." Another school leader wrote that if parents could see the true creativity that blossomed within their children when they were given intellectual freedom, they would "feel, quite rightly, that a report card is a swindle."[7]

The alternative school movement saw grading as the root of educational evils, and it worked to eliminate gold stars, letter grades, honor rolls, anything that gave the "ignoble satisfaction of feeling that one person is better than someone else." Some academics backed their skepticism of grades with scientific studies, like the researchers in 1972 who evaluated whether or not "the relationship between complex learning and competition-motivated is inverse or curvilinear" (they found that it was inversely related), or the 1974 study that examined how hundreds of elementary schoolchildren responded negatively to academic marks. An industry of pedagogical experts arose to promote their alternatives to traditional grading, among them such concepts as the "Personalized Achievement Reporting" and proposals to replace testing with math games. There was a consensus among alternative school advocates that academic grades were, fundamentally, about controlling children. Herbert Kohl concluded this while teaching in Harlem. He resigned from his public school to become a reformer, advocating that teachers unilaterally abandon the pretense behind report cards in favor of a truly egalitarian experience in which teacher and student would learn together. For some, the idealism paid off. One fourteen-year-old student at California's Valley Alternative School told a reporter that she enjoyed her new school because without grades "nobody outranks anybody." Others, however, such as a school board member in Sacramento, disagreed. He voted against the creation of an alternative school, holding firm to his belief that "competition is what the world is all about."[8]

The efforts to create democratic school communities reflected a far more radical break with precedent than classroom innovations. Students at one New Jersey alternative school wrote their own constitution with new attendance policies and codes of conduct. Inspired by Summerhill, one California alternative boarding school held weekly self-governance meetings that lasted up to three hours. Students voted on the allocation of funds, assigned each other chores, and offered each other critical feedback. A principal in Oregon took his office door off its hinges to make a statement about the school's commitment to transparency and "openness." Jonathan Kozol, rejecting public schools altogether, organized a community school in Boston entirely under the control of poverty-stricken parents. In more affluent Scarsdale, New York, parents attended public meetings that lasted hours, debating the ethics of whether a teacher should delay an assignment's due date for some students and not for others. The parents then formed a "fairness committee" that met periodically to resolve disputes between teachers and students.[9]

As the 1970s progressed, a distinction between two very different types of alternative schools emerged. On the one hand, gradeless and student-interest-driven schools—partly inspired by the utopian vision of *Summerhill*—sprang up for middle-class families. California's Wanderjahr, for instance, rested on a thousand-acre campus with a stable of horses, overlooking the Sacramento Valley. Tuition was $3,800 per year. On the other extreme was Evander Prep, a school within a school, which was located in the Bronx. Evander Prep dedicated its classes to remedial reading and math. School ended at 12:30 p.m. because most of the students had full-time jobs. Both Wanderjahr and Evander Prep were considered alternative, although the only thing that they had in common was a lack of grades and report cards. In another approach, attending Long Island's Village School was a stepping stone to Harvard, Yale, and MIT. Meanwhile, attending an alternative school in one of Chicago's southside neighborhoods was a last resort before incarceration. The contrast between the opposing visions for what an alternative school could and should be was striking for observers at the time. Jonathan Kozol, for one, made his views clear. "An isolated upper-class Free School for the children of the white and rich," he wrote in 1972, "is a great deal too much like a sandbox for the children of SS Guards at Auschwitz."[10]

Nearly every alternative school—whether for the elites or for those living in poverty—went to lengths to find new ways of communicating with parents beyond the traditional report card. Many schools experimented with the use of portfolios as a means of reflecting on a child's progress. The Newton Open School in Massachusetts replaced report cards with a four-page booklet that described each child's "well-being." In Miami, an alternative schoolteacher realized that banning report cards meant that, for the first time, her marginalized students were not deemed failures. In Indianapolis, teachers created an elaborate system of letters that narrated six individualized "competencies" for each child. In San Diego, a principal of an alternative school called report cards "blackmail cards," explaining to a journalist that they "have no other value other than to control students."[11]

Kirsten Albrecht was a fifth grader when she first enrolled at Wilson Campus School. Despite experiences of boredom at a traditional school, Kirsten's childhood was idyllic. She was a vegetable-farm kid, which distinguished her from the cattle-farm kids. Her parents were well-educated Minnesotans; her father taught engineering at a local vocational school and her mother was an occupational therapist who eventually published a book on hand therapy. They envisioned for their two daughters a life of agrarian self-reliance: Kirsten's days were spent picking and washing vegetables on their farm of 100 tillable acres, reading books, and playing board games with her older sister. She would wander for miles along southern Minnesota's deep ravines and fields of heavy, black soil that is the legacy of glacial deposits thousands of years earlier. Their home, built by Kirsten's parents, sat on a steep bluff overlooking the open plain of the Minnesota River Valley. Instead of watching television, the Albrechts listened to NPR all day long; after all, they were personally acquainted with Garrison Keillor.[12]

The Albrechts envisioned a back-to-the-earth life of self-reliance for their family. They did not consider themselves hippies, although they did not quite fit in with the cattle farmers nearby. They were independent Midwesterners, "God-damned independent," as the family liked to say. Kirsten and her older sister were put to work on the farm at an early age. They spent hours in the greenhouse preparing for planting season. In the spring, they dug 12,000 holes, one for each seedling, passing the time as they did so with word games and songs. By age eight, Kirsten was lifting hundred-pound crates of peppers and squash and organizing deliveries for the family's clients. By age nine, she was driving the family tractor. As a teenager, she supervised a team of farmhands, many of whom she defeated in periodic arm-wrestling competitions. Kirsten recorded in her diary that, on a typical day, "When I got home I had to plant onions. Onions, onions, onions or boring, boring, boring."[13]

Dealing with the traditional public school interrupted Kirsten's idyllic upbringing. One of her first memories was of first grade, when she brought home a report card with mostly As but also a C in handwriting. Her older sister had always had perfect scores, and her parents wanted to know what was wrong with their younger daughter. "I assumed that I was stupid," Kirsten remembered. "I knew that I wasn't smart like my sister and the report card proved it." Kirsten's most vivid memories of traditional public school were of laying her head on her desk to get through the day and of the principal publicly spanking students to maintain discipline. At another point, Kirsten lay on the classroom floor during nap time, staring at the ceiling, asking herself the existential question: "Why?"[14]

The Wilson Campus School rescued Kirsten. The school was in the heart of Mankato, a college town eighty-five miles south of the Twin Cities of St. Paul and Minneapolis but just ten miles from the Albrecht farm. Mankato experienced a population boom in the 1960s, growing by nearly 30 percent—or

Figure 6.2. Kirsten Albrecht at work on the farm near Mankato, Minnesota, c. 1973. Kirsten Albrecht Riehle private collection.

approximately 7,000 people—the highest rate of increase in the town's history. Around the time that Kirsten enrolled in Wilson, the population peaked at nearly 31,000 people before dipping and then plateauing in the 1980s. Mankato was the soybean capital of Minnesota and home to the state's two main processing plants. Mankato State College had grown to 12,500 students by the 1970s. The college-town feel of Mankato accentuated the existing disparities of wealth: about half of the city either lived in poverty or were considered working class; the other half was either affiliated with the college or held management positions in the railroad industry or the soybean processing plants. The town included two hotels, eight motels, three movie theaters, one hospital, and thirty-eight churches.[15]

Mankato State College's 300-acre campus stood on the bluffs overlooking the town's business district. The campus included the Wilson school building, which was nondescript, rectangular, and constructed in the ranch style of the 1950s. For the first few years of the school's existence, townsfolk viewed Wilson as a supplement to the district's two public high schools. Wilson was considered an excellent—albeit traditional—school, overseen by the college's education department, while funded by the Mankato public school district. The kindergarten through twelfth-grade school emphasized reading, writing, and arithmetic, all while training young undergraduate students of education in the art of classroom management.[16]

All of that changed in the fall of 1968 with the arrival of Don Glines, Wilson's new director. A wiry, red-headed California native, Glines was thirty-seven at the time. He had earned a PhD in education from the University of Oregon before heading an international school in Haiti. Because the Haitian school lacked resources and a formally trained faculty, Glines was forced to innovate, experimenting with a school without any tests. As the 1960s progressed, Glines became increasingly inspired by the idealism of the antiwar and civil rights movements. He looked up to John F. Kennedy, Martin Luther King Jr., and Robert F. Kennedy, all of whom, Glines wrote, "dreamed of a better world." Before he took the helm at Wilson, Glines visited Philadelphia's Parkway School, which was a national trendsetter in the alternative school movement. Like hundreds of thousands of educational reformers from the era, Glines took A. S. Neill's *Summerhill* very seriously.[17]

Glines unveiled his radical vision for the Wilson Campus School during two all-school meetings in August 1968: one assembly for the teachers and the other for the students. From this point on, Glines explained, there would be no report cards, no tests, no comparison of children whatsoever. Education would not be a competition. Instead of report cards, children would periodically meet with their parents and advisor to establish their learning goals for the semester. Each child would form his or her own "learning sessions," as Glines preferred to call classes. Each child would also choose his or her own teachers. Together, small groups of students and teachers would then go on learning journeys. These journeys might last three days or the entire school year. There were no truancy rules. Students only had to check in with their advisor before 10 a.m., as required by state law. After that, they were free to pursue their curiosity.[18]

Many in the Wilson Campus School community were shocked. One teacher remembered her students looking dazed as they filed out of the assembly, turning to her and asking, "What do we do now?" The teacher responded: "I have no idea." Parents called Glines' predecessor, pleading with him to do something about the "free wheelie operation." Seventy-five children, or nearly 15 percent of the student body, left the school as a result of the changes. One parent, a Mankato State professor, lived just three blocks away; but the school seemed so chaotic and unorganized that he preferred to send his children miles on the bus to the nearest traditional school. The music teacher—like many of the math teachers and elementary teachers—struggled with the new system. He tried to explain to Glines that learning a musical instrument, like math and reading, was sequential, and therefore required regular attendance. The basketball coach protested that he just could not run his team as a democracy. Some of the faculty were former combat veterans of World War II and the Korean War who were prone to instilling discipline in high schoolers. But Glines insisted that teachers expand their knowledge base, respond to the inherent curiosity of each child, and abandon the idea of dividing children by age. If there were 600 children attending the school, then there needed to be 600 different educational plans. To some students, Glines was "over the top," even "a wild man" at the first assembly. One townsperson considered Glines "straight from LSD-guru Timothy Leary."[19]

Despite some teachers describing Glines as "a pain in the royal derriere," most of the faculty grew to respect his conviction. In one instance, a teacher made the mistake of stopping Glines in the hallway to ask him an open-ended question. Ninety minutes later, Glines was still talking, enthusiastically trying to convince his employee of the ideals behind alternative schools. "It was endless if he ever got a hold of you," the teacher remembered. Glines also had a knack for public relations. He published two books that outlined the transformation of Wilson and sent copies of those books to Hubert Humphrey and

Walter Mondale, who were high-profile and potentially sympathetic politicians. He embarked on periodic speaking tours, seeking more converts to his vision. He presented his methods to sixty principals in Wisconsin, for instance. He traveled to Kansas and gave a presentation to an entire district's teachers. He believed that his brand of alternative schools could work for rich and poor alike. In Chicago, he spoke to the North Suburban Area Service Center for Gifted Children. At the Pine Ridge Reservation in South Dakota, he tried to persuade the leaders of the dropout prevention program to adopt his system.[20]

But Glines' transformation of Wilson faced some stiff opposition. He admitted in a memo to the faculty that his leadership was dictatorial, even though he believed in a democracy at all levels of society. Unfortunately, he explained, "Rapid, dramatic change needs a dictatorial approach in the early stages." The faculty despairingly labeled Glines "the redhead," especially when they were informed just a week before school that they would be expected to oversee ninety individualized educational plans. Teachers formed a committee to combat the expanded workload, which was primarily due to the additional contact hours they were expected to spend with students. Some townspeople admitted to seeing Glines as either "the devil" or "an instrument of the communist party." In a survey conducted at the end of the year, many students admitted to not working nearly as hard as they had under the traditional approach. One student concluded: "Wilson Campus School is a farce!"[21]

Ultimately, Glines converted most of the Wilson community to his vision. The change of heart among the faculty was significant and visible. As one teacher put it, prior to 1968, Wilson Campus School had "great traditional teachers"; after 1968, those same teachers became "great innovators." Students also bought into Glines' approach. By the end of the second year, they almost universally reported lower rates of anxiety, better relations with teachers, and greater joy in learning. While parents were harder to win over, quite a few echoed the sentiment of one father who called Wilson "the greatest educational opportunity" their child could have hoped for. Visitors began arriving on the bluffs overlooking Mankato to study Glines' experiment. In the spring of 1969, *National Observer* labeled Glines as "one of the foremost apostles of educational innovation" and Wilson "the most innovative school in America."[22]

Replacing report cards with goal sheets was the linchpin of the system. For Glines, report cards embodied everything that was wrong with traditional public schools. Glines wrote that "the nurturing of caring, warm persons and parents who could live in harmony with themselves, nature, and societal conditions" was antithetical to "the need to graduate youth who received A report

Figure 6.3. Don Glines, turning off the bells at the Wilson Campus School, Mankato, Minnesota, 1968. Photo courtesy of University Archives at Minnesota State University, Mankato.

cards." A year into his experiment at Wilson, Glines observed that conventional report cards destroyed any chance that an education could be individualized to fit each child's innate curiosity, and that children should therefore create their own goal sheets based on their natural interests. Complete transparency was required. The advisor was not there to spring evaluative traps on the student in the form of quizzes or tests. Instead, at the end of the semester, the advisor and student would work together to reflect on the child's progress.[23]

The new system—built around goal sheets and not report cards—required more work on the part of the teachers. In a memo, Glines pushed his faculty to get inside each student's brain, to determine not only what ignited each student's intellectual curiosity but also how each functioned cognitively. Teachers were expected to spend at least two hours with each advisee each week, which would be documented on goal sheets. Advisors wrote narratives on each child's self-image, the degree of their responsibility, their creativity, and an analysis of their "psychomotor domain." The goal sheets were to be sent home at least four times a year. Above all, Glines explicitly forbade teachers from using any form of grading or comparison of students on the goal sheets.[24]

The Wilson Campus School tended to attract mostly middle-class students. Many children who fit the typical profile had parents who were looking for cutting-edge pedagogical innovations, such as the dyslexic son of a professor or the teacher's son who, on the other hand, was already reading in kindergarten and was bored with traditional school. One student explained that her college-educated parents were drawn to Wilson because they thought it "was cool." According to Wilson's own data, about half of the students were categorized as coming from the "business professional" class. Most of this group, which constituted about a third of the student body, were the children of Mankato State faculty. On the other hand, about half of the parents were farmers, railroad mechanics, truck drivers, and "laborers." One working-class student had been concerned that "Wilson was an elite school catering to professors" but realized once she arrived that "they let people like me in." Pregnant teenage girls also tended to enroll in Wilson, enhanced by its reputation as an unusually caring, judgment-free school.[25]

Kirsten attended Wilson for two reasons. First, she disdained the grading systems of traditional schools, like the report card that she received that labeled her a C student in handwriting. Second, she attended because her older sister, Liz, was having a hard time fitting in socially at the traditional public school, being a bit too intellectual for the mainstream crowd.[26] When Kirsten arrived at her new school, Wilson was five years into its open school experiment, with the result being an environment dramatically different from the traditional school. Kirsten, for example, saw children roller skating in the hallways. One classroom had two pet monkeys—JoJo and Pepe—that tried to steal people's glasses. There was a pet boa constrictor named Ferdinand. On a typical day, a group of boys might be playing cards in the hallway, or children might be feeding mice to a Ferdinand, and "batches of three-year olds roam[ed] everywhere." On a single day, Kirsten chronicled in her diary attending musical theater, puppet theater, sculpture, lunch, and an advising session called "interpersonal communication." The school day culminated with piñata making. Her greatest source of anxiety that day occurred when the teenage director of the puppet show, a classmate, did not choose Kirsten's puppet for the lead as King Arthur.[27]

Students organized classes on women's history, traveled off campus to learn about nursing homes, or spent six weeks in Mexico for Spanish immersion. There was an entire class, or "learning session," on *Macbeth*. Chemistry classes tended to emphasize explosions, and one semester was dedicated to learning the art of TV magic. Students requested the creation of an African Studies course that would be open to children from ages seven through fifteen. A class on death offered students field trips to the town coroner, funeral home, and crematorium. One student spent the entire year making a purple paper mâché hippopotamus the size of a Volkswagen. As Kirsten explained, after a few traumatic years in traditional school, the student simply needed to take some time off to do that. Some students spent their entire career at Wilson almost never sitting at a desk. Other students skipped their learning sessions altogether, preferring to hang out at the Mankato State Student Union shooting pool.[28]

Kirsten thrived at Wilson. The stresses she had felt in her previous school were replaced by an enthusiasm for learning as well as opportunities to stretch and push herself. Her entries in Wilson's creative writing magazine often addressed existential questions. In one of her pieces, she lamented that "when this precious day is gone, it will be gone forever," and in another she reflected on a nuclear explosion, writing that "the end had come for all men—but the world lives on. Amen." Because of a natural affinity for math, Kirsten finished algebra in just a few months and became a de facto math instructor to help her classmates. Acting out of a deep sense of curiosity and empathy, Kirsten organized a learning session on sightlessness, recruiting a blind Mankato State student to teach her Braille and instruct her how to walk blindfolded.[29]

Glines' goal for Wilson was to blur the lines between who was the teacher and who was the student. "Everyone will be a teacher of whatever talent he has," Glines wrote in 1972. Given the fact that students, not teachers, chose the content of their learning sessions, in many cases teachers knew less about a subject than their pupils. Another key ingredient in creating an egalitarian learning community was allowing students to choose their own teachers and advisors. Having many advisees therefore became a status symbol among the faculty and a reflection of a teacher's merit. Without a good "match between the teacher and student," Glines believed, "positive learning does not occur." Eventually, Glines' vision came to fruition and teachers became "friends and helpers." Power dynamics shifted. Teachers left tests on shelves for students to take whenever they were ready. Even one of Wilson's World War II combat-veteran teachers had a revelation: if teachers would be willing to give up control, real learning would take place among the students. One student, articulating this experience from another point of view, explained, "You can talk to them [teachers] now. You feel like they're on your level." And another student told an interviewer, "You know, now, your teacher is considered as a person, a friend." The student added, "I feel like everybody is more relaxed—haven't got this rigid position between students and teachers."[30]

Even some teachers who were originally skeptical of Glines were impressed with the lack of discipline problems at Wilson. When a child misbehaved, a teacher would typically ask the student to leave or to go to the canteen for a "Coke break." Cheating did not occur because there were no grades and no class rank, which also led to surprisingly high levels of cooperation among the students. When one student arrived each day barefooted, there was no reprimand. When another boy annoyed his peers by compulsively flicking lights on and off, the faculty placed the boy in charge of theater lighting. Children were not angels, though. They still behaved cruelly and formed cliques, especially during the drama over lunchroom seating. There was one incident when a group of boys returned to their old public school and ran through the halls shouting obscenities. In another incident, older white boys hurled racial epithets at one of the few Black students at the school. There were also concerns about drug abuse. The clique of drug users was known as "the dirt" and they hung out by the entrance to the gym. Most of the time, however, students handled their newfound independence without discipline problems.[31]

Parents tended to be a bigger problem for Glines. Many parents were "extra hard core about report cards," Glines wrote in 1969. Despite holding open-house meetings at night to "preach no report cards," parents still insisted on some form of documentation of their children's academic performance, deportment, and attendance. In 1970, the school formed a Parent Advisory Committee to give parents an outlet for their concerns. The experience, however, left many of the participants frustrated and polarized. One father who was supportive of Glines' reforms admitted that most parents wanted Wilson to return to its former system. The comments in a parental survey reflected the parents' chagrin. One parent felt that "most children would welcome an adult who says they must do this so and so," and another claimed that her child was "utterly lost and confused at Wilson." A third admitted that "noise, lack of supervision, lack of organization, and uncleanliness were factors which influenced our decision to leave." Even Kirsten's father, who was an enthusiastic supporter of Wilson, wondered if the school was "demanding enough."[32]

Above all, parents seemed concerned that their children were falling behind on traditional academic benchmarks such as reading, writing, and arithmetic. Glines wrote to dozens of college admissions offices to ensure that Wilson graduates could still enter institutions of higher learning. Nearly all colleges and universities that responded were open to admitting Wilson students, but they wanted detailed documentation of each applicant's learning as well as results from an SAT test. Once again, goal sheets became essential, providing evidence that children were, in fact, learning something. But the data were inconclusive on the impact that Wilson had on its pupils' test scores. For instance, Wilson graduates outperformed other Mankato State freshmen on most standardized tests but underperformed on writing assessments.[33]

In part thanks to Glines' public relations skills, Wilson Campus School hosted over 1,000 visitors each year: teachers-in-training from Mankato State, educators from across the region, journalists, and pedagogues from across the country. Observers arrived from Australia, England, South Africa, and France. One student referred to the periodic visits as "zoo days." As many as twenty visitors might be watching a single learning session with just a handful of students. The school installed video cameras so that lessons could be studied outside of class time. Eventually, one student recalled, "we got used to it."[34]

Figure 6.4. Hallway meeting at the Wilson Campus School, Mankato, Minnesota, 1973. Photo from the *Tomahawk* yearbook courtesy of the University Archives at Minnesota State University, Mankato.

Not everyone had a great experience at Wilson Campus School. There was a tendency for students who transferred to Wilson late in their school careers to struggle in their new environment. They typically entered Wilson "angry and unhappy," slow to trust their new teachers, and lacking self-motivation. In 1970, a team of six professors of education voiced their concern about the "extreme permissiveness" at Wilson. Unfortunately, they concluded, the reality was that most teenagers "won't be that motivated" to accomplish high levels of learning. Many graduates came to the same conclusion. One teacher's son wished that he would not have been allowed to "coast through" Wilson. He eventually dropped out of college and worked at Radio Shack for a few years before joining the navy. Another student, even as an adult, struggled to do basic math because "it was a lot easier to go to the gym and shoot baskets than it was to go to math class." The child of a Mankato State physics professor said that he "got left behind" because Wilson was too unstructured for his level of maturity. The daughter of a farmer said that she "lacked the self-discipline" necessary for Wilson and wished that she had had more guidance to prepare her for college. Another graduate, a cheerleader, said that she attended Wilson for years without ever taking English, and she continued to struggle with grammar years later while writing memos at work. Despite these concerns, most graduates had fond memories of Wilson: 80 percent said that the alternative school had a positive impact on their lives. And yet, several graduates admit that they would not send their own children to a school with so much student autonomy.[35]

The goal sheets, Glines' replacement for report cards, also had its flaws. One boy set a goal to complete ten chapters in math, a bit too much of a challenge for his liking, and he never again "set the goals overly aggressive." Teachers sometimes cut corners with goal sheets, as they were overwhelmed by the extra amount of narrative writing necessary to complete the sheets for each student. Besides, one phys ed teacher admitted, "parents didn't know what the heck [the narratives on goals sheets] meant," since it all ended up sounding like a bunch of "googly gook." One student's goal sheet outlined her desire to meet with a different poet once a week for the entire semester and then to write her own poetry. The meetings took place, but the poems never materialized. The advisor's comment simply stated, "Not complete." Another goal for the spring of 1975 was to read Dee Brown's *Bury My Heart at Wounded Knee*. The extent of the advisor's evaluation of the semester was "Great job!" Glines' original vision for entering the mind of each pupil became a casualty to busy workloads.[36]

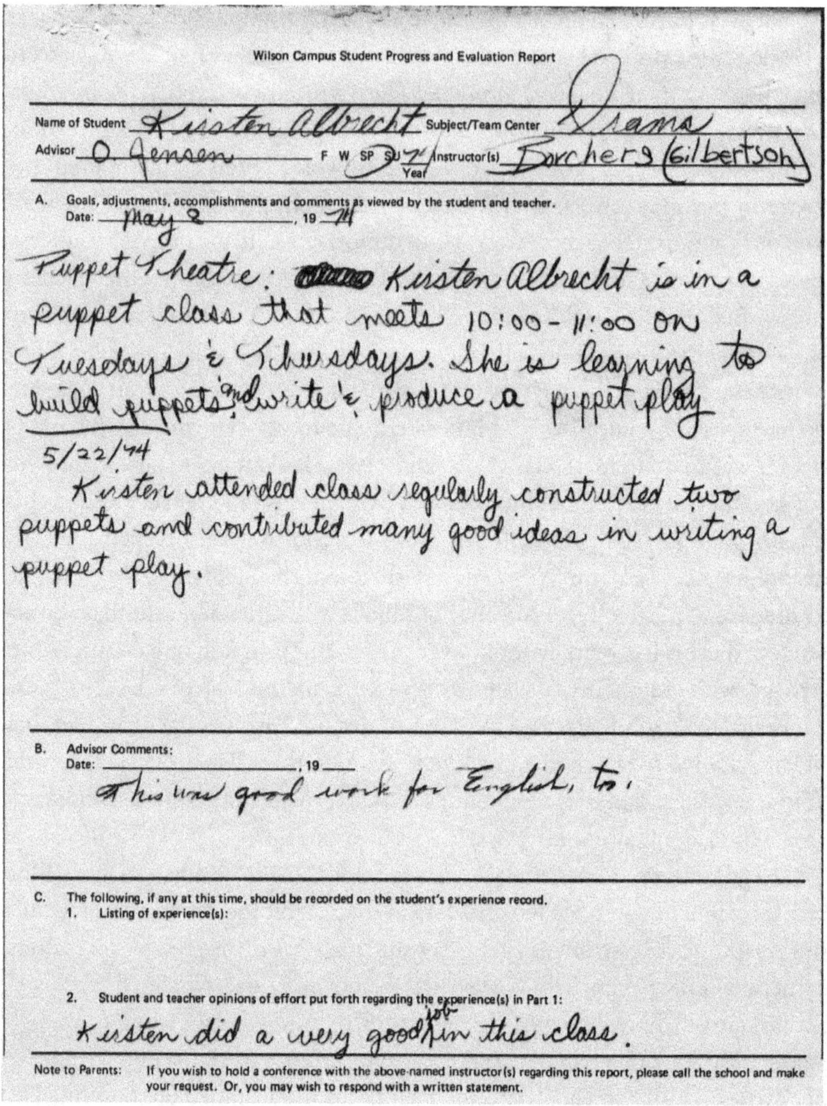

Figure 6.5. One of Kirsten Albrecht's goal sheets, 1974. Kirsten Albrecht Riehle private collection.

Kirsten, though, loved nearly every aspect of her experience at Wilson. Wilson prepared Kirsten well for traditional schooling, giving her the foundation to graduate in the top 10 percent of her high school class after she left the alternative school. Where some students now remember too much freedom, Kirsten described the autonomy to pursue things she was genuinely curious about. While some students blamed Wilson for their struggles in college, Kirsten blamed the bureaucracy of college for getting in the way of real learning. While a few students saw goal sheets as just as artificial a construct as report cards, Kirsten insisted that the goal sheets imprinted lifelong habits of self-awareness and self-discipline. Creating goal sheets was the first time in her life that she could sit down with an adult, as an equal, and say, "Here is what I'd like to learn." It forced her to metacognitively reflect on her own interests, intellectual strengths, and weaknesses. "It was earth shattering," Kirsten remembered. Finding not only specific topics but setting specific outcomes was also a skill that Kirsten found useful as an adult. She, as the student, decided what workload was reasonable but also challenging. "The goal sheets gave us freedom," she concluded.[37]

Just as the alternative school movement reached its high-water mark in the mid-1970s, a backlash ensued. In 1975, a pro-alternative school professor warned his students that "conditions are bad for open education," noting the rise in "campaigns for back to basics, more discipline." At the same time, federal grants seemed to switch their focus away from arts education and toward traditional reading. Even alternative school advocates such as Mary Anne Raywid acknowledged that their movement had lost momentum and that the tide had turned toward "formality, deference to authority, drill education, and rote learning." As usual, debates over the report cards became a proxy war for larger ideological differences. In 1975, for instance, one mother in upstate New York fumed that her child's narrative reports misled her into believing that her child was doing fine academically, only to be rudely awakened when her child left the friendly confines of an open school.[38]

In the mid-1970s, as many as 4,000 books or articles were published that promoted educational accountability. The literature reflected the US public's general sense that schooling had gotten too soft. In 1975, only 5 percent of responders to a Gallup poll said that they believed children worked too hard at school; 49 percent said that they believed children did not work hard enough. In 1980, 61 percent of parents and 78 percent of nonparents claimed that schools failed to "pay enough attention to reading," up from 48 percent who believed that in 1955. The historian William Reese, reflecting on the short-lived alternative school movement, concluded that "open schools were more of a mouse than a lion."[39]

One cause for the collapse of the movement was the stigmatization of alternative schools. Liberal reformers were concerned that a resegregation of schools was occurring in which mainstream education—with its emphasis on test scores—was being reserved for wealthy white elites, while Black and Brown children were being siloed away in a low-status alternative. That seemed increasingly to be the conclusion of school boards and district administrators in the late 1970s. In 1977, a Texas school board member called the district's alternative program "a dumping ground for problem students—an Alcatraz." In 1979, a New Jersey district administrator closed its alternative school because of de facto segregation. That same year in Connecticut, a district board met to discuss how its alternative school had become synonymous with "poor academic performance." One of South Dakota's alternative schools that was designed for children who struggled academically closed when federal funding dried up. As one administrator remembered, "for the vast majority of parents letter grades provide the knowledge and security that children are learning."[40]

The rapid expansion of alternative schools also caused a watering-down of the movement's classroom radicalism. There did not seem to be enough well-trained, energetic, idealistic classroom teachers to provide a truly student-interest-driven experience. One leader of the movement was concerned about teacher burnout, arguing that the present level of teacher "vitality and energy and anger and sacrifice" was unsustainable. The leader of a Portland, Oregon, alternative school developed ulcers due to the "stress of challenging the status quo" each day, and he ultimately stepped down from his post in 1975. Without his leadership, the school reintroduced testing a few years later. Around the same time, a New York City reporter visited an alternative school and left underwhelmed, writing that "the classroom instruction and subject matter are not essentially different from what might be found in many conventional high schools." In 1977, a member of the Wichita, Kansas, school board argued that the city's alternative school had become "redundant."[41]

In the end, teaching at an alternative school had become too hard, too energy-draining, too time-consuming to be sustained for decades. Leaders of the movement were asking teachers to innovate constantly and to never rest on their laurels, all while being especially sensitive to each child's emotional well-being. On top of it all, the movement required its teachers to eschew traditional systems of authoritarian control, including the efficient use of report cards. The result was a relentless "headache" of narrative descriptions that replaced the tidy columns of markings on school reports. Ultimately, that led to serious problems with teacher resignations. One Chicago teacher, while committed to revolutionizing schools, admitted that there probably were not enough "secure, emotionally healthy, open-minded teachers to allow children to question, to doubt, to express divergent opinions, and to create ideas."[42]

There was also a fundamental contradiction at the heart of publicly funded alternative schools, which Jonathan Kozol recognized when he renounced the entire education system. Although the movement advocated for a radical overhaul of 150 years of traditional education, it still had to rely on traditionalist school boards as its source of funding. Advocates for alternative schools tended to proselytize, as they couched their beliefs with messianic arguments and criticized traditionalists in morally righteous terms. In other words, they tended to alienate the very people who determined the existence of their newly born schools. Some leaders within the movement recognized this problem. At one conference in 1973, a professor of education admitted that alternative schools were already a relic of the 1960s; they had failed to "become the wave of the future" and probably never would.[43]

Perhaps the most insightful criticism of the alternative school movement came from the most righteous and idealistic within the movement itself. Joel Denker and Steve Bhaerman were young private school teachers in the late 1960s, when, inspired by Jonathan Kozol, they created an independently funded street school for African Americans living in Washington, DC. In 1983, they published a book about their failures, admitting to being "chastened rebels." They wrote, "Students came to us confused and left more bewildered and shellshocked than when they arrived." In hindsight, Denker and Bhaerman acknowledged that they should not have assumed that children would act more responsibly when given more freedom. They should not have assumed that "kids were always right, and parents were always wrong." They learned that excessive communication with students did not always lead to consensus, and that teachers frequently competed for the approval of their students instead of focusing on their well-being. "Our vicarious identification with adolescence, our fascination with youth culture," they wrote after the fact, "mirrored our own lack of confidence in our skills and experience." The greatest lesson they learned from the failure of their alternative school: "Love is not permissiveness."[44]

The death of the Wilson Campus School came slowly, and it was never clear who, exactly, killed it. As early as the fall of 1974, there were rumblings that Wilson's future was in danger. Douglas Moore, the new president of Mankato

State, labeled Wilson a "declining program" when he appeared before the state legislature's committee of education, despite the fact that there were nearly 200 children on the school's waiting list. A year later, news arrived that the state legislature was planning to consolidate two properties of Mankato State College—the upper and lower campuses, as they were known—into one central campus. As a result, the Wilson Campus School building would be transformed into the new home of the physical education department of the college.[45]

Initially, all the powerbrokers—Mankato State's administration, state legislators, and the district school board members—claimed that they wanted Wilson to survive. However, each group deflected responsibility for the funding of the school. By the fall of 1975, the frustrations of the Wilson community had turned toward the state legislature, which controlled the funding of Mankato State College and, by extension, the building that housed Wilson. In November 1975, students organized a caravan and drove two hours to St. Paul to meet with their representatives. Kirsten's mother testified before the House Appropriations Committee that the Wilson Campus School had transformed the lives of her children. Some parents and students raised their voices and several broke down in tears.[46]

In the end, the legislature refused to appropriate the $6.9 million needed to construct a new building for Wilson. Instead, the representatives voted to lease a gym on Mankato State's lower campus. They did not, however, appropriate the funds to retrofit the gym into a functional school building. The fundraising responsibilities were therefore imposed on Mankato's public school board. Wilson needed $756,000 to renovate its newly assigned space. As the school board debated whether to appropriate the funds, students marched from their campus down the hill to Mankato's district offices. Kirsten wrote the lyrics to the protest song that they sang while marching along the way: "The people of Mankato / Came dancing round and round / And all agreed the open concept / Was the best they'd ever found."[47]

The arguments against funding the Wilson Campus School were multilayered. The school district was experiencing a precipitous drop in enrollment of its traditional schools, as was the case in much of the country at the end of the postwar baby boom. Teachers at Mankato's traditional public schools were being laid off and the school board was paying for its $9 million loan for the recent construction of Mankato East High School. The broader national tide against alternative schooling was also a factor. One school board member cited the "many periodicals and newspaper articles" that were "seriously questioning alternative educational approaches." The board members added that the popular backlash among taxpayers had put politicians in no "political mood" to support alternative schools.[48]

There is also evidence that the leaders of the Wilson Campus School had alienated too many of the town's supporters of traditional schooling. Don Glines was the most obvious offender. While he had left Mankato in 1974, he still cast a shadow over the proceedings. The board chair recalled that years earlier, a traditionalist had asked Glines whether Mankato State offered classes in humility, and suggested that if so, Glines should enroll in them. Wilson's faculty sensed the schadenfreude among the traditionalists, and they pleaded for support from the board in a petition. "To be supportive of alternative education," they wrote, "does not mean to be anti-traditional education." But those words were a bit disingenuous. For nearly a decade, Mankato's citizens—most of them unaffiliated with the Wilson Campus School—had read about Glines' crusade against their system of education. On several different occasions, Glines claimed to be on a mission to "eliminate the evils" of public schools, arguing that the traditional classroom was "the worst place to learn" and that traditionalists were "doing a lousy job of running our schools." The traditionalists responded by calling Glines an unwelcome zealot, expressing disapproval of all the "crazy things that are going on up there," claiming Wilson was "wild and had kooky teachers," and insisting that "something must be done about that place." The antagonism between the Wilson community and the traditionalists was felt in Kirsten's family. In an article she wrote in 1974, Kirsten's older sister expressed her feeling that the school board did not want the "Wilsonites." They cared more about reducing costs and increasing enrollment in the traditional schools.[49]

On May 24, 1976, the school board rejected the measure to fund the Wilson Campus School's renovation. The final point of persuasion was that the board did not want to pay for a building that the state, not the school district, owned. A few days later, Wilson's newest director gave his thirty-three teachers their notices. The school would continue for the 1976–1977 school year but would close permanently in the summer of 1977. Kirsten and all of Wilson's other approximately 500 students had to find another school.[50]

Anticipating the school closure in the spring of 1977, Kirsten left Wilson early and enrolled in her local public school, but she loathed the experience of going to school each day. Kirsten, who was labeled a weird "Wilson kid," felt like a second-class citizen. The volleyball coach told her that no Wilson kid would play on his team. Her chemistry teacher asked her to sit on the floor when there were not enough desks for everyone, arguing that Wilson kids did not like to sit in desks. After a few weeks, Kirsten begged her mother to allow her to return to the Wilson Campus School, even though the school would be closing in nine months. She wanted to go down with the ship. "I didn't care that Wilson was closing," Kirsten remembered decades later. "I wanted to spend every last minute there." Her mother eventually allowed Kirsten to re-enroll for Wilson's final year.[51]

The 1976–1977 school year was bittersweet. Much of Kirsten's time was spent preparing for her final transition back to the traditional public school. As a tenth grader, Kirsten threatened that she would rather drop out of high school than spend two years at a traditional public school. The adults reached a compromise with Kirsten. If Kirsten promised to get through one year of traditional school, the Wilson administration would claim that Kirsten was a rising twelfth grader, meaning that she could graduate a year ahead of schedule. After Wilson closed, Kirsten gritted her teeth through that final year of high school, infuriated by the deluge of rules, restrictions, and rankings imposed on her.[52]

After graduating from high school, Kirsten enrolled in the University of Minnesota. While at the university, she fell in love with a "city boy," married, and moved to northern Minnesota to become an independent "citizen farmer." In the 1980s, she and her husband grew cauliflower and broccoli and started to raise their three children. In 1991, when their oldest daughter was five, Kirsten became involved in the local public elementary school. Although she had her misgivings about traditional schools, she still believed in public education, and she wanted her family to be part of the community.[53]

However, during her first two years as a school mom, Kirsten became disillusioned with the direction of public education. No works of student art were allowed to be posted on the school walls because of the fire hazard, which gave the institution a prison-like feel. When a shipment of workbooks arrived in the middle of her daughter's kindergarten year, the teacher ended creative play exercises in favor of rote memorization. The teacher acknowledged that her lessons had been a huge success without the workbooks but explained that she had to prepare her pupils for upcoming aptitude tests. In another incident, the principal tasked Kirsten, as a parent volunteer, to oversee photographing the "student of the week." Kirsten was disgusted with the concept. "It was an artificial meritocratic construction," Kirsten explained, channeling her inner-Wilsonian principles. "It was false. It did not have integrity to me." Then her daughter started to develop stomach pains because of the stress of report cards and began taking antacids. The final straw was when school canceled recess because of scheduling conflicts.[54]

Kirsten was parenting in a new age of formal testing. A wave of back-to-basics education had been sweeping the nation since the collapse of the alternative school movement. This new wave became the counterrevolution that some have labeled the accountability movement. The movement began at the district level, with the passing of state laws that required the tracking of "progress" through minimum competency testing programs. From 1975 through 1982—the year before the publication of the seminal study, *A Nation at Risk*—thirty-six states passed accountability laws for their schools. Until 1992, Minnesota granted local school districts the autonomy to devise their own system of testing. Even while in kindergarten, Kirsten's daughter began preparing for one of these district-level tests. In 1993, when Kirsten's oldest daughter was entering first grade, the Minnesota legislature passed a law mandating a statewide results-oriented graduation rule and directing the state's department of education to devise a Minnesota Basic Standards Test (MBTS). Advocates for universal testing argued that they wanted to ensure that no child would "slip through the cracks." Throughout Minnesota, the pressure was now on teachers to show high scores on centrally created exams, even in Kirsten's small farming community near the Canadian border.[55]

By the time that Kirsten's oldest daughter was entering middle school, the stakes of Minnesota's universal testing were raised even higher. In 1996, the legislature created the state's first "exit exam," which attached high school graduation requirements to periodic reading, writing, and mathematics tests. To unveil the new system, the legislature created the Office of Educational Accountability and mandated performance benchmarks that were designed to prepare children for the penultimate graduation exam: a third-grade reading and mathematics exam, a fifth-grade writing exam, and an eighth-grade exam designed to closely mirror the graduation requirements. There were massive problems. In 2000, 7,989 students were misinformed that they had failed the Minnesota Basic Standards Test and that they would not be graduating. It turned out to be a testing error, but the scandal highlighted the flaws in using high-stakes tests to grant or withhold diplomas.[56]

Kirsten seemed to have instinctively understood the direction that Minnesota's public education was heading. She could sense that public school teachers, responding to the state-mandated incentive structure, found themselves caring more about obtaining a "good record of academic achievement for

their class" than the emotional well-being of their students. Disillusionment combined with a personal tragedy led Kirsten to reassess her entire
life. In 1993, a drunk driver slammed into the family minivan that Kirsten's
husband was driving, causing him to suffer a traumatic brain injury. There-
after, running the family nursery business and berry farm in northern Minnesota became too challenging. Kirsten felt a sudden urge to change her life
and perhaps to teach, but not at a school built around the periodic testing of
children. She wanted to teach in a place that felt like the Wilson Campus School.
Kirsten also wanted to give her daughters the same type of education that she
had had, where school report cards did not cause ulcers. When Kirsten
searched for an alternative school that was still in existence, she stumbled upon
a brochure for the Minnesota Waldorf School.[57]

The Waldorf School movement dates to the early twentieth century in Ger-
many; it was a product of an earlier alternative school movement within the
European context. The brand of education then spread worldwide and to every
state in the United States. Waldorf schools were more structured than Wilson,
which had built its curricula around the immediate intellectual curiosities of
each child. Waldorf schools, on the other hand, began each morning with
music, which segued into movement activities, followed by intellectual challenges that reflected the rhythms and cycles of the four seasons. While the
schools do not provide complete student freedom, as there had been at Wilson, Waldorf did build its schools around learning for learning's sake. There
were no tests, no comparison of students, and no academic competition. Waldorf Schools never considered issuing data-driven, quantifiable report cards.[58]

The more Kirsten learned about Waldorf, the more she became intrigued.
At the age of thirty-four, she left the farm for a Waldorf teacher-training
program in California. When she returned three weeks later, the Minnesota
Waldorf School hired her as an assistant kindergarten teacher, where she
earned six dollars per hour. Kirsten then loaded her daughters into a pickup
truck, drove the three hours to Minneapolis, and began her new life in the
big city. She rented a second-floor, two-bedroom apartment near the school.
Kirsten taught at Waldorf for twenty-eight years. All three daughters attended
the school through eighth grade and have grown into responsible, functional,
and happy adults—all without report cards.[59]

In January 2001, President George W. Bush signed into law the No Child Left
Behind Act (NCLB), a bipartisan piece of legislation that many educational
historians see as a turning point in the history of American schools. The law

required that all schools that received federal assistance institute comprehensive formal testing. If test scores drop below certain benchmarks, funding would be removed.

Ninety senators voted in favor of the law. Among the few senators who voted against NCLB was Minnesota Senator Paul Wellstone (D). Wellstone was the scrappy son of Ukrainian immigrants and a championship college wrestler. As a child, Wellstone hated tests. In fact, his dyslexia made school incredibly difficult. Through grit and genuine curiosity, Wellstone earned his PhD in political science, and he then moved to Minnesota to become a professor at Carleton College.[60]

To Wellstone, something seemed horribly wrong about NCLB. He explained to a reporter at the time, "I think this [NCLB] oversteps, if not the authority, the sort of boundaries of congressional decision making on education." He added, "I'm convinced that I never would have received my doctorate if I had taken the results of standardized tests too seriously or listened to those who put so much credence in what they measured."[61] Tragically, Wellstone died in a plane crash just nine months after he voted against NCLB.

Since 2002—the year of both Wellstone's death and the enactment of NCLB—the term report card expanded its meaning. As required by NCLB, "report card" became a metaphor for evaluating entire education systems: individual schools, school districts, and state school systems. In 2004, the New York Board of Regents began issuing its "New York State Report Card," which showed, not surprisingly, that a child's test scores correlated with familial wealth, which correlated with race. Texas, like many states, issued report cards for individual school districts, categorizing each school as having "met standard" or "not met standard." In 2006, Illinois' school report cards made available mountains of aggregated data; for instance, 33 percent of the state's students met expectations on the PARCC test and 27.9 percent on the DLM-AA test. State education departments issued so-called report cards evaluating their sex education programs (New Jersey gave its teachers a C for their lack of training), their digital learning/technology classes (only Florida and Utah received As), and their efforts at diversity, equity, and inclusion (61 percent of third graders in Hermosa Beach, California, responded "favorably" when asked about diversity and inclusion).[62]

In the wake of No Child Left Behind, everyone seemed to be surveilling, evaluating, and reporting on everyone else: teachers issued report cards on students, principals evaluated teachers, districts reported on the performance of individual schools, state departments published report cards on districts, and news agencies like *U.S. News & World Report* and *Education Weekly* ranked each state. The zeitgeist seemed to be moving further and further away from Don Glines' vision of alternative schooling half a century before.

Meanwhile, student report cards started to go online. In the 2010s, dozens of new school databases exploded onto the educational marketplace; entrepreneurs and technology advocates sometimes called these databases "learning management systems" (LMS) or "learning community management systems" (LCMS) or "digital school performance platforms" (DSPP). Companies with names like FreshGrade, Canvas, Blackboard, Moodle, NetClassroom, iParent, and MyBackPack promised to revolutionize education, make online teaching more customized for each learner, and streamline grading for teachers. And, of course, these LMSs/LCMSs/DSPPs promised to transform the nineteenth-century relic of the paper school report card.[63]

In 2010, the US Department of Education encouraged local school districts to adopt online forms of report cards, issuing a paper called "The National Educational Technology Plan." The plan promoted a variety of databases that were "powerful" in "measuring student achievement in more complete, authentic, and meaningful ways." These databases, the department argued, could be used to produce a continuous flow of data on students, with daily updates for teachers and parents to track student progression. Online report cards began to include graphs in which parents could more easily compare their child's test scores to averages within the school, the district, and across the nation. The explicit goal of the new online report cards was to blur the lines between the home and the school, with prompt and continuous feedback. One company called Alberta Education created a system in which teachers could track and store student "performances" in "leadership skills, group process management, or multicultural interactions." Moodle offered its clients "automatic forum discussion grading" that parents could monitor instantaneously. Lane Merrifield, founder of FreshGrade, promoted his online grading system as "an immediate window into the classroom," in which parents are alerted whenever a digital portfolio grade has been updated.[64]

As the 2010s ended, the results of the new databases were mixed at best. Critics noted that online grading was essentially "static," glorified versions of paper copies of report cards. There was little evidence that the new levels of constant surveillance and instantaneous reporting helped students learn anything, despite the boosterism of companies and school officials alike. Meanwhile, some parents reflected on their new obsessive "hovering," logging in every day to check on their child's homework grades and in-class projects.

Channeling the nineteenth-century creators of report cards like George Willson, one founder of an EdTech company explained that daily surveillance was exactly the point. Rob Wilson promised that his database, Edupoint, would get "parents involved not just at the end of the quarter at report card time" but at each moment of progress. Paul Wellstone's comments from 2002 seemed increasingly prescient. A dyslexic kid like him, living through the age of digital surveillance and perpetual testing, may not have been given much of a chance to discover and then pursue a passion for political science.[65]

And then there is Kirsten, who taught in her gradeless school throughout the 2010s. She has not given up hope of carving out dignity for children in schools. She was lucky to find a niche for herself, holding firm to her belief that "human beings can't be quantified by numbers." She adds, "We have to be able to stomach the fact that every person is unique in what they can learn and accomplish."[66] That position appears to be increasingly countercultural.

Pulling Weeds and Foucault Fatigue

Patrick [pseud.] and I are friends. Our children attend the same public elementary school, a Title I school with about 60 percent of the children living at or below the poverty line. We are active school dads, not just dropping off and picking up our kids but also volunteering to help however we can. On one sunny afternoon, while I was researching the final chapter of this book, Patrick and I noticed a problem as we walked to school. The playground was becoming overrun with weeds and poison oak, swallowing up benches and play equipment. My instinct was to put on bug spray and start weeding. Patrick disagreed. He saw the encroaching weeds as a metaphor for the institutional incompetence of Atlanta Public Schools (APS), alleging graft, mismanagement, and laziness on the part of officials. He was angry. Angry that our children were schooled virtually for the first eleven months of the coronavirus pandemic, angry that students continued to wear masks, and angry that APS lacked the resources to clear weeds from the school playground.

A lot had changed in the years since my trip to Beirut and my serendipitous discovery of the stack of 1982 report cards. Multiple waves of COVID-19 had passed through Atlanta. Our city, like much of the country, had gone through a racial reckoning during the protests sparked by the death of George Floyd. A presidential election had come and gone, followed by an insurrection, and the systematic attack on our elections, with Georgia playing a leading role in the unfolding drama. Throughout these events, our children learned virtually. My daughters missed their friends and teachers. The entire family missed the daily hellos of drop-off and pickup. My wife and I missed volunteering with the PTA. We missed the deepening friendships that we had formed with the other parents. The pandemic highlighted how much our lives revolved around our school community and how much school was the main source of social interaction for children and adults alike.

Everyone seemed exhausted by the time that Patrick and I discussed the problem of the weeds. We had returned to in-person learning, but life was different. Part of the challenge was caused by the necessity to maintain social distancing: no more school events and no more parents inside the building.

Many families from our school had been uprooted by the pandemic, vanishing without saying goodbye. Politics had created divisions too. A small group of parents became frustrated when our principal recommended a children's book that explained the history of enslavement in the United States. I watched parents lose their tempers at the request to wait in line to pick up their children. Some parents were upset that they were asked to test their children for COVID; other parents were frustrated by the parents who resisted that testing. In another incident, I saw a community member refuse to remove her dog from the school playground. Instead of following the district rule, she pulled out her camera and began to videotape the adult who made the request, berating the person about tax dollars and personal freedom.

We were all on edge, and the institution of the school became the focal point for people's frustrations. My friend Patrick was a great example: a reasonable, responsible adult, his displeasure at all forms of authority pushed him toward supporting a burgeoning secessionist movement, in which the wealthiest part of our city, known as Buckhead, threatened to break away from the rest of Atlanta. Small grievances like unpulled weeds merged with larger grievances like the rise in crime.

I could not help but think that Michel Foucault—the darling of post-modern French intellectuals—was capturing the zeitgeist of this moment: the loss of faith in local institutions and the perception that small acts by authorities were sinister attempts at authoritarian control. Scholars have noted similar trends. Mask mandates and promotion of vaccinations, issues over which Foucault would gaze upon with suspicion, became hallmarks of the culture wars. Progressives found themselves on the opposing side of Foucault's legacy, as conservatives adopted Foucault's rhetoric of mistrust and suspicion of scientific experts. One unapologetic Foucauldian scholar, the Italian philosopher Giorgio Agamben, cited Foucault in his criticism of the "techno-medical despotism" of epidemiologists. The populist right, in a strange confluence, adopted Agamben's rhetoric of Foucauldian paranoia. Georgia Congresswoman Marjorie Taylor Greene, as one example, pointed out that Anthony Fauci, director of the US National Institute of Allergy and Infectious Diseases, was "not elected by the American people" and that his efforts to promote vaccines was akin to "medical brown shirts showing up at [your] door ordering vaccinations." Foucault, who inspired my research, seemed increasingly tiresome.[1]

The mistrust of medical expertise was just the latest episode in the larger decline of institutional trust in the United States. In 2021, survey results showed all-time lows in trust of government, religious institutions, journalists, and the criminal justice system. Included in these institutions experiencing a wave of suspicion were public schools. According to Gallup's 2021 polls, just 32 percent of respondents placed "quite a lot" of trust in public schools, down 9 percentage points from the year before and roughly half of the peak amount of trust in public schools that Gallup documented in the 1970s. An increase in mistrust typically leads to an increase in disengagement with institutions; data reflect this phenomenon, as well. In 2001, Robert Putnam noted the generational decline in rates of participation in civil society, including organizations like the PTA. Two decades later, the declines continue. Nationwide, the pandemic led to more than a million students dropping out of public schools altogether, with 340,000 kindergarteners not showing up at all.[2]

Speaking with Patrick, I wondered whether our school community really needed my Foucauldian analysis of report cards. Identifying ways in which schools extended disciplinary power into the lives of pupils seemed to have become a bit of an academic trope. Extracurricular sports like football, outdoor education like ropes courses, and even pep rallies have all been subject to Foucauldian analysis, characterized by academics as authoritarian attempts to control adolescents. My study of the origins and evolution of the school report card seemed too much part of a larger cliché, piling onto the criticism of our schools when they were already suffering from low morale. I was metaphorically kicking a person when they were down.[3]

The great paradox is that I cannot help but think that Foucault was right. Seemingly small acts, like sending home a school report card, are indeed attempts at control: control of the child and the child's family. This goal was made explicit in the antebellum period. Report cards were also incredibly effective. Throughout the nineteenth and twentieth centuries, teachers, parents, and students alike noted how school report cards caused neurosis, fear, and anxiety. The problem is that I was surrounded by neurosis, fear, and anxiety that sometimes seemed misplaced or misdirected.

Like a lot of histories, much of what I wrote was autobiographical. I loved being part of schools, both as a student and a teacher, yet I recognize their shortcomings. I can relate to George Willson, a career classroom teacher struggling to command respect from the parents of his pupils. In report cards, he leveraged the little power that he had to persuade parents to support his pedagogical efforts. I relate to William Matthews. Like young William, I brought home high marks on report cards. I also believed, like Matthews, in the transformative power of schooling to serve as a means for social mobility. I did not stop to question the report card. I believed in it, that it could instill individual discipline and healthy self-analysis, that it could be a barometer for a child's progress. Like Martha McKay, I am an overly involved public school parent. My wife and I pay close attention to our daughters' report cards. Also like McKay, my parenting is full of contradictions. I loathe the academic anxiety that emerges in my elementary-aged children, but I am fond of data that sheds light on their learning. I hate tests, but I am fascinated by test results. There is also a bit of Kirsten Albrecht in me: her joy for learning and dedication to her career as a teacher. Her idealism, which has lasted for half a century, is something that I can only wish to emulate.

I have a harder time relating to Andrew Monroe and Daniel Schorr. I never mistrusted authority like Andrew. I never rejected schooling altogether, never ran away from my parents or teachers. If there were anyone from chapter 4 with whom I connected it would be Judge Ben Lindsey, the child-saver who believed that he could synthesize a compassionate legal system with the efficiency of school reports. For the most part, it appears that Lindsey had the character and skill to do just that in his Denver court. However, his system of reporting spread, and in the hands of a less patient judge it could be cruelly reductionist. Likewise, I cannot claim to have much in common with Daniel Schorr. The challenges that he overcame—poverty, losing a parent, discrimination—required a drive and intensity that I have never needed. He was an outsider. I am the quintessential insider within my community and perhaps within the United States more broadly. Both Monroe and Schorr provide a healthy perspective on the system of school reporting, rejecting report cards while at the same time never quite escaping their reach.

Philosophy also helped me make sense of the balance between an individual's free will and broader systems of social control. Building on Michel Foucault's work, the philosopher Mark Bevir concluded that there can be no "autonomous subject who stands outside of society," meaning that no individual can live, grow, and develop consciousness in isolation from their surroundings. My protagonists, in other words, were not "sovereign" over their own lives; they could not rule themselves "uninfluenced by others." The periodic nudging and incentives of report cards throughout the lives of Willson, Matthews, McKay, Monroe, Schorr, and Albrecht were therefore case studies for what a lack of autonomy looks like in microcosm. Yet each historical figure asserted their independence. They acted in "creative, novel ways," as Bevir wrote, to alter the social backdrop that attempted to control them. A study of their lives therefore offers insight into how many individuals navigated the disciplinary power of modernity.[4]

Upon reflection, a British documentary series titled *Up* might have been another source of inspiration for this project. *Up* is a nine-part documentary that has tracked the lives of fourteen individuals for over fifty-six years, dating back to 1964. The director, Michael Apted, identified fourteen seven-year-old children, interviewed them, and documented their daily lives. Every seven years, Apted returned to the same children as they became adults: fourteen, twenty-one, twenty-eight, and so on. The most recent episode of *Up* was released in 2019 when the protagonists were sixty-three years old. Before Apted died in 2021, he explained that the purpose of the documentary series evolved over the decades. Originally, Apted intended to unmask Britain's entrenched class system. He wanted to show how the children of elites received greater opportunities and how the children of the working class were limited in their development. The results of fifty-six years of documentation did not necessarily contradict Apted's hypothesis. The wealthy did indeed maintain their wealth and they did indeed experience more career opportunities. Meanwhile, the working-class participants continued to struggle financially. However, as the series evolved, the relevance of Britain's hierarchy became less and less interesting. Instead, the *Up* series is fascinating because it traces fourteen people's maturation, their struggle to find meaning in their careers, their families, and their communities. The series stopped being a Marxist interpretation of Britain's political-economy and became a humanist reflection on existence.

In a small way, I feel that the same evolution occurred in the years of researching this book. I began with the intention of examining the history of how power exerted itself within schools. I ended much more interested in how individuals navigated that power to find purpose and meaning in their lives. The protagonists were, at times, aware of the arbitrary nature of school reports and how the system of surveillance and record keeping was shaping them. But how they lived their lives and how they found—or failed to find—purpose is fascinating, much more fascinating than the evolution of disciplinary power, in my opinion.

Patrick, my fellow elementary school dad, and I are continuations of the history of education in the United States. We have inherited the system that Willson helped to create, that Matthews perpetuated, that McKay reinforced, that Monroe rejected, that Schorr survived, and that Albrecht worked so hard to avoid. If the current era in the history of US schools is one characterized by mistrust and exhaustion, then it is important to note how Patrick and I are also navigating these larger forces in a daily struggle to both parent and build community. Do we pull the weeds, or do we add the weeds to the long list of shortcomings in our school system, a list that includes report cards?

My daughters' fourth-grade teacher, Ms. Williams, noticed the same problem with weeds. On a crisp Saturday, she organized a cleanup crew. For four hours, several dozen students, parents, administrators, and teachers gathered to pull those weeds, rake leaves, and lay pine straw. At one point, as I was digging up the roots of a dead bush in the school courtyard, a group of students arrived. They were there to give Ms. Williams a hug. Ms. Williams saw a need within the school community, and she acted. She did not overanalyze who was to blame for the weeds, nor did she pause to reflect on power structures within our public school district. Instead, she asked her fourth graders to give up their Saturday to help her. And they responded. They said yes because they adore her.

Ms. Williams' Saturday cleanup was the first opportunity that I had to chat casually with many of the teachers since the early days of the pandemic, when my exploration of the report card's history began. I asked them what they thought about Atlanta Public Schools issuing report cards in elementary school. No one defended the practice. Consensus, even among the administrators, was that quantifying the progress of children is silly, at best. Yet we continue the system—parents and teachers alike—because school, like life, is full of contradictions. Cognitive dissonance is sometimes required to be functional adults. Within these contradictions between pedagogical belief and daily practices, teachers and students are still able to find meaning.

Depiction of African American Parents
in American Missionary, *1867–1881*

The data show that there was a marked decrease in the number of references to Black parents from 1867 to 1881 (figure A.I.1). In 1867, thirty-four articles in *American Missionary* mentioned or described how formerly enslaved adults in the South were parenting their children. By the late 1870s and early 1880s, the references were less than half their peak in the late 1860s, numbering as low as just nine references in 1876. There are several explanations. First, as the 1870s progressed, the American Missionary Association (AMA) either closed its schools for freed people or turned administrative responsibility over to newly created local school boards. Lewis High was unusual in that it remained entirely reliant on the AMA for funding and administrative support. Second, the AMA's focus turned toward its overseas ventures in West Africa and China, and schools for indigenous people within the United States. While each issue of *American Missionary* still described the AMA's work with freed people, the journal dedicated more and more space to other projects. However, part of the decrease in references to African American parents did reflect a change in attitude among the mostly white teachers. The regional director of AMA's schools in Georgia, overseeing Lewis High School, wrote that "the novelty" of education "had worn off" among freed parents and "there was a loss of interest and a decreased attendance" in Georgia's schools.[1]

I further divided the articles that referenced African American parents into three categories: positive, critical, or neutral. The results are shown in figure A.I.2, tracking the percentage of positive and critical references to parents from 1867 to 1881 in *American Missionary*. Neutral articles typically described the challenges that freed parents faced but did so without commentary; a tone of pity, and perhaps even condescension, pervaded neutral articles. As soon as the article mentioned a parent overcoming challenges, I counted it in the positive column. Positive references also included a description of parents supporting their child's school or the parental sacrifices made on behalf of education. Critical references, on the other hand, tended to focus on parental alcohol consumption, absent fathers, overreliance on physical punishment, and general disinterest in education among parents.

Once again, the results were striking. As time progressed, there was a noticeable decrease in the percentage of positive references to African American parents. As the

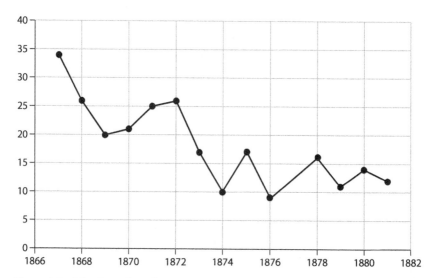

Figure A.I.1. Number of articles in *American Missionary* that mention the parenting of formerly enslaved people, from 1867 to 1881

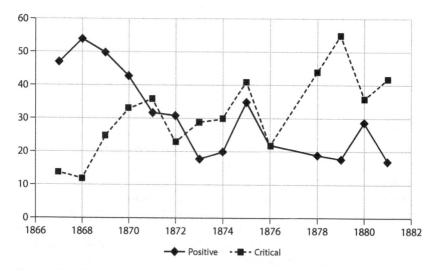

◆ Positive   ■ Critical

Figure A.I.2. Mentions of freed parents in *American Missionary* that were positive and critical, from 1867 to 1881 (in percentages)

1860s closed, typically about half of references to parents in *American Missionary* were explicitly positive, praising their enthusiasm for education and their resilience in the face of adversity. By the late 1870s and early 1880s, positive references to parents had dropped to below 20 percent. Meanwhile, criticism of African American parents jumped from 12 percent to 14 percent in the late 1860s, to as high as 55 percent in the late 1870s. To be sure, inherent in the data are the prejudices and racism of the authors. Also, the data reflect the general loss of enthusiasm in the North for the egalitarian crusade of Reconstruction. There are other factors, though, that are more peculiar to the AMA. In the late 1860s, schools for freed people were the main focus of the AMA's fundraising efforts. Thus, there was an incentive for editors and authors to celebrate freed people as worthy of and grateful to northern donors. In the 1870s, as the number of references to African Americans decreased and as the percentage of those references that were negative increased, there was less pressure on teachers to deliver fundraising propaganda.

NOTE

1. W. L. Clarke, "Transitions—Good Time Coming," *American Missionary* 16, no. 9 (September 1872): 196–97.

Ladies Home Journal *and the Defense of Teachers*

To what extent did the women's club movement lead to an increase in the defense of teachers? To help answer this question, I once again employed a content analysis. I examined each issue of two different monthly publications from the years 1885 to 1904. The first, *Ladies Home Journal*, was the most popular monthly magazine publicized primarily for white, upper-class female audiences. I chose the second journal, *Frank Leslie's Popular Monthly*, as a point of comparison. While not explicitly intended for wealthy white men, *Frank Leslie's Popular Monthly* did cater to male audiences and was also widely distributed across the United States. I tracked every article that referenced schoolteachers for a twenty-year period. I chose to begin in 1885, still the early period of the women's club movement, and ended in 1904, which was the year that G. Stanley Hall published his book *Adolescence* and represented the height of the child study movement.

I narrowed my focus on schoolteachers of grammar school through what was then beginning to be called "high school." I did not track references to college professors or Sunday school teachers. I excluded references to specialized teachers outside of school, what we might call tutors. There were hundreds of articles in *Ladies Home Journal* that mentioned piano, voice, and art tutors that I ignored. I also excluded descriptions of foreign teachers. *Frank Leslie's Popular Monthly* tended to publish long-form pieces describing European, African, and Asian cultures; many of these articles also described foreign educational traditions. However, if an article mentioned an American missionary teacher abroad, then I did include it in the data. One important point is that I was tracking the number of articles that referenced teachers, even if the reference was just in passing. I did not quantify the relative emphasis that each article placed on teachers. Therefore, an article that mentioned a teacher in a single sentence carried the same weight as an article dedicated to describing a teacher's working conditions in depth. Finally, I should note that each issue of *Frank Leslie's Popular Monthly* included about twice as many pages as *Ladies Home Journal*, and *Ladies Home Journal* also tended to include more images and advertisements. There were more opportunities, therefore, for *Frank Leslie's Popular Monthly* to mention schoolteachers.

The first goal of this content analysis was comparative. I wanted to see if a journal explicitly dedicated to women and largely written by women placed more of an emphasis on schoolteachers than a journal implicitly dedicated to male audiences. My hypothesis was that with the rise of women gaining a public voice, whether through the women's club movement or in a monthly magazine, the interests of a mostly female teaching workforce would be amplified. The second goal was to track change over time. Did references to schoolteachers become more sympathetic over these two decades, a period that correlated with an increase in participation in women's clubs? In order to answer this question, I categorized each reference to schoolteachers into four groups: positive, sympathetic, neutral, and critical. First, any reference to a teacher that mentioned a teacher's piety, patience, effectiveness, and so on was included in the positive group. Most important for testing William Reese's argument—that clubwomen became vocal defenders of teachers—was the "sympathetic" category.[1] I tracked all articles that mentioned the challenges that teachers faced, namely low pay, overcrowded classrooms, lack of supplies, and the like. I also created a category called "neutral" in which there was no editorializing about the teacher, good or bad. Finally, I tracked articles that were critical of teachers, their behavior in the classroom, lack of training, and so on. If William Reese's hypothesis was correct, then I would likely see an increase in the number of sympathetic references to teachers as the two decades progressed, as more and more women organized themselves into clubs and advocated for the interests of teachers.

It came as no surprise that the journal dedicated to women referenced teachers far more than the journal read by mostly men. From 1885 to 1904, *Ladies Home Journal* published 567 articles that mentioned schoolteachers. During that same period, *Frank Leslie's Popular Monthly* mentioned American schoolteachers in 188 articles. There were four times as many articles that included a positive reference to teachers in *Ladies Home Journal* but also twice as many articles that were critical of teachers. Most importantly for testing the Reese hypothesis, *Ladies Home Journal* was more than thirteen times more likely to include an article that was sympathetic to the challenges of school teaching than *Frank Leslie's Popular Monthly* (figure A.II.1). The typical refence to a teacher in *Frank Leslie's Popular Monthly* was in passing, such as a biography of William T. Sherman that described the general's childhood teacher.[2] Meanwhile, several of the authors in *Ladies Home Journal* were former teachers and it was not unusual for them to write with schoolteachers as the intended audience.[3] To be fair, however, *Ladies Home Journal* was not a publication dedicated to education. The journal published entire issues that did not reference teachers. The journal dedicated far more space to topics like opera, home decorations, floral arrangements, and cooking.

While the data show that *Ladies Home Journal* was more sympathetic to teachers than *Frank Leslie's Popular Monthly*, it is less clear that the increase in sympathetic references correlates with the increase in women's clubs. Three different peaks and valleys of articles that mention the challenges of teaching are shown in figure A.II.2. There were seven references in 1891, five references in 1898 and 1899, and then a spike in 1903 with thirteen articles. One of the main causes of concern in *Ladies Home Journal* was the poor physical condition of the classroom. In 1886, a teacher wrote about the "icy spare chambers" of her classroom; in 1888, the journal published

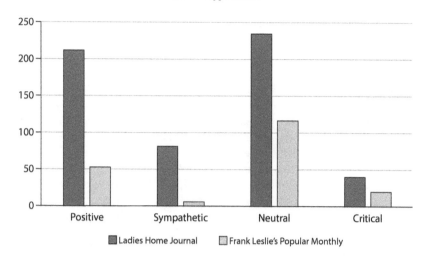

Figure A.II.1. Number of articles with references to teachers in *Ladies Home Journal* as compared to *Frank Leslie's Monthly Journal*, 1885 to 1904

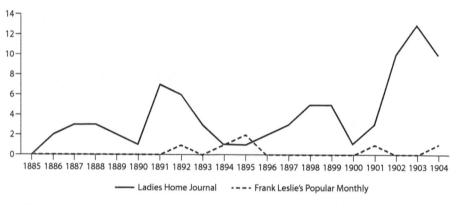

Figure A.II.2. Number of articles with sympathetic references to teachers in *Ladies Home Journal* as compared to *Frank Leslie's Monthly Journal*, 1885 to 1904

a fictionalized story in which the protagonist, a teacher, broke down with "nervous excitement" because of the crowded schoolroom that lacked lighting and ventilation; thirteen years later, in 1901, a veteran female educator detailed the "dreary" conditions under which teachers labored.[4] However, the most common sympathetic defense of teachers was about their low pay.

Many references to low pay were in passing, incidental to the main point of the article.[5] Yet on a few occasions, *Ladies Home Journal* published articles that bordered on political advocacy, denouncing the large workloads and low pay as an abuse of teachers. In 1890, one author criticized parents and society as a whole for allowing teachers to be "underrated, underpaid, and obtain[ing] no social recognition."[6] In 1899, the journal described teachers as a "noble army of martyrs" who "marched to the chambers of torture."[7] *Ladies Home Journal* veered closest to feminism, though, in 1889, when it protested the fact that female teachers were paid less than male teachers.[8]

It is difficult to conclude that the women's club movement caused the spike in such sympathetic references in the early 1900s. *Ladies Home Journal* did indeed publish stories on women's clubs, such as when it provided a detailed guide on how to establish a local club. However, there was rarely a link in the journal between the clubs and defense of teachers.[9]

One exception came in 1903 when the journal published a story about a club that raised money for teacher training and supplies.[10] However, editorial decisions best explain the dramatic rise in the early 1900s of sympathetic references. Beginning in the late 1890s, *Ladies Home Journal* dedicated more space to advice columns in which authors responded to reader mail. Many, but not all, of these readers were teachers or young women pondering whether or not to become teachers, asking for advice on how to navigate difficult working conditions.[11] Even though there is little evidence for a direct line of causation, William Reese's insight resonates. The more civically engaged women became, whether through a literary club or an advice column, the more visible the interests of women are to historians over a century later. Evidence suggests that mothers and teachers, particularly female teachers, did indeed become allies in the nineteenth century, albeit in a piecemeal, disconnected way that is difficult to track.

NOTES

1. William Reese noticed that the women's club movement prompted mothers to become vocal defenders of the rights of schoolteachers, a profession that was increasingly associated with women and poor working conditions. While Patricia Carter noticed a similar dynamic in the twentieth century, she focused on the impact that teachers made on the women's club movement, not vice versa. See Reese, *Power and the Promise of School Reform: Grassroots Movements During the Progressive Era* (Boston: Routledge & Kegan Paul, 1986), 46–49; Carter, *"Everybody's Paid But the Teacher": The Teaching Profession and the Women's Movement* (New York: Teachers College Press, 2002).

2. "Sherman and Porter," *Frank Leslie's Popular Monthly* 31, no. 5 (May 1891): 502–3.

3. In the early and mid-1890s, a columnist named "Aunt Patience" described her experience as a schoolteacher. As an example, see Aunt Patience, "Just Among Ourselves," *Ladies Home Journal* 9, no. 2 (January 1892): 24. In the late 1890s, *Ladies Home Journal* added a columnist who on several occasions responded to the letters of schoolteachers requesting advice. See Margaret Sangster, "Mrs. Sangster's Heart to Heart Talks with Girls," *Ladies Home Journal* 20, no. 7 (June 1903): 34. Note that *Ladies Home Journal* began each volume in December.

4. "More Bright Ideas," *Ladies Home Journal* 6, no. 3 (May 1886): 3; "The School Mistress," *Ladies Home Journal* 5, no. 2 (January 1888): 1; Mary Louise Graham, "My Boarding-School for Girls," *Ladies Home Journal* 18, no. 9 (August 1901): 5–6.

5. As an example, see "How We Went Abroad," *Ladies Home Journal* 6, no. 9 (August 1889): 4. This article, like several others, mentioned the challenges of how to survive on a teacher's salary.

6. Caroline B. LeRow, "Essential of a Good Teacher," *Ladies Home Journal* 7, no. 9 (August 1890): 11.

7. "The Murder of Modern Innocents," *Ladies Home Journal* 16, no. 3 (February 1899): 14.

8. "A Woman's Plan for Women," *Ladies Home Journal* 6, no. 11 (October 1889): 10.

9. Louise Stockton, "Organize a Literary Club," *Ladies Home Journal* 12, no. 12 (November 1895): 17.

10. "The World and His Wife," *Ladies Home Journal* 20, no. 4 (March 1903): 14–16.

11. For an example, see "Just Told in a Talkative Way," *Ladies Home Journal* 21, no. 7 (June 1904): 3.

Introduction · Civil War, Pandemic, and Report Cards

1. Reem Haddad, *I Am IC: A School's Journey from Smyrna to Beirut* (Beirut, Lebanon: Librairie Antoine S.A.L., 2019), 334–36.

2. Reem Haddad blacked out all proper names in the report cards to protect the anonymity of the students.

3. There is now over a half century's worth of literature on the shortcomings of Foucault's work. The historian Richard F. Hamilton, for one, outlined Foucault's methodological flaws, which included comparing noncomparable experiences, misleading readers into believing that Jeremy Bentham's panopticon was never built in England, and projecting intentionality despite a lack of evidence. Hamilton labels Foucault "paranoid" and his theories as "mock scholarship." In 1978, a panel of historians confronted Foucault with Hamilton's point about Bentham's panopticon, criticizing Foucault for implying that the new prison was ubiquitous when in fact none were ever built in Britain and only two modified versions were constructed in the United States. Foucault responded, "if I had wanted 'real life' in the prisons, I indeed wouldn't have gone to Bentham." Educational historian Ronald E. Butchart called Foucault "ethically suspect." Even worse were Foucault's disciples for using "speech that mystifies, that lords esoteric knowledge over its hearers" and for dismissing "most of history's audience as unworthy of its time." Keith Hoskin captured a moderate approach to Foucauldian analysis when he explained that, while *Discipline and Punish* was indeed "bad empirical history," on the other hand "bad data does not necessarily invalidate theory." See Richard F. Hamilton, "Michel Foucault: The Disciplinary Society," in *The Social Misconstruction of Reality: Validity and Verification in the Scholarly Community* (New Haven, CT: Yale University Press, 1996), 174–75, 181; Michel Foucault, "Questions of Method," in *Power*, ed. James D. Faubion, trans. Robert Hurley and others (New York: New Press, 1994), 232; Ronald E. Butchart, "What's Foucault Got to Do with It? History, Theory, and Becoming Subjected," *History of Education Quarterly* 51, no. 2 (May 2011): 242 and 246; Keith Hoskin, "Foucault Under Examination: The Crypto Educationalist Unmasked," in *Foucault and Education: Disciplines and Knowledge* (London: Routledge, 1990), 42–43.

4. See Michel Foucault, *Discipline and Punish: The Birth of the Prison*, trans. Alan Sheridan (New York: Vintage Books, 1995), 146–47; see also Foucault, "Truth and Juridical Forms," in *Power*, ed. James D. Faubion, trans. Robert Hurley and others (New York: New Press, 1994), 11–12.

5. Foucault, *Discipline and Punish*, 170; Foucault, *The History of Sexuality*, Volume I: *An Introduction*, trans. Robert Hurley (New York: Random House, 1990), 49.

6. See Michel-Rolph Trouillot, *Silencing the Past: Power and the Production of History* (Boston: Beacon Press, 1995), ch. 1.

Chapter 1 · *Rousing the Attention of Parents*

1. Noah T. Clarke, *Sixty Years Ago: Early History of Canandaigua* (Canandaigua, NY: Ontario County Times Steam Printing House, 1898), section XXXIII. Clarke's memoirs were published as a series in the *Ontario Repository*, a local newspaper. The Ontario County Historical Society collected these articles, which were published over the course of several months in 1898, as newspaper clippings in a folder. The call number for the folder is 974.786 C599s.

2. "Meeting of the Ontario County Lyceum," *Geneva (NY) Gazette*, September 23, 1835, 1. The meeting is briefly referenced in William C. Woodbridge, *American Annals of Education and Instruction*, Volume V (Boston: William D. Ticknor, 1835), 524–25. Jack Schneider and Ethan Hutt mention the passage within the larger context of the birth of systems of grading in the United States. See Jack Schneider and Ethan Hutt, "Making the Grade: A History of the A–F Marking Scheme," *Journal of Curriculum Studies* 46, no. 2 (March 4, 2014): 206–7.

3. A number of historians have examined the nineteenth-century origins of twentieth-century grading systems, yet the idea of the report card only received brief references. Jack Schneider and Ethan Hutt placed the rise of grading systems within the broader transatlantic context. See Schneider and Hutt, "Making the Grade," 203–10.

As an example of William Cutler's sources, in just a few pages he cited books by Charles Northend, a Massachusetts superintendent in the 1850s; J. J. Rerimensnyder, a Pennsylvania superintendent; and Paul H. Hanus, Harvard's first professor of education. Sources written by actual teachers were noticeably absent. See William W. Cutler III, *Parents and Schools: The 150-Year Struggle for Control in American Education* (Chicago: University of Chicago Press, 2000), 20–24.

William Reese detailed the tensions between Boston's schoolmasters and the administrative allies of Horace Mann. The power play between these two opposing sides, according to Reese, gave rise to the use of written examinations in secondary schools. Parents were not central to Reese's narrative, in either the birth of written examinations or in their spread beyond Massachusetts. See William J. Reese, *Testing Wars in the Public Schools: A Forgotten History* (Cambridge, MA: Harvard University Press, 2013), 40–43.

J. M. Opal touched on parent–teacher tensions when he wrote about one New England teacher's attempts in 1798 to create a system of rewards. Opal argued that parents resented the implication by teachers that "instead of following their parents' calling, children should seek distinction among their peers and within an expanded public." Joseph Kett explained that by the mid-to-late nineteenth century, as more children attended school during the planting and harvesting seasons, parents were increasingly aware of the sacrifice of potential earnings associated with longer school years. Parental expectations, therefore, increased as they demanded greater returns in future earnings for their children. Finally, Carl Kaestle recognized the ubiquity of parent–teacher animosity. According to Kaestle, prior to the common school era and the rise of educational bureaucracies, parents held more control over the running of local schools and the hiring and firing of teachers. That began to change in the mid-nineteenth century and with the change came an increase in complaints about teachers, and then teachers responded with their own list of grievances. See J. M. Opal, "Exciting Emulation: Academies and the Transformation of the Rural North, 1780s–1820s," *Journal of American History* 91, no. 2 (September 2004): 448–55. See also Joseph F. Kett, *Rites of Passage: Adolescence in America, 1790 to the Present* (New York: Basic Books, 1977), 170; finally, see Kaestle, *Pillars of the Republic: Common Schools and American Society, 1780–1860* (New York: Hill and Wang, 1983), 155 and 169.

The few histories that do emphasize parent–teacher dynamics typically do not link this dynamic with the rise of grading and record keeping. David Tyack and Larry Cuban alluded to written reports while discussing "academic bookkeeping." However, like Reese, Tyack and Cuban focused on the debate among educational reformers in the late nineteenth and early twentieth centuries. See David Tyack and Larry Cuban, *Tinkering Toward Utopia: A Century of Public School Reform* (Cambridge, MA: Harvard University Press, 1995), 89–93.

4. Nancy Beadie and Joseph Kett elaborated on the role of capitalism in classrooms like Willson's. For instance, Beadie detailed how free market capitalism made schools like Willson's Canandaigua Academy possible. Kett argued that education reformers modeled new systems of academic surveillance like report cards on merchant ledgers, engaging in capitalist accumulation. See Nancy Beadie, *Education and the Creation of Capital in the Early American Republic* (Cambridge: Cambridge University Press, 2010), 8–13. See also Joseph Kett, *Merit: The History of a Founding Ideal from the American Revolution to the Twenty-first Century* (Ithaca, NY: Cornell University Press, 2013), 106.

David Hogan and Bruce Curtis helped explain the context of how George Willson's use of the report card became a substitute for corporal punishment. See David Hogan, "Modes of Discipline: Affective Individualism and Pedagogical Reform in New England, 1820–1850," *American Journal of Education* 99, no. 1 (November 1990): 1–56. See also Bruce Curtis, "'My Ladies Birchely Must Needes Rule': Punishment and the Materialization of Moral Character from Mulcaster to Lancaster," in *Discipline, Moral Regulation, and Schooling: A Social History*, ed. Kate Rousmaniere, Kari Dehli, and Ning de Coninck-Smith (New York: Garland Publishing, 1997), 19–42.

Carl F. Kaestle and Rita Koganzon shed light on the impact of politics on Willson's educational ideology. Kaestle chronicled the missionary zeal of nineteenth-century reformers, men and women who believed that "public education could alleviate a host of worrisome problems and secure the nation's destiny." Koganzon described as the "unifying and homogenizing" goal of education in the new republic that would ensure political stability. See Kaestle, *Pillars of the Republic*, 72. See also Rita Koganzon, "'Producing a Reconciliation of Disinterestedness and Commerce': The Political Rhetoric of Education in the Early Republic," *History of Education Quarterly* 52, no. 3 (August 2012): 418–20.

5. Much of this chapter and chapter 3 reinforces the observations of William Cutler, whose central argument was that "in the nineteenth century, the balance of power shifted from home to the school." Meanwhile, David F. Allmendinger Jr., perhaps more than any other educational historian, recognized the *effects* of parental anxieties on the creation of educational technologies like grading systems and report cards. "Slowly, cumulatively, a transformation of great magnitude began to take place," Allmendinger wrote in *Paupers and Scholars*. "Hereafter, order would be imposed through a student's daily academic performance—and discipline through the influence of his own family. Scholarship would become a competitive activity and discipline an internalized matter of self-control and family watchfulness." Allmendinger, however, focused on New England colleges as the origin for educational innovations. I argue that report cards originated in grammar and secondary schools, independent from the influence of college professors. Willson, for example, had been experimenting with his system of weekly reports years before Amherst College adopted its report cards in 1838, which according to Allmendinger was the first time that colleges periodically sent home descriptions of student academic performance. See Cutler, *Parents and Schools*, 1; David F. Allmendinger Jr., *Paupers and Scholars: The Transformation of Student Life in Nineteenth-Century New England* (New York: St. Martin's Press, 1975), 121–24.

6. West Avenue Cemetery (Canandaigua, Ontario County, NY), George Willson grave marker, read and photographed by Wade Morris, June 27, 2020; Clarke, "Sixty Years Ago," section XVII; George S. Conover and Lewis Cass Aldrich, *History of Ontario County, New York with Illustrations and Family Sketches of Some of the Prominent Men and Families* (Syracuse, NY: D. Mason, 1893), 214; Ray Gunn, "Part IV. Antebellum Society and Politics (1825–1860)," in *The Empire State: A History of New York*, ed. Milton M. Klein (Ithaca, NY: Cornell University Press, 2001), 312, 315, and 34; Conover and Aldrich, *History of Ontario County*, 227.

Nancy Beadie pointed out that the funding did not work out as planned. She speculated that the abundance of land led to the need for even more revenue from other sources, hence the campaign for voluntary funding called "subscriptions." See Beadie, *Education and the Creation of Capital in the Early American Republic*, 130–31; George Frederick Miller, *The Academy System of the State of New York* (Albany, NY: J. B. Lyons, 1922), 25, 81, and 131.

7. West Avenue Cemetery (Canandaigua, Ontario County, NY), George Willson grave marker, read and photographed by Wade Morris, June 27, 2020; Kaestle, *Pillars of the Republic*, 132; Minute Book - Canandaigua School District #2, January 1, 1835, box 7, Ontario County Historical Society, Canandaigua, NY; George Willson Deeds, November 25, 1830, deed book 51, page 226, Ontario County Records, Archives and Information Management Services, Canandaigua, NY; Estate of George Willson, Deceased, Surrogate Court Records, December 3, 1859, pages 15–16, box: Ontario County Surrogate Court Records, folder: Willson, George_1859, Ontario County Records, Archives and Information Management Services, Canandaigua, NY; Last Will and Testament of Jared Willson, February 20, 1852, book 98, pages 112–113, the Ontario County Records, Archives and Information Management Services, Canandaigua, NY; Hogan, "Modes of Discipline," 6; Minute Book - Canandaigua Centre Lyceum, January 21, 1833, 1965.22, box 7, Ontario County Historical Society Archive, Canandaigua, NY; George Willson, *A Practical and Theoretical System of Arithmetic Containing Several New Methods of Operation and a New System of Proportion; with Theoretical Explanations of All the Principal Rules* (Canandaigua, NY: C. Morse, 1836), 36; "The Periodical Examination," *Ontario (NY) Repository*, April 13, 1831, 3.

8. Richard Lee Rogers, "The Urban Threshold and the Second Great Awakening: Revivalism in New York State, 1825–1835," *Journal for the Scientific Study of Religion* 49, no. 4 (December 2010): 694–96.

Paul E. Johnson characterized the religious revivalism in and around Rochester, New York, as distinct from New England for its "acceptance of an activist and millennialist evangelicalism as the faith of the northern middle class. New England revivals in the first quarter of the century had been quiet, decorous affairs, presided over by settled ministers who wanted only to reinstate conformity to God's laws among God's people. . . . Within a few years, free agency, perfectionism, and millennialism were middle-class orthodoxy." See Paul E. Johnson, *A Shopkeeper's Millennium: Society and Revivals in Rochester, New York, 1815–1837* (New York: Hill and Wang, 1978), 5–10.

Chad L. Anderson, "The Burned-Over District," in *History, Conquest, and Memory in the Native Northeast* (Lincoln: University of Nebraska Press, 2020), 156; Rogers, "The Urban Threshold and the Second Great Awakening," 694; Register of the First Congregational Church of Canandaigua Kept by O. E. Daggett, 1845, page 401, board room filing cabinet, First Congregational Church, Canandaigua, NY; Linda K. Pritchard, "The Burned-Over District Reconsidered: A Portent of Evolving Religious Pluralism in the United States," *Social Science History* 8, no. 3 (1984): 243–65.

9. Educational historians like David Labaree, Carl Kaestle, William Reese, and Benjamin Justice have linked the Second Great Awakening with a burst of enthusiasm in the northeastern United States for common schools. See Labaree, *The Making of an American High School: The Credentials Market and the Central High School of Philadelphia, 1838–1939* (New Haven, CT: Yale University Press, 1988), 13; Kaestle, *Pillars of the Republic*, 168; Benjamin Justice, *The War That Wasn't: Religious Conflict and Compromise in the Common Schools of New York, 1865–1890* (Albany: State University of New York Press, 2005) 35–36; Reese, *Testing Wars in the Public Schools*, 4. Also see Richard D. Birdsall, "The Second Great Awakening and the New England Social Order," *Church History* 39, no. 3 (September 1970): 355; Joseph Conforti, "The Invention of the Great Awakening, 1795–1842," *Early American Literature* 26, no. 2 (1991): 99.

James P. Jewett, "The Fight against Corporal Punishment in American Schools," *History of Education Journal* 4, no. 1 (Autumn 1952): 6–7. Also see Barbara Finkelstein, "A Crucible of

Contradictions: Historical Roots of Violence against Children in the United States," *History of Education Quarterly* 40, no. 1 (Spring 2000): 7; William Wordsworth, *Poems*, Volume I, ed. John O. Hayden (New York: Penguin Books, 1977), 522; Debra J. Rosenthal, "Temperance Novels and Moral Reform," in *The American Novel to 1870: The Oxford History of the Novel in English*, ed. J. Gerald Kennedy and Leland S. Person (Oxford: Oxford University Press, 2014), 517–31; see also Anna Pochmara, "Tropes of Temperance, Specters of Naturalism: Amelia E. Johnson's 'Clarence and Corinne,'" *Atlantis* 38, no. 2 (2016): 45–62; Nathaniel Hawthorne, "A Rill from the Town Pump," in *Twice Told Tales by Nathaniel Hawthorne* (London: J. M Dent & Sons, 1911), 100–105.

   10. Ansel D. Eddy, *Address on the Duties, Dangers, and Securities of Youth* (New York: Leavitt, Lord, 1836), 32; Charles G. Finney, *Memoirs of Charles G. Finney* (New York: A. S. Barnes, 1876), 300; Charles G. Finney, *Sermons on Gospel Themes* (Oberlin, OH: E. J. Goodrich, 1876), 118.

   11. George Willson, *The American Class-Reader; Containing a Series of Lessons in Reading; With Introductory Exercises in Articulation, Inflection, Emphasis and the Other Essential Elements of Correct Natural Elocution; Academies and Common Schools* (Canandaigua, NY: C. Morse, 1840), 4, 6–7; Estate of George Willson, Deceased, Surrogate Court Records, December 3, 1859, pages 15–16, box: Ontario County Surrogate Court Records, folder: Willson, George_1859, Ontario County Records, Archives and Information Management Services, Canandaigua, NY.

   Willson's book detailed the life of Pestalozzi, praising Pestalozzi's "benevolent desire to elevate the character and condition of the children of abject poverty. Willson, *The American Class-Reader*, 232–33; Johann Heinrich Pestalozzi, *Letters on Early Education* (London: Sherwood, Gilbert, and Piper, 1827), 30.

   Constitution, Ontario County Association of Teacher, 1833, box 6, catalog 2008.39, Educational Ephemera Collection, Ontario County Historical Society, Canandaigua, NY.

   12. Willson, *The American Class-Reader*, 40 and 12; Willson, *A Practical and Theoretical System of Arithmetic*, 3.

   13. Caroline Cowles Richards, *Village Life in America, 1852–1872* (New York: Henry Hold, 1908), 165; Minute Book - Canandaigua Centre Lyceum, October 3, 1835, 2003.61, box 7, Ontario County Historical Society Archive, Canandaigua, NY; "Extract from the Second Annual Report of the New York State Temperance Society," *Ontario (NY) Repository*, June 1, 1831, 3; Daggett, "Register of the First Congregational Church," 61–64; Clarke, "Sixty Years Ago," Section XXXVI; Willson, *The American Class-Reader*, 219; Charles F. Milliken, *A History of Ontario County, New York and Its People*, Vol. I (New York: Lewis Historical Publishing, 1911), 92.

   14. William H. Seward, who opposed the expansion of slavery, won large majorities in Ontario County during his 1838 election to become governor of New York. Milliken, *A History of Ontario County*, 79; "The Anniversary of Our National Independence," *Ontario (NY) Repository*, July 6, 1831, 3; Estate of George Willson, Deceased, Surrogate Court Records, December 3, 1859, pages 15–16, box: Ontario County Surrogate Court Records, folder: Willson, George_1859, Ontario County Records, Archives and Information Management Services, Canandaigua, NY; Willson, *The American Class-Reader*, 6–7; Daniel Webster, *Daniel Webster for Young Americans: Comprising the Greatest Speeches of the Defender of the Constitution* (Boston: Little, Brown, 1907), 22; Ansel D. Eddy, *The Christian Citizen. The Obligations of the Christian Citizen with a Review of High Church Principles in Relation to Civil and Religious Institutions* (New York: J. S. Taylor, 1843), 35–37; "Livingston County," *Common School Assistant* 1, no. 5 (May 1836): 36; Thomas Brainard, "Extract from an Address Delivered before the Association of Teachers of Hamilton Community Ohio," *Common School Assistant* 1, no. 2 (February 1836): 15.

15. "Meeting of the Ontario County Lyceum," *Geneva (NY) Gazette*, September 23, 1835. Schneider and Hutt place the spread of grading of individual students in the late nineteenth century, an evolution of Mann's written exams which were intended as an assessment of teachers and schools. See Schneider and Hutt, "Making the Grade," 210–18. "Ontario County Lyceum," *Ontario (NY) Repository*, July 13, 1831, 3.

16. Kaestle, *Pillars of the Republic*, 72; Cutler, *Parents and Teachers*, 16–30.

17. Joyce Appleby, ed., *Recollections of the Early Republic: Selected Autobiographies* (Boston: Northeastern University Press, 1997), 7–10; William James Stillman, *The Autobiography of a Journalist*, Volume I (Boston: Houghton, Mifflin, 1901), 61; "Communications," *Columbia (SC) Telescope*, May 29, 1824, 2; Edgar W. Knight, *A Documentary History of Education in the South Before 1860*, Volume V (Chapel Hill: University of North Carolina Press, 1953), 29.

18. "Parental Interest and Co-Operation," *Wisconsin Journal of Education* 1, no. 11 (January 1857): 324–26; Edgar W. Knight, *A Documentary History of Education in the South Before 1860*, Volume IV (Chapel Hill: University of North Carolina Press, 1953), 24; William A. Alcott, *Confessions of a School Master* (Andover, MA: Gould, Newman, and Saxton, 1839), 163–66; Hiram Orcutt, *Reminiscences of School Life* (Cambridge, MA: University Press, 1898), 17; Knight, *A Documentary History of Education in the South Before 1860*, Volume I, 729; Nelson Wheeler, "On the Relation of Common Schools to Higher Seminaries," *Transactions of the Massachusetts Teachers' Association* 1 (1853): 286.

19. "A Conversation," *Massachusetts Teacher* 1, no. 17 (September 1, 1848): 270; "Education," *Common School Journal* 7, no. 3 (February 1, 1850): 41; "Schools and Teachers," *Mountaineer* (Greenville, SC), November 26, 1847, 1; "Parents and Teachers," *Daily Evening Bulletin* (San Francisco, CA), March 26, 1858, 3; "Teachers' Rights," *Cleveland (OH) Daily Herald*, March 28, 1859, 1.

20. Warren Burton, *The District School as It Was by One Who Went to It*, ed. Clifton Johnson (Norwood, MA: Norwood Press, 1897), 116–17; J. Marion Sims, *The Story of My Life* (New York: D. Appleton, 1884), 55–57; "Disturbing a School," *Newburyport Herald* (Boston, MA), December 4, 1849, 3; Alcott, *Confessions of a School Master*, 162.

21. Stillman, *The Autobiography of a Journalist*, 68–72; A. B. Longstreet, *Georgia Scenes: Characters, Incidents, &c., in the First Half Century of the Republic* (Gloucester, MA: Peter Smith, 1970), 66–67; Hezekiah Prince, *Journals of Hezekiah Prince, Jr., 1822–1828* (New York: Crown Publishers, 1965), 350; J. E. Godbey, *Lights and Shadows of Seventy Years* (St. Louis, MO: Nixon-Jones, 1913), 69–70; Daris P. Page, "Duties of Parents & Teachers," *North American* (Philadelphia, PA), August 21, 1839, 1.

22. Willson, *The American Class-Reader*, 281; Clarke, *Sixty Years Ago*, sections XXXIII, LXII, and XIX.

23. Willson's lyceum subscribed to *Common School Assistant*. See Minute Book - Canandaigua Centre Lyceum, May 17, 1836, box 7, 1965.22, Ontario County Historical Society Archive, Canandaigua, NY; C. Moore, "Words of a Mother," *Common School Assistant* 1, no. 9 (September 1836): 68; "On Reading," *Common School Assistant* 2, no. 1 (January 1837): 4–5; "Teachers' Compensation, No. II," *Common School Assistant* 2, no. 5 (May 1837): 33–34; "Education - Temperance," *Common School Assistant* 2, no. 6 (June 1837): 46.

24. To guard against selection bias, however, I conducted a content analysis of *Common School Assistant*. Klaus Krippendorff defined content analysis as the "research technique for making replicable and valid inferences from texts to the contexts of their use." According to Krippendorff, replicability is the idea that multiple researchers working at different times should obtain the same results using the same techniques. I chose to focus on *Common School Assistant* because there is evidence that Willson read it, given that his lyceum subscribed to the journal in 1836 and 1837. To what extent did the *Common School Assistant* place a quantifiable emphasis on criticizing parents? What percentage of articles explicitly criticized parents? To answer these

questions, I counted the number of articles, excerpted speeches, poems, and letters to the editor that appeared in the twenty-four issues of *Common School Assistant*. This number served as the denominator. I then tracked references to the following words that appeared in each issue: "parents," "parent," "home," "father," and "mother." If these words appeared in the context of praise or in an uncritical way, then the article did not count in the numerator. If, though, the article was critical of parents, either attacking their indifference or emphasizing broader parenting flaws, then the article was included in the numerator. See Klaus Krippendorff, *Content Analysis: An Introduction to Its Methodology* (London: Sage, 2004), 18. See also Chara Haeussler Bohan, Lauren Yarnell Bradshaw, and Wade H. Morris, "The Mint Julep Consensus: An Analysis of Late Nineteenth Century Southern and Northern Textbooks and Their Impact on the History Curriculum," *Journal of Social Studies Research* 44 no. 1 (2020): 142.

25. Cutler, *Parents and Teachers*, 21–24; Hiram Orcutt, *Reminiscences of School Life* (Cambridge, MA: University Press, 1898), 154; "Teachers and Parents Must Co-Operate to Secure the Regular and Punctual Attendances of Scholars," *Connecticut Common School Journal* 2, no. 9 (February 15, 1840): 138; Knight, *A Documentary History of Education in the South Before 1860*, 112; "A Conversation," *Massachusetts Teacher* 1, no. 17 (September 1, 1848): 270–71; T. W. Curtis, "How Shall Parents and Children Be Made to Feel an Interest in Popular Education?," *Massachusetts Teacher* 3, no. 6 (June 1850): 176; "Parental Cooperation," *Massachusetts Teacher* 1, no. 4 (February 4, 1848): 58–59.

26. "Weekly Reports in Schools." *Common School Journal* 2, no. 12 (1840): 185–87; D. P. Galloup, "One of the Humbugs," *Massachusetts Teacher* 2, no. 4 (April 1849): 97–98.

27. Report Card, 1847, Wynne Family Papers.

28. Ariel Parish, "Lecture III. Management of the School-Room," *Transactions of the Massachusetts Teachers' Association* 1 (1853): 129; "To Parents," *Connecticut Common School Journal and Annals of Education* 1, no. 4 (April 1854): 117–18; Almira Seymour, "Motives to Be Urged in the Business of Education," *Massachusetts Teacher* 8, no. 1 (January 1855): 6; "Thirteenth Annual Meeting of the Massachusetts Teachers' Association," *Massachusetts Teacher* 11, no. 1 (January 1858): 17–18; "Meeting of the Ontario County Lyceum," *Geneva (NY) Gazette*, September 23, 1835, 1; "Tardiness and Irregular Attendance," *Illinois Teacher* 5, no. 4 (April 1859): 150.

29. Reese, *Testing Wars*, 3–9, 161; Hutt and Schneider, "Making the Grade," 205–6.

30. Daniel Calhoun, *The Intelligence of People* (Princeton, NJ: Princeton University Press, 1973), 62 and 78; Reese, *Testing Wars*, 78, 162–75.

31. Reese, *Testing Wars*, 1; William J. Shearer, *The Grading of Schools* (New York: H. P. Smith, 1898), 78.

32. For an entire chapter on the O.W.L.s, see J. K. Rowling, *Harry Potter and the Order of the Phoenix* (New York: Arthur A. Levine Books, 2003), 703–28; J. K. Rowling, *Harry Potter and the Sorcerer's Stone* (New York: Arthur A. Levine Books, 1997), 180–92; J. K. Rowling, illustrated by Jim Kay, *Harry Potter and the Goblet of Fire* (New York: Scholastic Inc., 2019), 18–24.

33. Shani Robinson and Anna Simonton, *None of the Above: The Untold Story of the Atlanta Public Schools Cheating Scandal, Corporate Greed, and the Criminalization of Educators* (Boston: Beacon, 2019); Annette Lareau, *Unequal Childhoods: Class, Race, and Family Life* (Berkeley: University of California Press, 2011), 157, 187, and 227–28; John J. Schmidt, "What Really Matters Is School Counselor Empowerment: A Response to Hipolito-Delgado and Lee," *Professional School Counseling* 10, no. 4 (April 2007), 338.

34. Gregory J. Palardy, "High School Socioeconomic Segregation and Student Attainment," *American Educational Research Journal* 50, no. 4 (August 2013), 714–54; Michael Thompson, *The Pressured Child: Helping Your Child Find Success in School and Life* (New York: Ballantine Books, 2004); Madeline Levine, *The Price of Privilege: How Parental Pressure and Material Advantage Are Creating a Generation of Disconnected and Unhappy Kids* (New York: Harper Collins, 2006).

her words, teachers compartmentalize the very thought process of their pupils into a
ny—remembering, understanding, analyzing, evaluating, and so on—in a way that
an inward gaze upon the pupils and their parents, all while justifying low scores on any
ᵤ   ₁ assignment. Brett Bertucio, "The Cartesian Heritage of Bloom's Taxonomy," *Studies in
Philosophy and Education* 36, no. 4 (July 2017): 478.

Chapter 2 · *Unity, Efficiency, and Freed People*

1. Report Cards, Lewis High School, 1881–1883, box 1, folder 9, William B. Matthews
Collection, the Atlanta University Center Robert W. Woodruff Library, Atlanta, GA (hereafter
cited as Report Cards, 1881–1883, Matthews Collection).

Michael Fultz published an article about the experiences of young African Americans who
were training to become teachers during the late nineteenth century. He shows that there
were 27,000 African Americans who were teaching in the South by 1900. See Michael Fultz,
"Determination and Persistence: Building African American Teacher Corps through Summer
and Intermittent Teaching, 1860s–1890s," *History of Education Quarterly* 35, no. 4 (February 2021): 4–34; Titus Brown, *Faithful, Firm, and True: African American Education in the
South* (Macon, GA: Mercer University Press, 2006), 33.

Historian Ronald E. Butchart was skeptical that the schools of freed people ever used
report cards. He wrote, "In forty years of tracking down every possible freed people's teacher,
I have never once found mention of, or even allusion to something vaguely like, a report
card." Ronald E. Butchart, email message to the author, October 26, 2020.

2. Kate Rousmaniere, *The Principal's Office: A Social History of the American School
Principal* (Albany: State University of New York Press, 2013), 28–32 and 79; Daniel Calhoun,
The Intelligence of a People (Princeton, NJ: Princeton University Press, 1973), 66; David B.
Tyack and Elizabeth Hansot, *Managers of Virtue: Public School Leadership in America,
1820–1980* (New York: Basic Books, 1982), 42 and 95; David F. Labaree, *The Making of an
American High School: The Credentials Market and the Central High School of Philadelphia,
1838–1939* (New Haven, CT: Yale University Press, 1988), 4, 118–25.

3. Calhoun, *The Intelligence of a People*, 96; Paul E. Peterson, *The Politics of School Reform,
1870–1940* (Chicago: University of Chicago Press, 1985), 166; Larry Cuban, *Teachers and
Machines: The Classroom Use of Technology Since 1920* (New York: Teachers College Press,
1986), 9–10; Raymond E. Callahan, *Education and the Cult of Efficiency: A Study of the Social
Forces That Have Shaped the Administration of the Public Schools* (Chicago: University of
Chicago Press, 1962), 2–23.

4. Labaree, *The Making of an American High School*, 97; A. P. Stone, "School Records,"
Massachusetts Teacher 17, no. 1 (January 1864): 56–65; "Monthly Reports," *Illinois Teacher* 14,
no. 12 (December 12): 391–92; "The Lewis High School - Closing Announcements," *Helping
Hand* 1, no. 9 (May 1882): 4.

5. See also James D. Anderson, *The Education of Blacks in the South, 1860–1935* (Chapel
Hill: University of North Carolina Press, 1988), 80 and 280.

6. Oakland Cemetery (Atlanta, GA), William Baxter Matthews grave marker, read and
photographed by Wade Morris, January 13, 2021; "Rites Will Be Held Here for Prof. Matthews," *Atlanta Daily World*, January 10, 1940; *History of Peach County, Georgia* (Atlanta, GA:
Cherokee, 1972), 23 and 356; Joseph P. Reidy, *From Slavery to Agrarian Capitalism in
the Cotton Plantation South: Central Georgia, 1800–1880* (Chapel Hill: University of North
Carolina Press, 1992), 63.

7. The source for much of Matthews' early life comes from a five-page document titled
"Tentative Biography." No date is given on the document. The context for its use and intended
audience is also unclear. It appears that someone wrote it while Matthews was still serving as
principal of Louisville's Central High School. The pages include handwritten corrections for a

number of details, including the dates for Matthews' birth and wedding. This suggests that the biography was written in consultation with Matthews. Perhaps the most likely explanation is that the biography was used as some form of retirement, celebrating his long career in education. See Tentative Biography: William Baxter Matthews, n.d., MS132.0283, Wade Hall Collection of American Letters, University of Kentucky Special Collections, Lexington, KY (hereafter cited as Tentative Biography, n.d., Wade Hall Collection).

David Eltis and David Richardson, "New Assessments of the Transatlantic Slave Trade," in *Extending the Frontiers: Essays on the New Transatlantic Slave Trade Database* (New Haven, CT: Yale University Press, 2008), 1–60, see Table 1.7; Michael A. Gomez, *Exchanging Our Country Marks: The Transformation of African Identities in the Colonial and Antebellum South* (Chapel Hill: University of North Carolina Press, 1998), 189; Sharla M. Fett, *Recaptured Africans: Surviving Slave Ships, Detention, and Dislocation in the Final Years of the Slave Trade* (Chapel Hill: University of North Carolina Press, 2017), 22–23; Fett, *Recaptured Africans*, 145; Ira Berlin, *Many Thousand Gone: The First Two Centuries of Slavery in North America* (Cambridge, MA: Harvard University Press, 1998), 190 and 314; Gomez, *Exchanging Our Country Marks*, 190; Peter Kolchin, *American Slavery, 1619–1877* (New York: Hill and Wang, 1993), 41; see also John W. Blassingame, *The Slave Community: Plantation Life in the Antebellum South* (New York: Oxford University Press), 39–40.

8. Death Certificate of William Baxter Matthews, January 8, 1940, file number 1778, registrar's number 195, Commonwealth of Kentucky, Bureau of Vital Statistics, Ancestry.com, accessed February 5, 2021; J. Britt McCarley, *The Atlanta and Savannah Campaigns, 1864* (Washington, DC: Center of Military History, 2014), 64; Edmund L. Drago, "How Sherman's March Through Georgia Affected the Slaves," *Georgia Historical Quarterly* 57, no. 3 (Fall 1973): 364; McCarley, *The Atlanta and Savannah Campaigns*, 70–72; McCarley, *The Atlanta and Savannah Campaigns*, 70–74; Drago, "How Sherman's March Through Georgia Affected the Slaves," 364; Yael A. Sternhell, "Bodies in Motion and the Making of Emancipation," in *Rethinking American Emancipation: Legacies of Slavery and the Quest for Black Freedom*, ed. William A. Link and James J. Broomall (Cambridge: Cambridge University Press, 2016), 23; Susan Eva O'Donovan, *Becoming Free in the Cotton South* (Cambridge, MA: Harvard University Press, 2007), 18.

9. Historians have noted that family obligations were a major disincentive for seeking refuge with approaching Union armies. Sternhell, "Bodies in Motion and the Making of Emancipation," 23; O'Donovan, *Becoming Free in the Cotton South*, 2. See also Ira Berlin and Leslie S. Rowland, eds., *Families and Freedom: A Documentary History of African-American Kinship in the Civil War Era* (New York: New Press, 1997), 22.

Michael Golay, *A Ruined Land: The End of the Civil War* (New York: John Wiley & Sons, 1999), 189; Andrew Ward, *The Slaves' War: The Civil War in the Words of Former Slaves* (Boston: Houghton Mifflin, 2008), 286–287; Gregory P. Downs, "Force, Freedom, and the Making of Emancipation," in *Rethinking American Emancipation: Legacies of Slavery and the Quest for Black Freedom*, ed. William A. Link and James J. Broomall (Cambridge: Cambridge University Press, 2016), 59.

10. Michael Perman, *Emancipation and Reconstruction*, 2nd ed. (Wheeling, IL: Harlan Davidson, 2003), 15; Downs, "Force, Freedom, and the Making of Emancipation," 43; Kristina Simms, *Macon: Georgia's Central City* (Chatsworth, CA: Windsor Publications, 1989), 17; Richard D. Iobst, *Civil War Macon: The History of a Confederate City* (Macon, GA: Mercer University Press, 1979), 22; Paul Michael Johnson, *The Negro in Macon, Georgia, 1865–1871* (Athens: University of Georgia, 1972), 1. For insight into the lives of enslaved people in and around Macon, see also William and Ellen Craft, *Running a Thousand Miles for Freedom; or, the Escape of William and Ellen Craft from Slavery* (London: William Tweedie, 1860), 15–17, 74, and 89. The Crafts describe the difficulties of their courtship and marriage while being

enslaved in Macon as well as white Maconites traveling to Boston to capture the Crafts. Clarence L. Mohr, *On the Threshold of Freedom: Masters and Slaves in Civil War Georgia* (Athens: University of Georgia Press, 1986), 205; Downs, "Force, Freedom, and the Making of Emancipation," 63; Carol Anderson, *White Rage: The Unspoken Truth of Our Racial Divide* (New York: Bloomsbury, 2016), 17. For a local history of Macon after the war, see Stephen Wallace Taylor and Matthew Jennings, *Images of Macon* (Charleston, SC: Arcadia Publishing, 2013), 41–59; O'Donovan, *Becoming Free in the Cotton South*, 174–75; Johnson, *The Negro in Macon*, 1–5.

11. Anderson, *White Rage*, 17; Johnson, *The Negro in Macon*, 2–4, 14, and 63; Simms, *Macon*, 17; Iobst, *Civil War Macon*, 423–24.

12. Leon F. Litwack, *Been in the Storm So Long: The Aftermath of Slavery* (New York: Alfred A. Knopf, 1979), 310–12; Reidy, *From Slavery to Agrarian Capitalism in the Cotton Plantation South*, 217–18 and 229; "The Colored People of Macon," *Helping Hand* (Macon, GA) 1, no. 1 (February 1881): 2.

13. Brown, *Faithful, Firm, and True*, 2–4 and 33; Paul A. Cimbala, *Under the Guardianship of the Nation: The Freedman's Bureau and the Reconstruction of Georgia, 1865–1870* (Athens: University of Georgia Press, 1997), 107–9; Susan F. Pressley, "'A Past to Cherish - A Future to Fulfill': Lewis High - Ballard Normal School, 1865–1900" (Master's thesis, Georgia Southern University, 1992), 46–49.

14. Joe M. Richardson, *Christian Reconstruction: The American Missionary Association and Southern Blacks, 1861–1890* (Tuscaloosa: University of Alabama Press, 1986), 58–62, 105, and 259.

15. Span, *From Cotton Field to Schoolhouse*, 9. Ronald E. Butchart, once again, complicates Span's narrative, emphasizing the high standards of the teachers of freed people. See Ronald E. Butchart, "Race, Social Studies, and Culturally Relevant Curriculum in Social Studies' Prehistory: A Cautionary Meditation," in *Histories of Social Studies and Race: 1865–2000*, eds. Christine Woyshner and Chara Haeussler Bohan (New York: Palgrave Macmillan, 2012), 19–36. See also Richardson, *Christian Reconstruction*, 113–14.

Ronald E. Butchart, *Schooling the Freed People: Teaching, Learning, and the Struggle for Black Freedom, 1861–1876* (Chapel Hill: University of North Carolina Press, 2010), 40, 96–117. A special thanks to Butchart for identifying my own AMA bias. Ronald E. Butchart, email message to the author, February 27, 2021. Historians tend to overstate the importance of the AMA in part because of the success of the Amistad Research Center, located in New Orleans, in organizing and making available AMA's records. Ironically, I could not find any report cards at the Amistad Research Center, despite several days of trying. Instead, I found Matthews' report card, which was issued by an AMA-managed school, in the Atlanta University Center's Woodruff Library. That discovery led me to focus on William Matthews' life at Lewis High and thus to reluctantly perpetuate the historical fallacy of overemphasizing the AMA. See Butchart, *Schooling the Freed People*, xvii; see also Report Cards, 1881–1883, Matthews Collection.

By 1970, Horace Mann Bond, building on the work of Carter Woodson, criticized the "extravagant claims" of education to serve as a panacea for African Americans in the South. In the 1990s, Ward McAfee labeled the good-faith efforts of postwar educational reformers as "cognitive dissonance." There was very little evidence that education could alleviate the plight of Black southerners, McAfee pointed out. Indeed, Ronald Butchart noted that the more education failed to provide economic opportunities for Black southerners, the more whites vocalized their support for publicly funded education of African Americans. To William Watkins, missionary schools, financed by northern industrialists and tolerated by former enslavers, were never about social equality or economic advancement. The education of African Americans in the South was always about securing an efficient labor source and maintaining a social order based on a racial hierarchy. Joseph Kett, among many others, examined this dynamic in non-racialized contexts. Both rich and poor, white and African American students were subjected to an educational system modeled on the industrial efficiency of Taylorism. See Anderson, *White Rage*, 15–16; Horace Mann Bond, *The Education of the Negro in the American Social Order*, Third (New York: Octagon Books, 1970), 12; Ward M. McAfee, *Religion, Race, and Reconstruction: The Public School in the Politics of the 1870s* (Albany: State University of New York Press, 1998), 12; Ronald E. Butchart, *Northern Schools, Southern Blacks, and Reconstruction: Freedmen's Education, 1862–1875* (Westport, CT: Greenwood Press, 1980), 205; Watkins, *The White Architects of Black Education*, 15; see Joseph F. Kett, "The Adolescent of Vocational Education," in *Work, Youth, and Schooling: Historical Perspectives on Vocationalism in American Education*, eds. Harvey Kantor and David B. Tyack (Stanford, CA: Stanford University Press, 1982), 79–109.

16. In the last fifty years, historians have constructed a complicated depiction of the northern schoolmarms who traveled south during Reconstruction. These northerners, with a web of goals, pedagogy, and motives, were the teachers who gave Matthews his report card in 1881. To historians Paul A. Cimbala and Horace Mann Bond, the fact that the northern teachers were attacked by white southerners is evidence in itself of their egalitarian idealism. Hilary Green recognized that the experience of teaching in a hostile environment created a bond between teachers and Black families. Robert C. Morris noted that teachers developed lessons explicitly designed to cultivate racial pride in freed people, including readings on Toussaint L'Ouverture and Phillis Wheatley. Ronald E. Butchart emphasized that only about a quarter of the teachers in southern Black schools were actually northern, white women. The majority of the teachers were neither northern nor white: a third were Black, and by the mid-1870s, a third were southern. Perhaps Adam Fairclough mounted the most sustained defense of teachers in postwar schools for freed people. While admitting that many southern Black families "bristled at the self-righteous arrogance" of the condescending northern teachers, Fairclough rejected the suggestion that northern teachers were harmful to the advancement of freed people in the decades after the Civil War. See Paul A. Cimbala, *Under the Guardianship of the Nation: The Freedman's Bureau and the Reconstruction of Georgia, 1865–1870* (Athens: University of Georgia Press, 1997), 113; Bond, *The Education of the Negro in the American Social Order*, 32; Hilary Green, *Educational Reconstruction: African American Schools in the Urban South, 1865–1890* (New York: Fordham University Press, 2016), 9; Robert C. Morris, *Reading, 'Riting, and Reconstruction: The Education of Freedmen in the South, 1861–1870* (Chicago: University of Chicago Press, 1976), 198–200; Butchart, *Schooling the Freed People*, 179–183; Adam Fairclough, *A Class of Their Own: Black Teachers in the Segregated South* (Cambridge, MA: Belknap Press of Harvard University, 2007), 22 and 82.

Meanwhile, the historiographical trend in the past four decades has been one of increasing criticism of northern teachers. Heather Andrea Williams noted how northern missionaries worked to sideline and subordinate Black teachers who, in the wake of the Civil War, had established their own schools. Christopher Span chronicled the effects that northern teachers' low expectations had on their Black students. Ward M. McAfee compared the northern missionaries to the former enslavers in the South. "[Northern teachers] exuded their cultural preferences for evangelical piety, self-control, and hard, steady work," McAfee wrote in 1998. "They were as ideologically opposed to true self-determination for African Americans as the former slave masters had been." Jacqueline Jones reinforced the depiction of northern teachers in Georgia's Black schools as narrowly self-righteous. Finally, after decades of researching thousands of missionary teachers, Ronald E. Butchart arrived at a similar conclusion to that of Jones and McAfee. Butchart, while emphasizing the high standards that teachers maintained in the schools for freed people, still admitted that northern teachers were too "insufficiently political and politically timid" for the task of combating white supremacy. Meanwhile, the work of William Watkins showed that racial prejudice permeated postwar philanthropic organizations, from the donor-class that supported the missionary associations, to the administrators who managed them with military efficiency, to the classroom teachers working with children each day. See Heather Andrea Williams, *Self-Taught: African American Education in Slavery and Freedom* (Chapel Hill: University of North Carolina Press, 2005), 95–99; Christopher M. Span, *From Cotton Field to Schoolhouse: African American Education in Mississippi, 1862–1875* (Chapel Hill: University of North Carolina Press, 2009), 9. Ronald E. Butchart, once again, complicates Span's narrative, emphasizing the high standards of the teachers of freed people. See Ronald E. Butchart, "Race, Social Studies, and Culturally Relevant Curriculum in Social Studies' Prehistory: A Cautionary Meditation," in *Histories of Social Studies and Race: 1865–2000*, eds. Christine Woyshner and Chara Haeussler Bohan (New York: Palgrave Macmillan, 2012), 19–36; McAfee, *Religion, Race, and Reconstruction*, 12–13; Jacqueline Jones, *Soldiers of Light and Love: Northern Teachers and Georgia Blacks, 1865–1873* (Chapel Hill: University of North Carolina Press, 1980), 9, 49–50, 138; William H. Watkins, *The White Architects of Black Education: Ideology and Power in America, 1865–1954* (New York: Teachers College Press, 2001), 81–96.

See Brown, *Faithful, Firm, and True*, 36–40, 243–45; "Lewis High School," *American Missionary* 34, no. 7 (July 1880): 212; S. E. Lathrop, "Georgia: A Beginner's Reflections - The Gospel - Congregationalism - The Negro," *American Missionary* 33, no. 4 (April 1879): 112; Theodore Burger Lathrop, Eulogy for Stanley Edwards Lathrop, 1928, box 1, file 1, Stanley Edwards Lathrop Collection, Congregational Library and Archive, Boston, MA; "Educating the Blacks," *Oshkosh (WA) Daily Northwestern*, July 23, 1884, 8; S. E. Lathrop, "Lewis High School," *American Missionary* 35, no. 8 (August 1881): 243–45.

17. Pressley, "'A Past to Cherish - A Future to Fulfill,'" 72–73, 111; Joe M. Richardson, *Christian Reconstruction: The American Missionary Association and Southern Blacks, 1861–1890* (Tuscaloosa: University of Alabama Press, 1986), 96–97, 226; William Sanders Scarborough, *The Autobiography of William Sanders Scarborough*, ed. Michele Valerie Ronnick (Detroit, MI: Wayne State University Press, 2005), 15.

18. Christopher Span examined how this process played out in Mississippi. Span showed how, by 1875, the state government had stripped Mississippi schools of funding, providing only a basic education for young Black children. Meanwhile, Adam Fairclough has complicated the narratives of Eric Foner and Span. While not denying that the Redeemers slashed school budgets, Fairclough emphasized that white opposition to Black education actually receded in the late 1870s. However, he admitted that the decline of white fears of Black schools correlated with southern whites seizing a degree of control over these schools. Either way, Black schools continued to "take root and grow" in the 1880s. On the other hand, Horace Mann Bond argued that this white compliance with the existence of Black schools was essentially conservative in its nature. New southern industrialists, Bond wrote, recognized the power of education to provide a docile labor force, restoring the prewar caste system. Wayne Urban wrote, "Bond's contribution to the historiography of education involved more than anticipating recent scholarship. . . . Bond noted that [Booker T.] Washington's personal influence in Alabama could not be considered apart from that of the white agent of the Peabody Fund, J. L. M. Curry. Bond carefully outlined Curry's conservative, privileged background and showed that Curry's commitment to philanthropic support of black education was never allowed to become a repudiation of his conservative political principles." Finally, John Hope Franklin pointed out that education was one of the few areas of northern reform that survived Reconstruction, albeit with fewer funds than were necessary. See Span, *From Cotton Field to Schoolhouse*, 152; Fairclough, *A Class of Their Own*, 138; Bond, *The Education of the Negro in the American Social Order*, 35; Wayne J. Urban, *Black Scholar: Horace Mann Bond, 1904–1972* (Athens: University of Georgia Press, 1992), 86–90; John Hope Franklin, *Reconstruction After the Civil War*, Second (Chicago: University of Chicago Press, 1994), 186.

See also James Anderson, *The Education of Blacks in the South*, 79–83. Anderson wrote on page 80 that "a coalition of northern philanthropists and southern whites viewed universal schooling for the laboring classes as complementary to a changing and modern political economy . . . universal education was not conceived of as transforming the social position of any laboring class, not to mention black southerners, but as a means to make society run more efficiently. Consequently, philanthropic and southern white crusaders for universal public education wished to substitute education for older and cruder methods of socialization and control."

Philip A. Klinkner and Roger M. Smith, *The Unsteady March: The Rise and Decline of Racial Equality in America* (Chicago: University of Chicago Press, 1999), 85; Eric Foner, *Forever Free: The Story of Emancipation and Reconstruction* (New York: Alfred A. Knopf, 2005), 201; Howard N. Rabinowitz, "Half a Loaf: The Shift from White to Black Teachers in the Negro Schools of the Urban South, 1865–1890," *The Journal of Southern History* 40, no. 4 (November 1974): 574–77; Green, *Educational Reconstruction*, 32, 91–92.

19. Numan V. Bartley, *The Creation of Modern Georgia* (Athens: University of Georgia Press, 1983), 68–79; "Prof. B. M. Zettler Drops Dead at Home," newspaper clip, n.d., B. M. Zettler Personality File, Atlanta History Center, Kenan Research Library, Atlanta, GA; B. M. Zettler, *War Stories and School-Day Incidents for the Children* (New York: Neale Publishing, 1912), 21, 32–33, 146–48; see also Ida Young, Julius Gholson, and Clara Nell Hargrove, *History of Macon, Georgia* (Macon, GA: Lyon, Marshall & Brooks, 1950), 315.

20. Reidy, *From Slavery to Agrarian Capitalism in the Cotton Plantation South*, 227–29; Richardson, *Christian Reconstruction*, 111; Brown, *Faithful, Firm, and True*, 64, 65–67; Pressley, "'A Past to Cherish - A Future to Fulfill,'" 94, 100–103.

21. Tentative Biography, n.d., Wade Hall Collection; W. E. B. Du Bois, *Souls of Black Folk* (Chicago: A. C. McClurg, 1903), 190; Albert J. Raboteau, *Slave Religion: The "Invisible Institution" in the Antebellum South*, Second (Oxford: Oxford University Press, 2004), 135–46, 231; Eugene D. Genovese, *Roll, Jordan, Roll* (New York: Pantheon Books, 1972), 256.

22. Tentative Biography, n.d., Wade Hall Collection; Butchart, *Schooling Freed People*, 9–11; Gomez, *Exchanging Our Country Marks*, 2–4.

23. Tentative Biography, n.d., Wade Hall Collection; Speeches Given by William B. Matthews, n.d., box 10, folder 16, MS132.0283, Wade Hall Collection of American Letters, University of Kentucky Special Collections, Lexington, KY.

24. Heather Andrea Williams, "'Clothing Themselves in Intelligence': The Freedpeople, Schooling, and Northern Teachers, 1861–1871," *Journal of African American History* 87 (Autumn 2002): 385; Jones, *Soldiers of Light and Love*, 9–10; "Alabama," *American Missionary* 11, no. 11 (November 1867): 255–56; "Extracts from Letters of Normal Class Teachers," *American Freedman* 3, no. 7 (July 1869): 9–12.

25. Jacqueline Jones described a teacher visiting the homes of freed people in Anderson-ville, making an analogy to modern social workers, and Chloe Merrick made regular visits to the homes of her pupils in Amelia Island, Florida, as well; see Jones, *Soldiers of Light and Love*, 60, 149–50.

Anderson, *The Education of Blacks in the South*, 31; Sarah Whitmer Foster and John T. Foster Jr., "Chloe Merrick Reed: Freedom's First Lady," *Florida Historical Quarterly* 71, no. 3 (1993): 285; Brown, *Faithful, Firm, and True*, 24–35; Butchart, *Schooling the Freed People*, 144; "Items from the Field: Macon, GA," *American Missionary* 33, no. 6 (June 1879): 166.

26. The goal of content analysis is to add a degree of objective quantification to textual analysis. In this case, I focused on the years between 1867 and 1881, beginning the year before Lewis High School was formally created and ending the year report cards first appeared at the school. I chose to focus on references to African American parents in the South because the creation of the report card in the North was in large part a response to tensions between

parents and teachers. I wanted to test whether or not the rise of the report card in the AMA's schools correlated with any noticeable change in teacher–parent relations. I first counted each explicit reference within the journal to the parenting of freed people. These references gave me a sense of any continuities and changes in the overall emphasis or interest among the mostly white AMA employees toward African American parents.

27. See Appendix I; W. L. Clarke, "Transitions - Good Time Coming," *American Missionary* 16, no. 9 (September 1872): 196–97.

28. Petition to E. P. Smith, May 23, 1867, item 6633, box 158, folder H6628-H6672, South Carolina Collection, Amistad Research Center, New Orleans, LA; Petition to Retain Mary D. Williams, July 6, 1868, item 101948, box 124, folder 101946-101973, North Carolina Collection, Amistad Research Center, New Orleans, LA.

29. The actions of Black parents during Reconstruction were, in some ways, a prequel to Vanessa Siddle Walker's history of segregated education in the mid-twentieth century. Walker chronicled how Black educators both publicly petitioned for equal access to education while also "quietly" and "secretly" fighting for resources. As an example, Black teachers in the South went beyond the official state curricula by "rewrit[ing] inclusion into American democracy." See Walker, *The Lost Education of Horace Tate: Uncovering the Hidden Heroes Who Fought for Justice in Schools* (New York: New Press, 2018), 9 and 153–58.

James Gross, Sutton Gross, and David Hardman to E. P. Smith, May 17, 1869, item 50310, box 64, file 50303-50351, Maryland Collection, Amistad Research Center, New Orleans, LA; L. White to Rev. E. P. Smith, July 29, 1869, item 22712, box 29, folder 22681-22727, Georgia Collection, Amistad Research Center, New Orleans, LA; L. P. McGaffey to E. M. Cravath, February 12, 1875, item 46357, box 59, folder 46342-46386, Louisiana Collection, Amistad Research Center, New Orleans, LA; Span, *From Cotton Field to Schoolhouse*, 80–82; Jones, *Soldiers of Light and Love*, 65; Anderson, *The Education of Blacks in the South*, 26.

The parents of one publicly funded school in Georgia even fought a seventeen-year battle with the school board that ultimately led to a lawsuit. See June O. Patton, "The Black Community of Augusta and the Struggle for Ware High School, 1880–1899," in *New Perspectives on Black Educational History*, ed. Vincent P. Franklin and James D. Anderson (Boston: G. K. Hall, 1978), 50. Also see Shanté' J. Lyons and Matthew D. Davis, "School Naming as Racial Resistance: Black School Principals and Critical Race Pedagogy in 1890 St. Louis," *Journal of Thought* 51, no. 1–2 (Spring/Summer 2017): 4–10.

30. William Scarborough, who attended Lewis High in the late 1860s, remembered his mother defending him at a disciplinary hearing. See Scarborough, *The Autobiography of William Sanders Scarborough*, 38–39; Reidy, *From Slavery to Agrarian Capitalism in the Cotton Plantation South*, 228–29; Pressley, "'A Past to Cherish - A Future to Fulfill,'" 95; Resolution of Lewis High School Parents, June 20, 1878, item 27220, box 35, folder 27187-27240, Georgia Collection, Amistad Research Center, New Orleans, LA; Richardson, *Christian Reconstruction*, 248; "The Colored People on Education," *Macon (GA) Telegraph and Messenger*, June 29, 1875, 7; J. D. Smith to M. E. Strieby, September 24, 1878, item 27402, box 35, folder 27382-27426, Georgia Collection, Amistad Research Center, New Orleans, LA.

31. A. P. Stone, "School Records," *Massachusetts Teacher* 17, no. 1 (January 1864): 56–65; "Monthly Reports," *Illinois Teacher* 14, no. 12 (December 12): 391–92; James Pyle Wickersham, *School Economy: A Treatise on the Preparation, Organization, Employments, Government, and Authorities of Schools* (Pennsylvania, PA: J. B. Lippincott, 1867), 57; "School Registers," *Maine Journal of Education* 4, no. 6 (June 1870): 204–205; "Intelligence," *Massachusetts Teacher* 28, no. 6 (June 1874): 256–58; "Publisher's Notes," *Illinois School Journal* 1, no. 11 (March 1882): 30; Thomas Lane's Report to Lawrence Public Schools, 1874, box 1, folder 1, RH MS P937, Thomas Lane Collection, Kenneth Spencer Research Library, Lawrence, KS; Preparatory School

Report of the Standing in Conduct and Studies of Will Talbot, 1874, MS170, Will Talbot Papers, C. L. Sonnichsen Special Collections Department, University of Texas, El Paso, TX.

32. James D. Anderson documented that African American families, from emancipation through the twentieth century, were at the forefront of efforts to expand public education in the South. See Anderson, *The Education of Blacks in the South*, 25–27; William Reese, *America's Public Schools: From the Common School to "No Child Left Behind"* (Baltimore: Johns Hopkins University, 2011), 45–47. See also Kyle P. Steele, *Making a Mass Institution: Indianapolis and the American High School* (New Brunswick, NJ: Rutgers University Press, 2020), 1–3; Raymond E. Callahan, *Education and the Cult of Efficiency: A Study of the Social Forces That Have Shaped the Administration of the Public Schools* (Chicago: University of Chicago Press, 1962), 7–8; David Tyack, *The One Best System: A History of American Urban Education* (Cambridge, MA: Harvard University Press, 1974), 45–49; Labaree, *The Making of an American High School*, 97.

33. "New Appointments," *American Missionary* 36, no. 2 (February 1882): 42; "Willard A. Hodge, Apoplexy Victim: Real Estate Man and Temperance Worker Dies After Fall Early in Week," *Wisconsin State Journal* (Madison, WI), March 23, 1917, 10; W. A. Hodge, "The South. Macon, Ga.," *American Missionary* 40, no. 6 (June 1886): 166; "The Lewis High School," *Helping Hand* 1, no. 8 (March 1882): 4; "Closing Exercises of Lewis Normal Institute," *Helping Hand* 4, no. 10 (June 1885): 2; "No License Vote Here This Spring," *Wisconsin State Journal* (Madison, WI), March 24, 1916, 14.

34. History of Ballard Normal School by Lester Sullivan, 1942, 83-36 ARB, Lewis High School / Ballard Normal School Collection, Middle Georgia Regional Archive, Macon, GA; W. A. Hodge, "The Lewis High School," *Helping Hand* 2, no. 1 (September 1882): 4; "Lewis High School - Closing Exercises," *Helping Hand* 1, no. 4 (June 1881): 4; "The Lewis High School - Closing Announcements," *Helping Hand* 1, no. 9 (May 1882): 4; "Closing Exercises of Lewis Normal Institute," *Helping Hand* 4, no. 10 (June 1885): 2; "The Lewis High School - Closing Announcements," *Helping Hand* 1, no. 9 (May 1882): 4.

35. Brown, *Faithful, Firm, and True*, 74–75; S. E. Lathrop, "Six Years in Macon," *Helping Hand* 4, no. 4 (December 1884): 4; W. A. Hodge, "Theory and Practice: A Township High School," *Wisconsin Journal of Education* 18, no. 10 (October 1888): 442–44; "The Land We Live In: What People Are Doing, Saying, and Thinking," *Atlanta (GA) Constitution*, December 28, 1881, 2; "The Nashville Conference," *American Missionary* 36, no. 2 (February 1882): 34–36.

36. Report Cards, 1881–1883, Matthews Collection.

37. Frank Lincoln Mather, *Who's Who of the Colored Race: A General Biographical Dictionary of Men and Women of African Descent*, Volume 1 (Detroit, MI: Gale Research Company, 1915). For more on the experiences of African American teachers like Matthews, see Fultz, "Determination and Persistence," 4–34; Recommendation for William Matthews by William N. Nelson, August 4, 1890, box 1, folder 34, OCLC 229150818, William B. Matthews Collection, Woodruff Library of the Atlanta University Center, Atlanta, GA; W. F. Slaton to W. B. Matthews, March 22, 1906, aarl89-011, William B. Matthews Papers, Auburn Avenue Research Library, Atlanta, GA; Letter from W. F. Slaton to W. B. Matthews, February 16, 1906, aarl89-011, William B. Matthews Papers, Auburn Avenue Research Library, Atlanta, GA; W. F. Slaton to W. B. Matthews, February 7, 1906, aarl89-011, William B. Matthews Papers, Auburn Avenue Research Library, Atlanta, GA; Letter to Asa Candler, July 6, 1909, aarl89-011, William B. Matthews Papers, Auburn Avenue Research Library, Atlanta, GA; Biographical Items on William B. Matthews, n.d., aarl89-011, William B. Matthews Papers, Auburn Avenue Research Library, Atlanta, GA.

38. W. B. Matthews to the Colored Branch of the Y.M.C.A., c. 1920, box 1, folder 6, MSS 439 6, Matthews Family Papers, Filson Historical Society, Louisville, KY; M. M. Reid to Mrs. William B. Matthews, February 11, 1906, aarl89-011, William B. Matthews Papers,

Auburn Avenue Research Library, Atlanta, GA; Daniel Levine, "A Single Standard of Civilization: Black Private Social Welfare Institutions in the South, 1880s–1920s," *Georgia Historical Quarterly* 81, no. 1 (Spring 1997): 64; W. S. Witham to International Committee of Young Men's Christian Associations, August 30, 1902, box 1, folder 34, OCLC 229150818, William B. Matthews Collection, Woodruff Library of the Atlanta University Center, Atlanta, GA.

39. Introduction for Florida Louise Matthews Speaking Engagement, n.d., box 9, folder 17, Wade Hall Collection of American Letters, University of Kentucky Special Collections, Lexington, KY; Letter from William B. Matthews to Ophelia Matthews, July 11, 1917, box 3, folder 13, Wade Hall Collection of American Letters, University of Kentucky Special Collections, Lexington, KY; Speeches Given by William B. Matthews, n.d., box 10, folder 16, Wade Hall Collection of American Letters, University of Kentucky Special Collections, Lexington, KY; Letter from William B. Matthews to Ophelia Matthews, August 7, 1922, box 3, folder 13, Wade Hall Collection of American Letters, University of Kentucky Special Collections, Lexington, KY.

40. Levine, "A Single Standard of Civilization," 77; Telegram from Booker T. Washington to William B. Matthews, n.d., folder: various letters and telegrams, aarl89-011, William B. Matthews Papers, Auburn Avenue Research Library, Atlanta, GA; W. E. B. Du Bois to William B. Matthews, October 16, 1905, box 1, folder 18, OCLC 229150818, William B. Matthews Collection, Woodruff Library of the Atlanta University Center, Atlanta, GA.

Decades later, Du Bois happened upon Matthews' daughter, which led to a happy reminiscence on the part of Du Bois about the time he spent with Matthews as young educators together in Atlanta. See Letter from Louise Matthews to Mother, February 25, 1917, box 1, folder 36, OCLC 229150818, William B. Matthews Collection, Woodruff Library of the Atlanta University Center, Atlanta, GA.

41. Report of the Findings Committee of State Inter-Racial Conference Held on the Call of Governor Morrow in Louisville, July 23, 1920, box 1, folder 2, M4392, Filson Historical Society, Louisville, KY; Preamble to the Constitution of the Crispus Atticus Chapter of the Sons and Daughters of the American Revolution, n.d., box 1, folder 3, MSS 439 3, Filson Historical Society, Louisville, KY.

42. Oakland Cemetery (Atlanta, GA), William Baxter Matthews grave marker, read and photographed by Wade Morris, January 13, 2021; Donovan X. Ramsey, "The Political Education of Killer Mike," *GQ Magazine*, July 8, 2020; for a biography of Killer Mike, see Samuel Momodu, "Michael Santiago 'Killer Mike' Render," *Black Past* (website), December 14, 2020, https://www.blackpast.org/african-american-history/michael-santiago-killer-mike -render-1975/; see also Gary M. Pomerantz, *Where Peachtree Meets Sweet Auburn: A Saga of Race and Family* (New York: Penguin Books, 1996), 67–78 and 112–14.

For more, see Maurice J. Hobson, *The Legend of the Black Mecca: Politics and Class in the Making of Modern Atlanta* (Chapel Hill: University of North Carolina Press, 2017) and Robert D. Bullard, Glenn S. Johnson, and Angel O. Torres, "Atlanta: A Black Mecca?," in *The Black Metropolis in the Twenty-First Century: Race, Power, and Politics of Place*, ed. Robert D. Bullard (Lanham, MA: Rowman & Littlefield, 2007), 160–83.

43. Kara Swisher, "Killer Mike Says He Has a Choice to Make: The Rapper and Activist on Transforming Fear into Power," *New York Times*, October 8, 2020. See also Sheldon Pearce, "Killer Mike Is Trigger Happy," *Pitchfork Magazine*, January 31, 2019; Mark Richardson, "'RTJ4' by Run the Jewels: Politics and Prose," *Wall Street Journal*, June 8, 2020; David Fear, "Run the Jewels Wish Their New Album Didn't Make So Much Sense Right Now," *Rolling Stone Magazine*, June 18, 2020; Sheldon Pearce, "Run the Jewels: RTJ4," *Pitchfork Magazine*, June 5, 2020.

44. See Fabian T. Pfeffer and Robert F. Schoeni, "How Wealth Inequality Shapes Our Future," *Russell Safe Foundation Journal of the Social Sciences* 2, no. 6 (October 2016): 2–21; Karen D. Lincoln, "Economic Inequality in Later Life," *Generations: Journal of the American*

Society on Aging 42, no. 2 (Summer 2018): 6–12; Shetay Ashford-Hanserd, Stephen B. Springer, Mary-Patricia Hayton, and Kelly E. Williams, "Shadows of *Plessy v. Fergusson*: The Dichotomy of Progress Toward Educational Equity Since 1954," *Journal of Negro Education* 89, no. 4 (Fall 2020): 410–22; Robynn Cox, "Mass Incarceration, Racial Disparities in Health, and Successful Aging," *Generations: Journal of the American Society on Aging* 42, no. 2 (Summer 2018): 48–55.

45. Michel Foucault, "Truth and Power," in *Power/Knowledge: Selected Interviews and Other Writings*, ed. Colin Gordon, trans. Colin Gordon, Leo Marshal, John Mepham, and Kate Soper (New York: Pantheon), 119; see also Foucault, "Technologies of the Self," in *The Essential Foucault: Selections from the Essential Works of Foucault, 1954–1984*, eds. Paul Rabinow and Nikolas Rose (New York: New Press), 146.

46. Carter G. Woodson, *The Mis-Education of the Negro* (New York: Clear Words Press, 2009), 17, 52–56, and 112–14.

The University of Kentucky has maintained a folder of William Matthews' public speeches. Almost all of the speeches are undated and untitled. They most likely served as Matthews' personal notes while addressing both his students as well as a variety of civic organizations. All of them support the notion of schooling as a means through which African Americans could advance themselves economically, socially, and legally. See "Speeches Given by William B. Matthews," n.d., box 10, folder 16, Wade Hall Collection of American Letters, University of Kentucky Special Collection.

Chapter 3 · Overworn Mothers and Unfed Minds

1. Report Card of Helen McKay, 1886, box 13, folder 2, M 1078, Brandt and Helen McKay Steele Collection, Indiana Historical Society, Indianapolis, IN; Report Card of Helen McKay, 1889, box 13, folder 2, M 1078, Brandt and Helen McKay Steele Collection, Indiana Historical Society, Indianapolis, IN. For a history of public schools in Indianapolis, see Kyle P. Steele, *Making a Mass Institution: Indianapolis and the American High School* (New Brunswick, NJ: Rutgers University Press, 2020).

2. Diary of Helen McKay, January 28, 1891, and May, 1, 1891, box 13, folder 2, M 1078, Brandt and Helen McKay Steele Collection, Indiana Historical Society, Indianapolis, IN (hereafter cited as Diary of Helen McKay, date of entry, McKay Steele Collection); Journal of Helen McKay, December 11, 1891, box 13, folder 8, M 1078, Brandt and Helen McKay Steele Collection, Indiana Historical Society, Indianapolis, IN (hereafter cited as Journal of Helen McKay, date of entry, McKay Steele Collection); Journal of Martha McKay, December 8, 1891, box 13, folder 8, M 1078, Brandt and Helen McKay Steele Collection, Indiana Historical Society, Indianapolis, IN (hereafter cited as Journal of Martha McKay, date of entry, McKay Steele Collection); Diary of Helen McKay, June 11, 1891, McKay Steele Collection; Martha N. McKay, "Theory of the True Science of Housekeeping," *Indianapolis (IN) Daily Sentinel*, May 18, 1879, 3.

3. Since Tocqueville, historians and social scientists have examined "the complex power relations and in social and economic contexts" between female-dominated work and work assigned to men. Linda K. Kerber, "Separate Spheres, Female Worlds, Woman's Place: The Rhetoric of Women's History," *Journal of American History* 75, no. 1 (June 1988): 28; Nancy F. Cott, *The Bonds of Womanhood: "Woman's Sphere in New England, 1780–1835* (New Haven, CT: Yale University Press, 1977), 67–72; see also Carroll Smith-Rosenberg, "The Female World of Love and Ritual: Relations between Women in Nineteenth-Century America," *Journal of Women in Culture and Society* 1, no. 1 (1975): 8–10.

Kerber's historiographical article challenges the dualism that historians have constructed with their use of the metaphor of separate spheres, labeling the phenomenon as a "trope" with "superficial vitality." See Kerber, "Separate Spheres, Female Worlds, Woman's Place," 30–35.

4. William Cutler recognized this trend in the late nineteenth century. He examined the rise of early parent–teacher groups in rural Michigan, which he shows later spread to urban

areas. See William W. Cutler III, *Parents and Schools: The 150-Year Struggle for Control in American Education* (Chicago: University of Chicago Press, 2000), 30–35.

5. See Katherine Badertscher, "Social Life and Social Services in Indianapolis: Networks During the Gilded Age and Progressive Era," *Indiana Magazine of History* 113, no. 4 (December 2017): 271–308; "Pushing the Fight: Local Council of Women Meets and Discusses Its Prospects of Success," *Indianapolis (IN) Journal*, June 6, 1894, 2.

6. Nancy M. Theriot labeled the first half of the nineteenth century the "maternal generation." A subtle shift occurred in the late nineteenth century as mothers adapted the "inherited script of suffering" to the new challenges of industrialization and urbanization. See Nancy M. Theriot, *Mothers and Daughters in Nineteenth-Century America: The Biosocial Construction of Femininity* (Lexington: University Press of Kentucky, 1996), 15; see also Jodi Vandenberg-Daves, *Modern Motherhood: An American History* (New Brunswick, NJ: Rutgers University Press, 2014), 135; Alice Boardman Smuts, *Science in the Service of Children, 1893–1935* (New Haven, CT: Yale University Press, 2006), 18–20; Vandenberg-Daves, *Modern Motherhood*, 114; Nancy F. Cott also links the roots of what became feminism to a similar dynamic of women expanding their autonomy in the private sphere to areas in the public sphere deemed maternalistic, such as education. See also Cott, *The Grounding of Modern Feminism* (New Haven, CT: Yale University Press, 1987), 16–20; Julia Grant, *Raising Baby by the Book: The Education of American Mothers* (New Haven, CT: Yale University Press, 1998), 5–17; Vandenberg-Daves, *Modern Motherhood*, 79; Peter N. Stearns, *Anxious Parents: A History of Modern Childrearing in America* (New York: New York University Press, 2003), 8–9, 19; Rima D. Apple, *Perfect Motherhood: Science and Childrearing in America* (Brunswick, NJ: Rutgers University Press, 2006), 2–3; Molly Ladd-Taylor, *Mother-Work: Women, Child Welfare, and the State, 1890–1930* (Urbana: University of Illinois Press, 1994), 15–18.

7. Vandenberg-Daves, *Modern Motherhood*, 95–97, 135; Peter N. Stearns, "Obedience and Emotion: A Challenge in the Emotional History of Childhood," *Journal of Social History* 47, no. 3 (Spring 2014): 607; Stearns, *Anxious Parents*, 18.

8. See Dorothy Ross, *G. Stanley Hall: The Psychologist as Prophet* (Chicago: University of Chicago Press, 1972) 292–95; Smuts, *Science in the Service of Children*, 3–7; Stearns, *Anxious Parents*, 41; Jacy L. Young, "G. Stanley Hall, Child Study, and the American Public," *Journal of Genetic Psychology* 177, no. 6 (2016): 198–203; G. Stanley Hall, *Adolescence: Its Psychology and Its Relations to Physiology, Anthropology, Sociology, Sex, Crime, Religion and Education*, Vol. 1 (New York: D. Appleton and Company, 1904), xv–xviii.

9. Theresa Richardson, *The Century of the Child: The Mental Hygiene Movement and Social Policy in the United States and Canada* (Albany: State University of New York Press, 1989); Ladd-Taylor, *Mother-Work*, 44–46. For a history of the anti-homework movement, see Brian Gill and Steven Schlossman, "'A Sin against Childhood': Progressive Education and the Crusade to Abolish Homework, 1897–1941," *American Journal of Education* 105 (November 1996): 27–66; Stearns, *Anxious Parents*, 86.

10. In 1984, Cowan won the Dexter Prize for scholarship. After two decades, her book had been cited by 319 scholarly articles and in the twenty-first-century professors continued to assign *More Work for Mothers* in sociology and women's history courses. Joy Parr, "Industrializing the Household: Ruth Schwartz Cowan's 'More Work for Mother,'" *Technology and Culture* 46, no. 3 (July 2005): 604–12; Ruth Schwartz Cowan, *More Work for Mother: The Ironies of Household Technology from the Open Hearth to the Microwave* (New York: Basic Books, 1983), 55–64.

In the 1990s and early 2000s, scholars debated the implications of Cowan's thesis. Juliet B. Schor, for instance, argued that businesses had economic incentives to sell more labor-producing (not saving) products to households. Joel Mokyr, an economist, disagreed with Schor. Mokyr thought that increasing knowledge about diseases created new incentives for women to spend more labor on cleaning. Other historians have incorporated Cowan's ideas into their nineteenth-century analysis of moral motherhood. Rebecca Jo Plant studied the discourse of women as the "angel of the house." Peter Stearns incorporated Cowan's ironic twist when he argued that decreasing fertility rates for middle-class women caused mothers to dedicate more attention to each child's emotional, educational, and psychological well-being. See Juliet B. Schor, *The Overworked American: The Unexpected Decline of Leisure* (New York: Basic Books, 1993), 101–2; Joel Mokyr, "Why 'More Work for Mother'? Knowledge and Household Behavior, 1870–1945," *Journal of Economic History* 60, no. 1 (March 2000): 13; Rebecca Jo Plant, *Mom: The Transformation of Motherhood in Modern America* (Chicago: University of Chicago Press, 2010), 2; Stearns, *Anxious Parents*, 13–18.

11. In her journal, Martha McKay kept a newspaper clipping advertising life-size portraits. On the back of clipping, McKay recorded her notes on prices. See Journal of Martha McKay, 1883–1906. For a description of the socioeconomic divisions within Indianapolis' neighborhoods, see Steele, *Making a Mass Institution*, 17–20.

"Mrs. M'Kay, Club Worker, Passes at 91," *Indianapolis (IN) Times*, March 5, 1934, 8; "M'Kay Funeral Set for Tuesday," *Indianapolis (IN) Sunday Star*, May 10, 1914, 9; Badertscher, "Social Life and Social Services in Indianapolis," 277; Journal of Helen McKay, January 1 and January 9, 1889, McKay Steele Collection; Steele, *Making a Mass Institution*, 1; Letter from Martha McKay to Father, January 8, 1877, box 37, folder 5, M 1078, Brandt and Helen McKay Steele Collection, Indiana Historical Society, Indianapolis, IN (hereafter cited as Martha McKay to Father, relevant date, McKay Steele Collection).

12. Diary of Helen McKay, March 20, 1891, McKay Steele Collection; Letter from Helen McKay to Sister, October 16, 1891, box 12, folder 12, M 1078, Brandt and Helen McKay Steele Collection, Indiana Historical Society, Indianapolis, IN; Journal of Helen McKay, March 31, 1887, McKay Steele Collection; Martha McKay to Father, January 8, 1877, McKay Steele Collection; Martha McKay to Father, November 7, 1880, McKay Steele Collection; Martha McKay to Horace McKay, August 1887, box 37, folder 5, M 1078, Brandt and Helen McKay Steele Collection, Indiana Historical Society, Indianapolis, IN; Journal of Martha McKay, December 8, 1891, McKay Steele Collection; Journal of Martha McKay, March 24, 1888, November 5, 1888, and December 31, 1888, McKay Steele Collection; McKay, "Theory of the True Science of Housekeeping," 3.

13. See Indianapolis Institute for Young Ladies, 1878, box 37, folder 4, M 1078, Brandt and Helen McKay Steele Collection, Indiana Historical Society, Indianapolis, IN; Journal of Martha McKay, June 6, 1883, McKay Steele Collection; Diary of Helen McKay, January 8, 1891, and April 13, 1891, McKay Steele Collection; Journal of Helen McKay, December 11, 1891, McKay Steele Collection; Helen McKay to Sister, October 21, 1891, box 12, folder 12, M 1078, Brandt and Helen McKay Steele Collection, Indiana Historical Society Library and Manuscripts Collection (hereafter cited as Helen McKay to Sister, October 21, 1891, McKay Steele Collection); Journal of Helen McKay, January 3, 1889, McKay Steele Collection; Journal of Helen McKay, January 20, 1888, McKay Steele Collection; Diary of Helen McKay, January 28, 1891, and May 1, 1891, McKay Steele Collection; Journal of Helen McKay, March 3, 1887, McKay Steele Collection; Diary of Helen McKay, January 9, 1891, McKay Steele Collection; Essay on Macbeth, January 1892, box 13, folder 9, M 1078, Brandt and Helen McKay Steele Collection, Indiana Historical Society, Indianapolis, IN.

14. Journal of Martha McKay, June 6, 1883, McKay Steele Collection; McKay, "Theory of the True Science of Housekeeping," 3; Journal of Martha McKay, December 5, 1890, McKay Steele Collection.

15. "Good Sense," *Illinois School Journal* 3, no. 9 (January 1884): 235–36; Emma Stebbins, ed., *Charlotte Cushman: Her Letters and Memories of Her Life* (Boston: Houghton, Osgood, 1878), 19; Laura C. Holloway, *The Mothers of Great Men and Women, and Some Wives of Great*

Men (Baltimore: R. H. Woodward, 1892), 400–401; Ellen LaGarde, "Jim Preston's Bicycle: A Story for Boys," *Ladies' Home Journal* 8, no. 3 (February 1891): 1–2; "New Marking System," *Milwaukee (WI) Journal,* June 11, 1890, 8; "The Teacher and the Child," *Macon (GA) Telegraph,* September 23, 1895, 8.

16. John G. Gittings, "School Work of the State," *The West Virginia School Journal* 6, no. 12 (December 1887): 11; "Notes," *Wisconsin Journal of Education* 12, no. 5 (May 1882): 226–32; Pearl Abel, "Ely School Report, '99," *Monroe City (MO) Democrat,* November 16, 1899, 4.

17. "Parent's Department," *Kindergarten Magazine* 7, no. 5 (January 1895): 370–75; Emerson White, *Promotions and Examinations in Graded Schools* (Washington, DC: Government Printing Office, 1891), 44–65.

18. Charleston Female Seminary Report Card, December 5, 1885, folder 4, MSS 110003062452, Aichel Family Papers, University of South Carolina Special Collections, Columbia, SC; Letter from William Burum to Mollie, November 25, 1898, box 2, folder 43, MS-1109, Burum and Gallagher Family Papers, University of Tennessee–Knoxville, Betsey B. Creekmore Special Collections, Knoxville, TN; Sam McNeely to Robert Whitehead McNeely, October 22, 1888, box 1, file 3, MSS 110003034494, Robert Whitehead McNeely Papers, University of South Carolina Special Collections, Columbia, SC.

19. "Noted Churchman and Scholar Passes," *Times-Star* (Cincinnati, OH), March 27, 1936, 1; Letter from M. McDermott to Albert Nast, March 1, 1883, box 1, folder 2, item 16, MSS fW567a, Marie Nast Wherry Papers, Cincinnati Museum Center, Cincinnati, OH; Letter from Albert Nast to Marie Nast, March 9, 1899, box 1, folder 8, item 72, MSS fW567a, Marie Nast Wherry Papers, Cincinnati Museum Center, Cincinnati, OH; Letter from William G. Nast to Albert Nast, January 20, 1889, box 1, folder 3, item 25, MSS fW567a, Marie Nast Wherry Papers, Cincinnati Museum Center, Cincinnati, OH; Letter from Albert Nast to Marie Nast, June 26, 1899, box 1, folder 7, item 67, MSS fW567a, Marie Nast Wherry Papers, Cincinnati Museum Center, Cincinnati, OH; Letter from Albert Nast to Marie Nast, May 3, 1899, box 1, folder 8, item 76, MSS fW567a, Marie Nast Wherry Papers, Cincinnati Museum Center, Cincinnati, OH.

20. The historian Nancy M. Theriot identified the nineteenth century's "idealized notion of powerful yet self-sacrificing and suffering motherhood." See Theriot, *Mothers and Daughters in Nineteenth-Century America,* 15–22; Diary of Emily Jane Winkler Bealer, 1876–1886, pages 6, 18–21, 25–26, and 41, folder 2, MSS814f, Emily Jane Winkler Bealer Collection, Atlanta History Center, Kenan Research Library (hereafter cited as Diary of Bealer, relevant pages, Bealer Collection.

21. Letter from Katherine Fletcher to Henrietta Fletcher, October 1886, box 063, folder 003, item 009, Fletcher Family Papers, University of Vermont Libraries, Burlington, VT (hereafter Katherine to Henrietta, October 1886, Fletcher Papers); Letter from Katherine Fletcher to Henrietta Fletcher, October 1, 1887, box 063, folder 019, item 011, Fletcher Family Papers, University of Vermont Libraries, Burlington, VT (hereafter cited as Katherine to Henrietta, October 1, 1887, Fletcher Papers); Letter from Henrietta Fletcher to Katherine Fletcher, September 17, 1886, box 063, folder 016, item 020, Fletcher Family Papers, University of Vermont Libraries, Burlington, VT (hereafter cited as Henrietta to Katherine, September 17, 1886, Fletcher Papers); Letter from Henrietta Fletcher to Katherine Fletcher, January 8, 1888, box 063, folder 020, item 002, University of Vermont Libraries, Burlington, VT (hereafter cited as Henrietta to Katherine, January 8, 1888, Fletcher Papers); Letter from Henrietta Fletcher to Katherine Fletcher, May 13, 1886 or 1887, box 063, folder 015, item 034, Fletcher Family Papers, University of Vermont Libraries, Burlington, VT; Henrietta to Katherine, September 17, 1886, Fletcher Papers; Letter from Katherine Fletcher to Henrietta Fletcher, October 7, 1886 or 1887, box 063, folder 015, item 013, Fletcher Family Papers, University of Vermont Libraries, Burlington, VT (hereafter cited as Katherine to Henrietta, October 7, 1886 or 1887, Fletcher Papers); Letter from Henrietta Fletcher to Katherine Fletcher, April 15, 1886

or 1887, box 063, folder 015, item 033, University of Vermont Libraries, Burlington, VT;
Henrietta to Katherine, January 8, 1888, Fletcher Papers; Katherine to Henrietta, Octo-
ber 1, 1887, Fletcher Papers; Katherine to Henrietta, October 7, 1886 or 1887, Fletcher Papers;
Katherine to Henrietta, October 1886, Fletcher Papers; Letter from Henrietta Fletcher to
Katherine Fletcher, c. 1885–1887, box 063, folder 015, item 044, Fletcher Family Papers,
University of Vermont Libraries, Burlington, VT; Henrietta Fletcher to Katherine Fletcher,
November 13, 1887, box 063, folder 019, item 014, Fletcher Family Papers, University of
Vermont Libraries, Burlington, VT.

    22. Letter from Herbert Bingham to R. S. McLucas, May 30, 1896, box 1, folder 6, MSS
2019.03.02 12055, McLucas Family Papers, University of South Carolina, Special Collections,
Columbia, SC; Letter from Effie McLucas to Roderick McLucas, March 19, 1886, box 1, folder
6, MSS 2019.03.02 12055, McLucas Family Papers, University of South Carolina, Special
Collections, Columbia, SC (hereafter cited as Effie to Roderick, March 19, 1886, McLucas
Papers); Letter from Effie McLucas to Roderick McLucas, April 5, 1886, box 1, folder 6,
MSS 2019.03.02 12055, McLucas Family Papers, University of South Carolina, Special
Collections, Columbia, SC (hereafter cited as Effie to Roderick, April 5, 1886, McLucas
Papers); Effie to Roderick, March 19, 1886, McLucas Papers; Effie to Roderick, April 5, 1886,
McLucas Papers; Effie to Roderick, March 19, 1886, McLucas Papers.

    23. "Ex-School Teacher, Principal's Rites, Held Monday," *Indianapolis (IN) Recorder*,
August 31, 1974, 9; J. Summers Report Card, 1898–1899, box 1, folder 2, M 1143, Jeannette
Summers Collection, Indiana Historical Society, Indianapolis, IN.

    24. Letter from Oblinger Family to Thomas Family, July 11, 1881, RG1346.AM.S01.l160,
Oblinger Family Collection, Library of Congress, Washington, DC (hereafter cited as Family
to Thomas, July 11, 1881, Oblinger Collection); Family to Thomas, July 11, 1881, Oblinger
Collection; Letter from Laura I. Oblinger to Uriah W. Oblinger, January 22, 1894, Oblinger
Family Collection, Library of Congress, Washington, DC (hereafter cited as Laura to Uriah,
January 22, 1894, Oblinger Collection); Letter from Laura I. Oblinger, Sadie Oblinger, Nettie
Oblinger to Uriah W. Oblinger, Stella Oblinger, and Maggie Oblinger, April 22, 1887, Oblinger
Family Collection, Library of Congress, Washington, DC; Laura I. Oblinger to Uriah W.
Oblinger, May 24, 1887, Oblinger Family Collection, Library of Congress, Washington,
DC; Laura to Uriah, January 22, 1894, Oblinger Collection; Laura I. Oblinger to Uriah W.
Oblinger, January 8, 1882, Oblinger Family Collection, Library of Congress, Washington, DC.

    25. David Hogan, "'To Better Our Condition': Educational Credentialing and 'The Silent
Compulsion of Economic Relations' in the United States, 1830 to the Present," *History of
Education Quarterly* 36, no. 3 (Autumn 1996): 251–56; Susan M. Brookhart et al., "A Century
of Grading Research: Meaning and Value in the Most Common Educational Measure," *Review
of Educational Research* 86, no. 4 (December 2016): 804.

    26. Thomas R. Guskey and Susan M. Brookhart, *What We Know About Grading: What
Works, What Doesn't, and What's Next* (Alexandria, VA: ASCD, 2019), 14; Thomas R. Guskey
and Jane M. Bailey, *Developing Grading and Reporting Systems for Student Learning* (Thousand Oaks, CA: Corwin, 2001), 26.

    27. Julius D'Agostino, "Concern for the Future, Ghosts from the Past for American High
Schools: The Carnegie Unit Revisited," *American Secondary Education* 13, no. 3 (1984): 3–4;
Sidney L. Besvinick, "The Expendable Carnegie Unit," *Phi Delta Kappan* 42, no. 8 (May 1966):
365.

    28. Paul E. Peterson, *The Politics of School Reform, 1870–1940* (Chicago: University of
Chicago Press, 1985), 161–66; Raymond E. Callahan, *Education and the Cult of Efficiency:
A Study of the Social Forces That Have Shaped the Administration of the Public Schools*
(Chicago: University of Chicago Press, 1962), 67–73; William J. Shearer, *The Grading of
Schools* (New York: H. P. Smith, 1898), 77.

29. Leroy D. Weld, "A Standard of Interpretation of Numerical Grades," *The School Review* 25, no. 6 (June 1917): 412; Brookhart, "A Century of Grading Research," 806; Jack Schneider and Ethan Hutt, "Making the Grade: A History of the A–F Marking Scheme," *Journal of Curriculum Studies* 46, no. 2 (March 4, 2014): 215.

30. Guy Stanton, "Educational Column," *Wood County (WI) Reporter*, November 11, 1897, 4; "Byron Farmers' Club," *Owosso (MI) Times*, April 22, 1898, 9; "School Reports That Puzzle Poor Parents," *Brooklyn (NY) Daily Eagle*, October 6, 1901, 3.

31. "Keystone Academy," *Scranton (PA) Tribune*, November 23, 1894, 8; "A Dry Teacher," *Southern Herald* (Liberty, MS), March 23, 1889, 2; "Friday, Jan. 31, 1896," *Times* (Owosso, MI), January 31, 1896, 5; "A School Incident," *Herald* (Los Angeles, CA), July 1, 1898, 7; "Missing from Home: Strange Disappearance of Pretty School Girl," *Seattle (WA) Post-Intelligencer*, March 10, 1895, 7.

32. Estelle Baker, "Little Arna and Her Selfishness," *San Francisco (CA) Call*, October 9, 1898, 31; "All Mothers," *Daily Chieftain* (Vinita, OK), December 8, 1900, 4; "Giving Medals in Schools," *San Francisco (CA) Call*, May 11, 1897, 14; Hall, *Adolescence*, xv–xviii.

33. "Rawlingsville Notes," *Lancaster (PA) Daily Intelligencer*, January 13, 1887, 1; "Giving Medals in Schools," *San Francisco (CA) Call*, May 11, 1897, 14; "School Reports That Puzzle Poor Parents," *Brooklyn (NY) Daily Eagle*, October 6, 1901, 3; "No More Report Cards," *Morris (MN) Tribune*, September 29, 1900, 1; S. G. Burked, "Co-Operation: An Address Given at the Opening of the Fifth Germ of the Lawrence Union School," *True Northerner* (Paw Paw, MI), May 12, 1871, 1; "School Board," *Wichita (KS) Eagle*, March 5, 1889, 5; "No Increase of Pay: The Public School Teachers Must Be Content with Their Salaries," *Atlanta (GA) Constitution*, August 23, 1895, 2; "Among Our Schools," *Sterling (IL) Daily Standard*, December 17, 1897, 5; "School Notes," *Red Cloud (NE) Chief*, April 12, 1895, 12; A. E. Winship, "That Deserving Case," *St. Johnsbury (VT) Caledonian*, April 21, 1887, 2.

34. "A Reply to 'Taxpayer,'" *Morning Journal and Courier* (New Haven, CT), July 31, 1880, 1; for more on the Victorian construct of female "nervous exhaustion," see Cynthia Eagle Russett, *Sexual Science: The Victorian Construction of Womanhood* (Cambridge, MA: Harvard University Press, 1989), 39–46; "Teacher Died from Overwork," *New York Times*, May 27, 1898, 8.
See Appendix II for a content analysis that traces sympathetic references to teachers in one of the most popular monthly newspapers, intended for middle-class mothers. Cutler makes a similar point in *Parents and Schools*. As an example, see Cutler, *Parents and Schools*, 88.

35. Historians mark the 1868 founding of New York City's Sorosis Club as the start of the women's club movement. Christine Woyshner, *The National PTA, Race, and Civic Engagement, 1897–1970* (Columbus: Ohio State University, 2009), 25; Sheila M. Rothman, *Woman's Proper Place: A History of Changing Ideals and Practices, 1870 to the Present* (New York: Basic Books, 1978), 64.
The groups were more formal and hierarchical than their predecessors in the antebellum period. The late nineteenth-century women's clubs relied on rules of order, official titles, and chairs of subcommittees, and they were increasingly interconnected through state and national federations. In 1890, Jane Cunningham Croly, a founding member of the Sorosis Club, spearheaded an effort to create the General Federation of Women's Clubs (GFWC). By 1898, the GFWC reported 60,000 members in thirty-five states. See Anne Firor Scott, *Natural Allies: Women's Associations in American History* (Chicago: University of Chicago Press, 1992), 121; Rothman, *Woman's Proper Place*, 328 and 64; Scott, *Natural Allies*, 126; Woyshner, *The National PTA, Race, and Civic Engagement*, 28; Theodora Penny Martin, *The Sound of Our Own Voices: Women's Study Clubs, 1860–1910* (Boston: Beacon Press, 1987), 92–112.
William Reese noticed that the women's club movement prompted mothers to become vocal defenders of the rights of schoolteachers, a profession that was increasingly associated with women and poor working conditions. While Patricia Carter noticed a similar dynamic in the twentieth century, she focused on the impact that teachers made on the women's club

movement, not vice versa. See William J. Reese, *Power and the Promise of School Reform: Grassroots Movements During the Progressive Era* (Boston: Routledge & Kegan Paul, 1986), 46–49; Patricia A. Carter, *"Everybody's Paid But the Teacher": The Teaching Profession and the Women's Movement* (New York: Teachers College Press, 2002). For more on the link between the women's suffrage movement and school board elections, see Gaylynn Welch, "Suffrage at the School House Door: The 1880 New York State School Suffrage Campaign," *New York History* 98, no. 3/4 (Summer/Fall 2017): 329–42; Marilyn Schultz Blackwell, "The Politics of Motherhood: Clarina Howard Nichols and School Suffrage," *New England Quarterly* 78, no. 4 (December 2005): 570–98; Kristin Mapel Bloomberg, "A Vast Host of Consecrated Women: New Scholarship on Minnesota's Woman Suffrage and Women's Rights Movement," *Minnesota History* 67, no. 3 (Fall 2020): 88–93.

36. In the very first meeting of the Atlanta women's club, one of the founding members stated that she wanted "to study the schoolteacher's problems and find out why she is not paid as much as the men who do exactly the same work." In the early 1870s in Memphis, a school-wage controversy mobilized the city's elite women who presented to the city leaders a plan of not only equal pay but also equal representation for women on the school board. The Memphis women even proposed a female candidate for superintendent. Patricia Carter chronicled the equal pay campaign in New York City, from 1900 to 1911. In 1898–1899, the Chicago Women's Club allied with the Chicago Teachers' Federation to prevent the passage of a bill in the Illinois legislature. The bill would have limited the opportunities of many working-class women from entering the teaching profession. See Atlanta Woman's Club Scrapbook, 1895–1900, page 2, MSS 353, box 3.73, Atlanta Woman's Club Collection, Atlanta History Center, Kenan Research Library, Atlanta, GA; Carter, *"Everybody's Paid But the Teacher,"* 34–41; Marsha Wedell, *Elite Women and the Reform Impulse in Memphis, 1875–1915* (Knoxville: University of Tennessee Press, 1991), 14–15; Rousmaniere, *Citizen Teacher*, 52.

Carter, *"Everybody's Paid But the Teacher,"* 14; Jackie M. Blount, *Fit to Teach: Same-Sex Desire, Gender, and School Work in the Twentieth Century* (Albany: State University of New York Press, 2005.). School districts explicitly designed protocols for promotion from classroom teaching to the principal's office to appeal to males. See Kate Rousmaniere, *The Principal's Office: A Social History of the American School Principal* (Albany: State University of New York Press, 2013), 50–53. See also Joel Perlman and Robert A. Margo, *Women's Work?: American Schoolteachers, 1650–1920* (Chicago: University of Chicago Press, 2001), 120.

Even though the path to promotion was limited, the profession of school teaching offered modest financial security for working-class and immigrant women. However, between the years 1880 and 1900, the teaching workforce became increasingly associated with middle-class women. In 1880 Chicago, for instance, half of teachers were working class but by 1900 just one-third were working class. See Carter, *"Everybody's Paid But the Teacher,"* 14; Kate Rousmaniere, *Citizen Teacher: The Life and Leadership of Margaret Haley* (Albany: State University of New York Press, 2005), 14–27; Reese, *Power and the Promise of School Reform*, 46–49; "The School House Teachers' Issue," *Philadelphia (PA) Inquirer*, February 14, 1892, 7.

37. Dozens of clubs followed the IWC: the Clio Club, the Inter Nos Club, and the Magazine Club, to name just a few. Each held similar mission statements for the "social and literary advancement" of their members. Club membership was typically between thirty and fifty women, with between twelve and twenty-four attending meetings on a regular basis. Buried in their meeting minutes were references to their interests in schools. In January 1889, for instance, the Clio Club met to discuss educational history as well as listen to a presentation on "Schools of Today." Six years later, the Clio Club established a subcommittee to examine conditions in local schools and report back to the larger group. Interest in local education sometimes became public in the form of letters to the local newspaper, as in 1885, when an Indianapolis public school parent wrote that teachers were being "literally worked to death."

The letter was framed in gendered terms, focusing on the how a "woman cannot be worked 12 to 15 hours a day," and called for an earlier end to the school day in order to give female teachers time to rest. See Indianapolis Woman's Club Registers, 1875, box 37, folder 1, M 1078, Brandt and Helen McKay Steele Collection, Indiana Historical Society, Indianapolis, IN; Badertscher, "Social Life and Social Services in Indianapolis," 286–89; Clio Club Minutes, January 1889, box 1, folder 1, L471, Clio Club Collection, Indiana State Library, Manuscripts and Rare Books Division, Indianapolis, IN; Clio Club Minutes, November 1895, box 1, folder 2, L471, Clio Club Collection, Indiana State Library, Manuscripts and Rare Books Division, Indianapolis, IN; "Why So Much Sickness Among Our Teachers?," *Indianapolis (IN) Journal,* April 14, 1885, 3; "Teacher Salaries," *Indianapolis (IN) Journal,* January 13, 1900, 3.

38. "Pushing the Fight; Local Council of Women Meets and Discusses Its Prospects of Success," *Indianapolis (IN) Journal,* June 6, 1894, 2. See also Scott, *Natural Allies,* 136–42. Scott showed how suffragists had their first success in securing voting rights in the 1870s and 1880s for the right to vote in school board elections. In 1872, women voted in school board elections in New Hampshire and in Boston, and in 1882 they voted for Philadelphia's school board. See also Carter, *"Everybody's Paid But the Teacher,"* 80–83; Martha Nicholson McKay, *Literary Clubs of Indiana* (Indianapolis, IN: Bowen-Merrill, 1894), 19, 30, 48; Story of Martha and Horace, n.d., box 12, folder 9, M 1078, Brandt and Helen McKay Steele Collection, Indiana Historical Society, Indianapolis, IN; Laura Sherin Gaus, *Shortridge High School, 1864–1981: In Retrospect* (Indianapolis: Indiana Historical Society, 1985), 65.

39. Steele, *Making a Mass Institution,* 12, 16–19; Gaus, *Shortridge High School,* 44, 63–65; "Death of Miss Cornelia McKay," *Indianapolis (IN) Journal,* August 14, 1893, 8.

40. "Frenzel's Fine Hand: Working Hard to Retain Control of the Board - His Candidates in Several Districts-Boundaries," *Indianapolis (IN) Journal,* June 8, 1894, 8; "Cut Short," *Indiana (IN) Woman: An Illustrated Journal,* April 11, 1896, 3; "School Election Results," *Indianapolis (IN) News,* June 11, 1894, 8.

41. Tiffany Benedict Browne, "Sunday Prayers: McKay Home," *Historic Indianapolis,* April 24, 2011, https://historicindianapolis.com/sunday-prayers-mckay-house/; Libby Cierzniak, "Indianapolis Collected: The Mystery of the Missing Mantels," *Historic Indianapolis,* July 11, 2015, https://historicindianapolis.com/indianapolis-collected-the-mystery-of-the-missing-mantels/; Breanna Cooper and Tyler Fenwick, "We've Been Gentrified," *Indianapolis (IN) Reporter,* July 23, 2020; Brandon Drenon, "This Is How the Racial Makeup of Indianapolis Has Changed Since 1970," *Indianapolis (IN) Star,* July 12, 2021.

42. Francis A. Pearman II and Walker A. Swain found that high-income white families were much more likely to gentrify "communities of color" when given opportunities of school choice. Chase M. Billingham and Shelley McDonough Kimelberg conducted a qualitative study of a group of middle-class parents in Boston gentrifying an urban school. The authors concluded that school-based engagement led to deeper loyalties to and engagement with their neighborhoods among middle-class parents. See Francis A. Pearman II and Walker A. Swain, "School Choice, Gentrification, and the Variable Significance of Racial Stratification in Urban Neighborhoods," *Sociology of Education* 90, no. 3 (July 2017); Chase M. Billingham and Shelley McDonough Kimelberg, "Middle-Class Parents, Urban Schooling, and the Shift From Consumption to Production of Urban Space," *Sociological Forum* 28, no. 1 (March 2013): 85–108. "General Information," *Center for Inquiry Schools,* accessed July 22, 2021, https://myips.org/cfischools/cfi-school-70/; "Our Mission and Vision," *Center for Inquiry Schools,* accessed July 22, 2021, https://myips.org/cfischools/cfi-school-70/; "Center for Inquiry Family Handbook," *Center for Inquiry Schools,* accessed July 22, 2021, https://myips.org/cfischools/wp-content/uploads/sites/203/2019/06/CFI-Family-Handbook-2017-2018_Final.pdf.

43. Arika Herron, "'Straight Up Segregation': Parents, Principals Ask for Change to IPS Enrollment Policies," *Indianapolis (IN) Star,* June 23, 2021; Elizabeth Gabriel, "This IPS School

'Feels Like Segregation' Say Parents Who Demand Enrollment Changes," *NPR: WFYI Indianapolis*, June 23, 2021, https://www.wfyi.org/news/articles/ips-school-feels-like -segregation-parents-demand-enrollment-changes; "Quick Facts: Indianapolis, Indiana," *United States Census*, accessed July 22, 2021, https://www.census.gov/quickfacts/fact/table/indi anapoliscitybalanceindiana,US/PST045219.

Annette Lareau's longitudinal ethnography captures much of the education-fueled anxiety among twenty-first-century middle-class parents. See Lareau, *Unequal Childhoods: Class, Race, and Family Life*, 2nd ed. (Berkeley: University of California Press, 2011).

44. Michel Foucault deserves some credit for noting the peculiarity of this nineteenth-century parenting paradox in which parents complained about education while at the same time seeking more of it. In a November 1973 lecture at the Collège de France, Foucault pontificated on the "apparatus" of disciplinary systems. Essential to the systems, Foucault explained, was familial compliance. At one point, Foucault stated that "the family is the instance of constraint that will permanently fix individuals to their disciplinary apparatuses." Foucault went on to explain that it was the parents, after all, who delivered their children to the schools in compliance with nineteenth-century truancy laws. "The family plays a full role," he wrote, in "consigning [their children] to pathology." See Foucault, *Psychiatric Power: Lectures at the Collège de France, 1973–1974*, ed. Jacques Lagrange, trans. Graham Burchell (New York: Palgrave Macmillan, 2006), 80–82. See also Chloë Taylor, "Foucault and Familial Power," *Hypatia* 27, no. 1 (2012): 201–18.

Chapter 4 · The Eye of the Juvenile Court

1. Colorado's Department of Human Services requested that I use a pseudonym for the protagonist in this chapter.

2. William A. Fischel, *Making the Grade: The Economic Evolution of American School Districts* (Chicago: University of Chicago Press, 2009), 57; Tracy L. Steffes, *School, Society, and State: A New Education to Govern Modern America, 1890–1940* (Chicago: University of Chicago Press, 2012), 126; David Tyack and Michael Berkowitz, "The Man Nobody Liked: Toward a Social History of the Truant Officer, 1840–1940," *American Quarterly* 29, no. 1 (Spring 1977): 32.

3. Tyack and Berkowitz, "The Man Nobody Liked," 43; Steffes, *School, Society, and State*, 127; Julia Grant, *The Boy Problem: Educating Boys in Urban America, 1870–1970* (Baltimore: Johns Hopkins University Press, 2014), 26–27; 91–92.

The more recent histories are building on the work of Michael Katz, Anthony M. Platt, and Steven Mintz. Katz dedicated a chapter to a single Massachusetts reform school's history, when reformers "took off their velvet gloves" and made explicit that "education was to be a key weapon in a battle against poverty, crime, and vice." Platt, writing around the same time as Katz, argued that progressive reformers, in their effort to help marginalized children, "invented new categories of youthful misbehavior which had been hitherto unappreciated." More recently, Mintz chronicled how the efforts of the urbanized elite to create juvenile corrections systems led them to "universalize the middle-class ideals of child-hood." Katz, *The Irony of Early School Reform: Educational Innovation in Mid-Nineteenth Century Massachusetts* (Cambridge, MA: Harvard University Press, 1968), 164; Platt, *Child Savers: The Invention of Delinquency* (Chicago: Chicago University Press, 1969), 3–4; Mintz, *Huck's Raft: A History of American Childhood* (Cambridge, MA: Belknap Press of Harvard University Press, 2004), 184.

Sarah E. Igo chronicled the "percolating anger over intrusive psychological testing" among school parents and the efforts of those parents to reduce the amount of educational book-keeping. See Igo, *The Known Citizen: A History of Privacy in Modern America* (Cambridge, MA: Harvard University Press, 2018), 129–34.

See also Ethan L. Hutt, "Formalism Over Function: Compulsion, Courts, and The Rise of Educational Formalism in America, 1870–1930," *Teachers College Record* 114, no. 010301 (January 2012): 1–27.

4. See Tera Eva Agyepong, *The Criminalization of Black Children: Race, Gender, and Delinquency in Chicago's Juvenile Justice System, 1899–1945* (Chapel Hill: University of North Carolina Press, 2018), 4 and 37; "Andrew Monroe [pseud.] Says It's No Use to Try; He Cannot Live Down the Past His Wife Accuses," *Des Moines (IA) News*, June 18, 1913, 1.

5. This development of juvenile courts using report cards reflects a broader trend noted by Ethan Hutt and Jack Schneider. Hutt and Schneider identified the 1870s as the beginning of an era in which grades, originally intended for internal communication between parents and students, became a means through which to communicate a child's merit beyond the school community. "Unlike ordered rankings, which only communicated a student's relative standing within his or her class," Hutt and Schneider wrote, "grades also promised to serve as an external communication device—to admissions boards, employers and others." I am arguing that the list of external recipients of grades should include juvenile court judges, truant officers, and parole boards. Schneider and Hutt, "Making the Grade: A History of the A–F Marking Scheme," *Journal of Curriculum Studies* 46, no. 2 (March 4, 2014): 209.

6. Carl Abbott, Stephen J. Leonard, and David McComb, *Colorado: A History of the Centennial State* (Niwot: University Press of Colorado, 1994), 162; Richard Hogan, *Class and Community in Frontier Colorado* (Lawrence: University of Kansas Press, 1990), 82.

7. William Wei, *Asians in Colorado: A History of Persecution and Perseverance in the Centennial State* (Seattle: University of Washington Press, 2016), 55; David Schor, *The Colorado Doctrine: Water Rights, Corporations, and Distributive Justice on the American Frontier* (New Haven, CT: Yale University Press, 2012), 49; Peggy Ford Waldo, *Greeley: Images of America* (Charleston, SC: Arcadia Publishing, 2016), 59–60; "Greeley's Potato Day," *Gastronomica* 7, no. 4 (Fall 2007): 126; Abbott, Leonard, and McComb, *Colorado*, 138; Waldo, *Greeley*, 8–22; Duane A. Smith, *The Trail of Silver and Gold: Mining in Colorado, 1859–2009* (Boulder: University Press of Colorado, 2009), 242–43; Program: First Concert of the Greeley High School Orchestra, March 28, 1890, 1983.44.22-.32, The Family Records of A. B. Copeland, Hazel E. Johnson Research Center, Greeley History Museum; Mollie Copeland to A. B. Copeland, 1886, 1981.41.0013B.1-9, A. B. Copeland Family Records, Greeley History Museum, Hazel E. Johnson Research Center, Greeley, CO; 1900 US Census, Daniel and Ervilla Monroe [pseud.], Phillips County, precinct 4, Colorado, page 5, line 94, Ancestry.com; "A Long Time About It," *Rifle (CO) Telegram*, January 22, 1915, 6.

8. David M. Henkin, "The Traveling Daguerreotype: Early Photography and the U.S. Postal System," in *Photography and Other Media in the Nineteenth Century* (University Park, PA: Penn State University Press, 2018), 49; Beaumont Newhall, *The History of Photography: From 1839 to the Present* (Boston: Little, Brown, 1982), 63–64; Mark Osterman, "The Technical Evolution of Photography in the Nineteenth Century," in *The Focal Encyclopedia of Photography*, ed. Michael R. Peres, 4th ed. (New York: Focal Press, 2007), 33–34; May Warner Marien, *Photography: A Cultural History* (London: Lawrence King, 2002), 166; "Cabinet Photographs," *Greeley (CO) Tribune*, April 7, 1892, 4; "Photographs," *Greeley (CO) Tribune*, April 7, 1892, 1.

9. Fortune telling became a popular Victorian pastime in the late nineteenth century. See Stanley Weintraub, "'The Hibernian School': Oscar Wilde and Bernard Shaw," *Shaw* 13, no. 1 (1993): 27–28; Michael D. Bailey, *Magic and Superstition in Europe: A Concise History from Antiquity to the Present* (Lanham, MD: Rowman & Littlefield, 2007) 218; Joan Navarre, "Oscar Wilde, Edward Heron-Allen, and the Palmistry Craze of the 1880s," *English Literature in Transition, 1880–1920* 54, no. 2 (2011): 174–77.

Female fortune tellers were common at the time, particularly because palm reading was seen as upholding traditional gender roles of mystic intuition, the antithesis of masculine reason. See Jeremy C. Young, "Empowering Passivity: Women Spiritualists, Houdini, and the 1926 Fortune Telling Hearing," *Journal of Social History* 48, no. 2 (Winter 2014): 347–56; Navarre, "Oscar Wilde, Edward Heron-Allen, and the Palmistry Craze," 176–77; Stanley Finger, "Mark Twain's Life-Long Fascination with Phrenology," *Journal of the History of Behavioral Sciences* 55, no. 2 (April 2019): 109; "Palmistry," *State Herald* (Holyoke, CO), January 19, 1900, 1.

10. The census lists Monroe's profession as palmistry. There is also a Holyoke newspaper advertisement that names "Mrs. Sheldon" as the fortune teller. See "Untitled," *State Herald* (Holyoke, CO), February 2, 1900, 1; 1900 US Census, Daniel and Ervilla Monroe [pseud.], Phillips County, Precinct 4, Colorado, page 5, line 94, Ancestry.com.

The Homestead Act of 1862 allowed for individual applicants to claim 160 acres of public lands in exchange for residing on the property and putting it to agricultural use. The railroad company also launched a public relations campaign that attracted migrants like Daniel and Ervilla Monroe, who may have seen the positive reports of Phillips County in the Greeley newspaper. Richard Edwards, Jacob K. Friefeld, and Rebecca S. Wingo, *Homesteading the Plains: Toward a New History* (Lincoln: University of Nebraska Press, 2017), 6–12; Abigail Christman, "United States Department of the Interior, National Park Service, National Register of Historic Places, Multiple Property Documentation Form" (Boulder: Center for Preservation Research, University of Colorado, 2017), 5; Paul W. Gates, "Homesteading in the High Plains," *Agricultural History* 51, no. 1 (January 1977): 116; "To Pueblo and Back," *Greeley (CO) Tribune*, June 20, 1895, 7; Jean Gray, *Homesteading Haxtun and the High Plains: Northeastern Colorado History* (Charleston, SC: History Press, 2013), 37–38; "Photographs," *State Herald* (Holyoke, CO), May 19, 1899, 2.

11. Gary Libecap and Zeynep Kocabiyik Hansen, "'Rain Follows the Plow' and Dryfarming Doctrine: The Climate Information Problem and Homestead Failure in the Upper Great Plains, 1890–1925," *Journal of Economic History* 62, no. 1 (March 2002): 96; Rena K. Fowler, "Settling Down and Proving Up on an Eastern Colorado Homestead: The Correspondence of Estelle Siglin and Home Evans, 1906–1911," *Great Plains Quarterly* 36, no. 3 (Summer 2016): 211–13; Gates, "Homesteading in the High Plains," 121; "Palmistry," *State Herald* (Holyoke, CO), May 18, 1900, 1.

There are several important histories of schooling in the West. David Wallace Adams studied the factionalism among the faculty and administrators at the Fort Defiance Indian Agency. Steven Mintz described the lives of children in western mining towns, struggling through poverty while also enjoying less supervision than their urban middle-class counterparts. Elliott West analyzed the layers of complexity of how growing up on the frontier changed the experience of childhood. West explained that, "The lines between childhood and adulthood became vague and imprecise on the frontier." Finally, David A. Gamson, once again, clarifies the greater context of Denver's schools. Through the leadership of superintendents like Jesse Newlon, Denver's public schools developed a reputation for valuing teacher feedback with curriculum reform in the 1920s. See David Wallace Adams, "Blood and Ice: Intimacy and Factionalism at Fort Defiance Indian Agency, 1887–1888," *Western Historical Quarterly* 50, no. 3 (Autumn 2019): 209–31; Mintz, *Huck's Raft*, 149–52; Elliott West, *Growing Up with the Country* (Albuquerque: University of New Mexico Press, 1989), xix; David A. Gamson, *The Importance of Being Urban: Designing the Progressive School District, 1890–1940* (Chicago: University of Chicago Press, 2019), 141–47.

12. William Philpott, *Vacationland: Tourism and Environment in the Colorado High Country* (Seattle: University of Washington Press, 2013), 15–16; The hills surrounding the village of Glenwood Springs became a site of conflict between cattle and sheep grazers, followed by fruit farms and spotted with coal mines. Andrew Guilford, *The Woolly West: Colorado's History of Sheepscapes* (College Station: Texas A&M University Press, 2018), 46, 49–50; Jim Nelson, *Glenwood Springs: The History of a Rocky Mountain Resort* (Ouray, CO: Western Reflections, 1999), 44–45, 123.

Nearby towns bore the brunt of labor-capital strife over miners' wages in an era of "open industrial warfare." While the Glenwood Springs region was a hub for coal mines, the focal points of the labor unrest were over 150 miles away in towns like Leadville and Cripple Creek. See Carl Ubbelohde, Maxine Benson, and Duane A. Smith, *A Colorado History* (Boulder, CO: Pruett Publishing, 1976), 232; Smith, *The Trail of Silver and Gold*, 187–92; Nelson, *Glenwood Springs*, 123; Abbott, Leonard, and McComb, *Colorado*, 111.

Melanie Shellenbarger, *High Country Summers: The Early Second Homes of Colorado, 1880–1940* (Tucson: University of Arizona Press, 2012), 32–33; Nelson, *Glenwood Springs*, 86–87, 122, 128–29; Lena M. Urquhart, *Glenwood Springs: Spa in the Mountains* (Glenwood Springs, CO: Taylor, 1970), 68.

Glenwood High School was already in existence and had been graded for over a decade. Evidence that Willard Monroe [pseud.] attended high school in Glenwood Springs comes from a photograph of the 1907 high school football team that lists Willard as one of the players. Likewise, the local historical society contains periodic report cards from Glenwood High School. See Photograph of Glenwood Football Team, 1907, subject file: Sports-Football, Glenwood Springs Historical Society, Frontier Museum and Archive, Glenwood Springs, CO; Cynthia Hines, *Early Glenwood Springs: Images of America* (Charleston, SC: Arcadia Publishing, 2015), 50–51; Glenwood Springs High School Diploma and Report Card, Bertram J. Cross, 1905, box: Original School Documents, Diplomas, Report Cards, etc., Glenwood Springs Historical Society, Frontier Museum and Archive, Glenwood Springs, CO; Glenwood Springs Schools, Report of Earl Hopkins, 1916, box: Original School Documents, Diplomas, Report Cards, etc., Frontier Museum and Archive, Glenwood Springs, CO.

The circus' tarot cards survived in the local historical society. See Tarot Cards, c. 1905, Al G. Barnes Show Company Collection, Permanent Public Display, Frontier Museum and Archive, Glenwood Springs, CO; Dave Robeson, *Al G. Barnes: Master Showman* (Caldwell, Idaho: Caxton Printers, 1936), 456.

13. "Partners Disagree," *Avalanche–Echo* (Glenwood Springs, CO), July 3, 1902, 1; "Monroe [pseud.] in Jail," *Eagle County Blade* (Red Cliff, CO), October 15, 1903, 1; "Monroe [pseud.] in Jail," *Glenwood Post* (Glenwood Springs, CO), October 10, 1903, 1; "Nonpariel Notes," *New Castle Nonpareil* (Nonpariel, CO), October 16, 1903, 1; "Nonpariel Notes," *New Castle Nonpareil* (Nonpariel, CO), October 30, 1903, 1; "Advertisement," *Yuma (CO) Pioneer*, October 7, 1904, 8; State Industrial School, Record of Examinations [RESTRICTED], 1906, box 18485 C, book 3, State Industrial School for Boys Collection, Colorado State Archive, Denver, CO (hereafter cited as Record of Examinations, 1906, Industrial School).

14. Michael Katz, Anthony M. Platt, and Steven Mintz wrote foundational histories of the "child-savers" like Lindsey. Katz dedicated a chapter to a single Massachusetts reform school's history, when reformers "took off their velvet gloves" and made explicit that "education was to be a key weapon in a battle against poverty, crime, and vice." Platt, writing around the same time as Katz, argued that progressive reformers, in their effort to help marginalized children, "invented new categories of youthful misbehavior which had been hitherto unappreciated." More recently, Mintz chronicled how the efforts of the urbanized elite to create juvenile corrections systems led them to "universalize the middle-class ideals of childhood." Katz, *The Irony of Early School Reform*, 164; Platt, *Child Savers*, 3–4; Mintz, *Huck's Raft*, 184.

By the early 1900s, Denver was in the midst of a remarkable period of growth. In 1870, the city counted a population of 4,759. Fifty years later, about 200,000 people resided in Denver. The city served as a kind of port, where the mountain mines met the railroads that stretched east across the plains. At the juncture of mountains and plains, "diabolical conditions" existed in Denver's smelter plants, which employed thousands of immigrant laborers. Thomas G. Andrews, *Killing for Coal: America's Deadliest Labor War* (Cambridge, MA: Harvard University Press, 2008), 59–63.

Ben B. Lindsey, "Moral Training, No. 4," *Denver (CO) Weekly Post*, December 14, 1912, 1. Typically, over 90 percent of the juveniles who appeared before the court were white. About 15 percent of the total were the children of Irish immigrants, 12 percent were Italian, and 20 percent were labeled as "Jewish." Between 5 percent and 10 percent were categorized as "Negro." For the gender breakdown, typically between 10 percent and 15 percent of the juveniles who appeared before the court were female. See *Report of the Denver Juvenile Court* (Denver, CO: Published by the City and County of Denver, 1909), 11–16; *Report of the Denver Juvenile Court* (Denver, CO: Published by the City and County of Denver, 1910), 9–12; D'Ann Campbell, "Judge Ben Lindsey and the Juvenile Court Movement, 1901–1904," *Arizona and the West* 18, no. 1 (Spring 1976): 9–10.

15. Some historians argue that these new courts became tools through which the middle class could impose their value systems onto the laboring classes. Political scientist Andrew J. Polsky called this phenomenon the rise of the "therapeutic state," a moment when government assumed that "some people are unable to adjust to the demands of everyday life," and therefore required the help of experts like Judge Lindsey. Polsky applied Michel Foucault's theories to "normalizing intervention," in which the discourse of experts in the late nineteenth and early twentieth centuries—clinicians, social workers, and educators—led to "increasingly invasive moralizing intervention." Polsky, though, recognized the agency of marginalized groups who sought to "manipulate intervention to achieve their own purposes." Polsky described a performance in which the moralizing elites pretended to act as caring matriarchs/patriarchs, while the recipients of the therapy pretended to reform themselves. Polsky, *The Rise of the Therapeutic State* (Princeton, NJ: Princeton University Press, 1991), 4–70.

Sherri Broder argued that the industrialized working class in America's cities were far from passive recipients of middle-class values. Instead, the relationship between the recipients of the new therapeutic state and the operators of that system was much more fluid, one in which the laboring poor resisted, shaped, and manipulated the values of the middle-class reformers. Emma Watkins and Barry Godfrey documented the fears that middle-class elites held toward working-class youth. Ken McGrew detailed the Chicago police's tactics of arresting children en masse, focusing on efficient and cost-saving measures. To David Tanenhaus, the juvenile courts reflected new levels of unchecked power. See Sherri Broder, *Tramps, Unfit Mothers, and Neglected Children: Negotiating the Family in Nineteenth-Century Philadelphia* (Philadelphia: University of Pennsylvania Press, 2002), 6–8; Emma Watkins and Barry Godfrey, *Criminal Children: Researching Juvenile Offenders, 1820–1920* (Philadelphia, PA: Pen & Sword Books, 2018), 4–5; Ken McGrew, *Education's Prisoners: Schooling, the Political Economy, and the Prison Industrial Complex* (Bern, Switzerland: Peter Lang Publishing, 2008), 26–29. David S. Tanenhaus, *Juvenile Justice in the Making* (Oxford: Oxford University Press, 2004), 35.

In New York City in the 1820s, the idea of rehabilitating juvenile criminals through institutionalization emerged with the New York House of Refuge. In 1855, the Cook County government opened the Chicago Reform School. See Christopher J. Menihan, "Criminal Mind or Inculpable Adolescence? A Glimpse at the History, Failures, and Required Changes of the American Juvenile Correction System," *Pace Law Review* 35, no. 2 (Spring 2015): 766; Joseph E. Illick, *American Childhoods* (Philadelphia: University of Pennsylvania Press, 2002), 89.

For the impact that progressive reformers had on the instruction of classroom teachers, see Larry Cuban, *How Teachers Taught: Constancy and Change in American Classrooms* (New York: Teachers College Press, 1993); see also Barbara Finkelstein, *Governing the Young: Teaching Behavior in Popular Primary Schools in Nineteenth-Century United States* (London: Falmer, 1989). Both historians conclude that progressive efforts to push teachers to create more student-centered classroom experiences were only marginally effective; McGrew, *Education's Prisoners*, 29.

Alice Boardman Smuts highlighted the alliance between female reformers and child psychologists in the first few decades of the twentieth century. She wrote, "progressive reformers believed that scientifically validated facts were an essential preliminary to effective social action. Adherents of the child development movement hoped, through scientific research, to discover optimum child-rearing methods and, through parent education, to foster their application. Philanthropic sponsors of the child development research institutes believed that scientific child rearing would produce a new kind of child who would grow into a new kind of adult, free of most of the afflictions and deficiencies of their progenitors." Elizabeth Brown also examined the intersection of science and the child-saving movement in her study of Seattle's juvenile corrections. Experts in Seattle created categories like "accidental delinquents" and "recidivist" based on a child's physique and intellectual testing. The pseudo-science of testing was also at the center of Miroslava García-Chávez's history of juvenile justice in California. See Alice Boardman Smuts, *Science in the Service of Children* (New Haven, CT: Yale University Press, 2006), 7; Elizabeth Brown, "The 'Unchildlike Child': Making and Marking the Child/Adult Divide in the Juvenile Court," *Children's Geographies* 9, no. 3–4 (2011): 366–67; Miroslava García-Chávez, *States of Delinquency* (Berkeley: University of California Press, 2012), 72–95. See also Rima D. Apple, *Perfect Motherhood: Science and Childrearing in America* (Brunswick, NJ: Rutgers University Press, 2006), 2–3; Anthony M. Platt, *Child Savers: The Invention of Delinquency* (Chicago: Chicago University Press, 1969), 9 and 143.

16. Paul Colomy and Martin Kretzmann, "Projects and Institution Building: Judge Ben B. Lindsey and the Juvenile Court Movement," *Social Problems* 42, no. 2 (May 1995): 197–99; Tanenhaus, *Juvenile Justice in the Making*, 35.

According to one report, Lindsey sent just fifty boys to the reform school in Golden during his career. Indeed, a Denver newspaper reported in 1914 that 200 out of the 200 probationers in that year received positive school reports and therefore avoided reform school. See Campbell, "Judge Ben Lindsey and the Juvenile Court Movement," 8; "The Youthful Delinquent: A New Way to Deal with Him," *New York Times*, February 25, 1906, SM3; Joseph M. Hawes, *Children in Urban Society: Juvenile Delinquency in Nineteenth-Century America* (New York: Oxford University Press, 1971), 232; "The Youthful Delinquent: A New Way to Deal with Him," SM3. Lindsey's approach became typical among progressive judges. In New York, Jacob Panken expanded the power of his municipal court to deal with family violence while maintaining the "leeway in deciding case outcomes" based on his principles of "love, sympathy, understanding, and kindliness." See Britt P. Tevis, "'The People's Judge': Jacob Panken, Yiddish Socialism, and American Law," *American Journal of Legal History* 59, no. 1 (March 1, 2019): 58 and 61; A. E. Winship, "Ben B. Lindsey," *Journal of Education* 59, no. 19 (May 12, 1904): 291; Ben B. Lindsey, "General Discussion," in *Proceeding of the National Conference of Charities and Correction at the Twenty-Ninth Annual Session Held in the City of Detroit*, ed. Isabel C. Barrows (Boston: Geo. H. Ellis, 1902), 436.

17. Ben B. Lindsey, "The Bad Boy: How to Save Him," *American Motherhood* 11, no. 6 (October 1905): 231–38; Ben B. Lindsey, *The Juvenile Court Laws of the State of Colorado* (Denver, CO: Juvenile Improvement Association of Denver, 1905), 68–71; Lindsey, *The Juvenile Court Laws of the State of Colorado*, 13.

18. Ben B. Lindsey, "Probation Work," *Juvenile Record* 4, no. 6 (June 1903): 13–14. Lindsey cultivated a network of progressive reformers, which fits with another theme in David A. Gamson's book. Gamson studied educational reformers in four different cities but, in doing so, he revealed the interconnectedness of their ideas and efforts. As an example, see Gamson, *The Importance of Being Urban*, 114–21; "The Youthful Delinquent: A New Way to Deal with Him," *New York Times*, February 25, 1906, 3; Ben B. Lindsey, "Denver's Juvenile Court; Its Successful Operation," *Atlanta (GA) Constitution*, April 3, 1904, 1; Ben B. Lindsey, "The Child and the State," in *Proceedings of the Third California State Conference on Charities and*

Corrections (San Francisco, CA: Preston School of Industry, 1904), 12–27; "King's Daughters Hold Interesting Session: The Conference Was Addressed Last Night by Judge Ben Lindsey, of Denver," *Atlanta (GA) Constitution*, November 17, 1907, 1; Frederic Almy, "Juvenile Courts and Probation," *Juvenile Record* 3, no. 1 (January 1902): 8–9; Geo. L. Sehon, "Address of Geo. L. Sehon of Kentucky Children's Home Society," *Juvenile Record* 6, no. 11 (November 1905): 5–7; "Trials of Boyhood Told Gentle Judge," *Los Angeles Herald*, April 13, 1908, 3; "Schools Ask Help with Defectives," *New York Times*, January 27, 1913, 7; Minnie L. Bauldauf, "The History of Juvenile Court Movement in Cleveland," *Juvenile Record* 11, no. 5 (May 1910): 14.

   Report cards were most directly impactful in tracking truancy cases. In Michigan, truancy cases represented a higher and higher percentage of juvenile cases. In 1885, just 3.6 percent of minors appeared before criminal court because of absence from school. By 1900, 24 percent of juvenile cases were for truancy. In Utah, over 20 percent of the minors arrested from 1905 through 1906 were for truancy. A North Dakota judge wrote that he relied on weekly reports from teachers in order to keep track of truants. The judge of Lyon County, Kansas, ranked the most important conditions for parole. At the top of this list was school attendance, followed by obedience to teachers, and ending with submitting regular reports from school. One Kentucky teacher reported that a truant child was indeed finally attending school but requested in a report that the minor be sent to reform school for disobedience instead of truancy. Thomas J. Homer, *Juvenile Court Laws in the United States* (New York: Russell Sage Foundation, 1910); Lorna F. Hurl and David J. Tucker, "The Michigan County Agents and the Development of Juvenile Probation, 1873–1900," *Journal of Social History* 30, no. 4 (Summer 1997): 913; "Juvenile Court Annual Report: Judge Willis Brown Gives Out Statement of the Work Done," *Desert Evening News* (Salt Lake City, UT), December 17, 1906, 5; "Juvenile Court—What It Is Doing," *Fargo (ND) Forum and Daily Republican*, October 3, 1911, 5; Report of the Juvenile Court of Lyon County, Kansas, June 30, 1921, box: Misc. Reports, folder: Report of Delinquent, Dependent and Neglected Children, Office of Governor Collection, Kansas State Historical Society, Topeka, KS.

   19. "Shindlebower Hearing in Juvenile Court," *Arizona Republican* (Phoenix, AZ), October 2, 1910, 5; "Teacher Saves a Colored Boy," *Daily Home* (New Brunswick, NJ), July 12, 1905, 1; "A Day in the Chicago Juvenile Court," *Juvenile Record* 3, no. 5 (May 1902): 12–13; "New York: Report on the System of Probation in Operation in the Court of Special Sessions in the City of New York, First Division," *Juvenile Record* 9, no. 5 (May 1908): 5–8.

   20. "Detroit Juvenile Court: Some of Judge Rohnert's Views of the Delinquent Problem and His Methods of Handling the Children," *Juvenile Record* 10, no. 2 (February 1909): 4–5; Henry W. Thurston, "What Should a Probation Officer Do for the Child?" in *Proceeding of the Annual Congress of the American Prison Association* (Indianapolis, IN: Wm. B. Burford, 1908), 45–55. Joseph L. Tropea studied the "backstage rules that guided urban school authorities in dealing with difficult pupils." Essentially, Tropea found that teachers and administrators in the Progressive Era selectively used formal programs to segregate troublesome children. See Tropea, "Bureaucratic Order and Special Children: Urban Schools, 1890s–1940s," *History of Education Quarterly* 27, no. 1 (Spring 1987): 29–30; Emma Shaw-Love, "That Angel Boy," *Juvenile Record* 17, no. 6 (November 1917): 10–11.

   21. Charles Larsen, *The Good Fight: The Life and Times of Ben B. Lindsey* (Chicago: Quadrangle Books, 1972), 32–35; Evidence of Lindsey-style juvenile system can be found from as far away as the town of Wray in the eastern edge of Colorado to Cañon City, closer to the New Mexico border. See "Paroled Youth Taken on Booze Charge," *Wray (CO) Gazette*, October 27, 1927, 1; "Taken to the State Industrial School This Morning," *Canon City (CO) Record*, July 15, 1909, 4.

   Locating surviving school report cards used in juvenile courts is not an easy task. First and most obviously, most courts seal the case files for minors. In the few instances that a judge will unseal a minor's records from the early 1900s, what remains in the file is a cursory summary of the charges against the juvenile and the sentencing. Additional documentation like school reports is typically missing. The example of Ben Lindsey is reflective of judges who went to lengths to protect the anonymity of his probationers. In 1927, Lindsey publicly burned his files on juvenile cases, which included thousands of school report cards. As juvenile courts grew in size, teachers submitted report cards to probation officers, not judges. Identifying the records of probation officers is a bit more difficult than official court documents. The Kansas State Historical Society maintained the papers of one probation officer in Leavenworth County, Kansas, including a handful of school reports documenting the conduct of probationers. The report card is a standard page-size, front and back. The questions that teachers answered were a series of two-word binary choices: "deportment: good or bad," "unruly or otherwise," "dull or bright," "stubborn or yielding," "untruthful or truthful," and so on. The report card is a case study in efficiency. Probation officers tended to be overworked and underpaid. There was no time for elaboration. As an example, Michigan struggled to fill it probation officer positions. Two-thirds of the jobs were unfilled by the early 1900s. School Record of [RESTRICTED], State of Kansas, Leavenworth County, Juvenile Court, December 19, 1919, box 13, folder 3, #28-11-06-06, Confidential Records of Courts in Leavenworth County, Kansas State Historical Society, Topeka, KS; Hurl and Tucker, "The Michigan County Agents and the Development of Juvenile Probation," 905; "Sentenced for Incorrigibility," *Western Slope Criterion* (Olathe, CO), August 5, 1909, 1; "Girl's Confession Involved Fifteen," *Colorado Statesman* (Denver, CO), November 6, 1915, 3.

There has been quite a lot of scholarship on the regulation and criminalization of adolescent girls' sexual activity. In 1978, Steven Schlossman and Stephanie Wallach published their essay that highlighted how girls in the Progressive Era received more severe punishment than boys, an effect of progressives trying to "purify society." More recently, Tera Eva Agyepong dedicates the third chapter of her book to African American girls who the Chicago courts deemed "sex delinquents" and the psychological impact that racial discursive practices had on those girls. Karin L. Zipf examined a North Carolina female reform school, tracing the increasing reliance on sterilization of girls in the 1930s and 1940s, all within a broader defense of whiteness. Anne Meis Knupfer conducted a case study of a female reform school in Geneva, Illinois. She noted the new medicalization of the reform school while also centering the narratives around the agency of the girls who were incarcerated for their "sexual misbehaviors." Finally, Tamara Myers' 2006 book focused on the juvenile court in Montreal, which served as a "disciplinary instrument" to "maintain and uphold the subordination of adolescent girls." See Steven Schlossman and Stephanie Wallach, "The Crime of Precocious Sexuality: Female Juvenile Delinquency in the Progressive Era," *Harvard Educational Review* 48, no. 1 (1978): 65–94; Agyepong, *The Criminalization of Black Children*, 70–95; See Karin L. Zipf, *Bad Girls at Samarcand: Sexuality and Sterilization in a Southern Juvenile Reformatory* (Baton Rouge: Louisiana State University Press, 2016), 158–64; Anne Meis Knupfer, "'To Become Good, Self-Supporting Women': The State Industrial School for Delinquent Girls at Geneva, Illinois, 1900–1935," *Journal of History of Sexuality* 9, no. 4 (October 2000): 420–45; Tamara Myers, *Caught: Montreal's Modern Girls and the Law, 1869-1945* (Toronto, ON: University of Toronto Press, 2006), 8.

22. The local newspaper in Montrose did not have many misgivings in publishing the names and misdeeds of boys appearing before the court. Judge Lindsey, in Denver, meanwhile, made an effort to protect the anonymity of the minors in his court. Modern-day Montrose County is also more relaxed in sharing its court filings than other municipalities; "Delinquent Boys in Court," *Montrose (CO) Press*, September 13, 1907, 7; *People of the State of Colorado v. Earl Sutherland*, Court Proceedings, August 31, 1907, Montrose County Court Records, Montrose, CO; "Sent to Industrial School," *Montrose (CO) Daily Press*, April 17, 1908,

2; *People of the State of Colorado v. Earl Sutherland*, Court Proceedings, August 31, 1907, Montrose County Court Records, Montrose, CO; "Sent to Industrial School," *Montrose (CO) Daily Press*, April 17, 1908, 2.

23. "Winding Up Business," *Avalanche–Echo* (Glenwood Springs, CO), January 15, 1903, 1; "Current Events: Town and County," *Avalanche–Echo* (Glenwood Springs, CO), July 2, 1903, 1; "Fell to His Death," *Glenwood Post* (Glenwood Springs, CO), July 11, 1903, 1.

24. "Drowned," *Avalanche* (Glenwood Springs, CO), July 9, 1903, 1.

25. "Local News," *Palisades (CO) Tribune*, August 18, 1906, 3; "Week's Local News," *Avalanche–Echo* (Glenwood Springs, CO), June 8, 1905, 3; "Local Happenings," *Daily Avalanche* (Glenwood Springs, CO), April 28, 1906, 4; "Local News," *Palisades (CO) Tribune*, August 18, 1906, 3; Advertisement," *Palisade (CO) Tribune*, June 27, 1903, 1; see also "Local News," *Palisades (CO) Tribune*, August 18, 1906, 3.

26. Record of Examinations, 1906, Industrial School.

27. There is a wide-ranging list of secondary literature on reform schools during the Progressive Era. Khalil Gibran Muhammad studied how "ideas of racial inferiority and crime became fastened to African Americans," leading to disproportionate incarceration rates for Black adolescents and "an enduring statistical discourse of black dysfunctionality." Likewise, Carl Suddler examined how reform schools led to the "racialized construction of youth criminality in [postwar] New York City." Geoff K. Ward examined the increasing rates of African American juvenile incarceration in reform schools. As an example, by 1910 in North Carolina, Black males were incarcerated at four times the rate of non-immigrant white males. Karin L. Zipf chronicled the history of a female reform school in North Carolina called Samarcand Manor, an institution that was "explicitly designed to protect and uphold white womanhood." Anne Meis Knupfer chronicled the history of resistance at the Illinois State Industrial School for Delinquent Girls. See Khalil Gibran Muhammad, *The Condemnation of Blackness: Race, Crime, and the Making of Modern Urban America* (Cambridge, MA: Harvard University Press, 2010), 6–7; Carl Suddler, *Presumed Criminal: Black Youth and the Justice System in Postwar New York* (New York: New York University Press, 2019), 5; Geoff K. Ward, *The Black Child-Savers: Racial Democracy and Juvenile Justice* (Chicago: University of Chicago Press, 2012), 88; Zipf, *Bad Girls at Samarcand*, 162; Knupfer, "'To Become Good, Self-Supporting Women,'" 420–45.

State-sponsored reform schools in the United States predate juvenile courts. Philanthropists established early versions of reform schools in New York City, Boston, and Philadelphia in the 1820s. They were known as Houses of Refuge, and they separated juvenile criminals from adult inmates. In the 1830s, the Massachusetts legislature created a system of publicly funded reformatory institutions. They were followed by Pennsylvania (1851), Maine (1853), Ohio (1856), Wisconsin (1860), and New Jersey (1864). Western states like Kansas (1879) and Colorado (1882) adopted state-sponsored reform schools, and by the late nineteenth century the system moved south to Tennessee (1895) and Georgia (1902). McGrew, *Education's Prisoners*, 23–24; Paul D. Nelson, "Early Days of the State Reform School," *Minnesota History* 63, no. 4 (Winter 2012): 134; Fifteenth Biennial Report of the State Industrial School for Boys, June 30, 1910, folder: Biennial Reports, SP 364 K13t, Boys Industrial School Collection, Kansas State Historical Society, Topeka, KS; Randall G. Shelden, "A History of the Shelby County Industrial and Training School," *Tennessee Historical Society* 51, no. 2 (Summer 1992): 96; "Grand Jury Presentments," *Atlanta (GA) Constitution*, June 25, 1904, 8.

Historians have noted that the rise of reformatory schools correlated with concerns about urban poverty and immigration. From this perspective, truancy and incorrigibility laws were the criminalization of the realities of poverty. For girls, their sexuality was also criminalized. See McGrew, *Education's Prisoners*, 23–29; Menihan, "Criminal Mind or Inculpable Adolescence?," 766; Nelson, "Early Days of the State Reform School," 132–38; Shelden, "A History of the Shelby County Industrial and Training School"; Knupfer, "'To Become Good, Self-Supporting Women,'" 420–45.

For more on compulsory education laws, see Tracy Steffes' fourth chapter in *School, Society, and State*. Steffes argued that compulsory education "justified and even necessitated greater contacts between home and school, and prompted school oversight and involvement in issues of health, welfare, and work once deemed wholly private, family decisions." Steffes, *School, Society, and State*, 141.

In Tennessee, 80 percent of the children sent to reform schools were guilty of status offenses. About two-thirds of the boys incarcerated in Minnesota's system of industrial schools were there because of conviction for truancy or incorrigibleness. Meanwhile, New York City was overwhelmed with the perceived problem of truancy. One journalist in 1912 estimated that that at least 10,000 minors were habitually truant each day in the city, causing concern about "gangs of half-grown boys" wandering the streets, smashing windows, and engaging in petty theft. Meanwhile, in Iowa, local notables called for an expansion of truant schools to bring order to the hundreds of children who "run the streets at night and then are allowed to remain in bed late into the morning." Not everyone agreed with the mixing of truant, incorrigibles, and violent juvenile offenders into the same system of schooling. The superintendent of Michigan's industrial school formally protested the incarceration of truants in his report to the governor. Truants, he wrote, "should be a problem for the public schools." See Shelden, "A History of the Shelby County Industrial and Training School," 97–99; Menihan, "Criminal Mind or Inculpable Adolescence?," 766; "Tens of Thousands Truant Schoolboys," *New York Times*, December 2, 1912, 5; "Detention School Needed," *Dubuque (IA) Telegraph-Herald*, July 5, 1910, 8; *Tenth Biennial Report of the State Board of Charities and Corrections of Colorado* (Denver, CO: Smith-Brooks, 1910); *Biennial Report of the Board of Trustees of the Industrial School for Boys of Michigan* (Lansing, MI: Wynkoop Hallenbeck Crawford, 1908); "Grand Jury Presentments," *Atlanta (GA) Constitution*, June 25, 1904, 8; "Alabama Industrial School Is Leading Many: Wayward Lads to Happy Citizenship," *Atlanta (GA) Constitution*, May 10, 1903, 5.

28. Some states like Alabama had small enough systems that the decision about release from the institutions was left entirely to the discretion of the superintendent. See "Alabama Industrial School Is Leading Many," 5; *First Annual Report of the Trustees of Massachusetts Training Schools* (Boston: Wright & Potter, 1912); Seventh Biennial Report of the State Industrial School for Boys at Kerney, Nebraska, 1902, file: reports, State Industrial School for Boys at Kerney Collection, Nebraska State Historical Society. In Michigan, the point system was turned into a competition, in which each company's report cards were totaled, with the possibility of obtaining trophies and ribbons. *Biennial Report of the Board of Trustees of the Industrial School for Boys of Michigan* (Lansing, MI: Wynkoop Hallenbeck Crawford, 1908); O. E. Lewis, "After the Reformatory—What?," *New York Times*, February 27, 1910, 7.

29. *First Annual Report, Virginia Home and Industrial School for Girls* (Richmond, VA: Davis Bottom, Superintendent of Public Printing, 1915); Fifteenth Biennial Report of the State Industrial School for Boys, Topeka Kansas, June 30, 1910, SP 364 K13t, Kansas State Historical Society, Topeka, KS; Report on Boys Industrial School to Governor W. R. Stubbs by M. F. Amrine, May 5, 1909, box 19, folder 7, Records of the Governor's Office, Gov. Walter R. Stubbs, Kansas State Historical Society, Topeka, KS.

30. Record of Examinations, 1906, Industrial School.

31. "Charities Board Reports," *Colorado Farm & Ranch* (Denver, CO), March 24, 1916, 7; *Tenth Biennial Report of the State Board of Charities and Corrections of Colorado* (Denver, CO: Smith-Brooks, 1910); "Settlement Work," *Jewish Outlook* (Denver, CO), March 1906, 7; *Colorado: Images of America* (Charleston, SC: Arcadia Publishing, 2002), 51–77.

32. "School News," *Daily Pickings* (Golden, CO), December 18, 1907, 4, SER.2606, State Industrial School Collection, History Colorado Museum, Stephen H. Hart Research Center,

Denver, CO (hereafter cited as "School News," *Daily Pickings* (Golden, CO), relevant date, page number); "School News," *Daily Pickings* (Golden, CO), February 17, 1908, 4; "School News," *Daily Pickings* (Golden, CO), February 17, 1908, 3; "School News," *Daily Pickings* (Golden, CO), April 7, 1908, 4; "State Industrial School: Report of the Board of Charities Urges Removal of Superintendent," *Carrizo (CO) Weekly Miner*, January 24, 1902, 2; Carey Southwell, *The History of Golden's Schools* (Golden: Published by the State Historical Fund Grant from the Colorado Historical Society, 1997); "State Industrial School: Report of the Board of Charities Urges Removal of Superintendent," 2; "Charges Filed Against Jones," *Jefferson County Republican* (Golden, CO), February 11, 1926, 1.

33. "Settlement Work," *Jewish Outlook* (Denver, CO), March 1906, 7; Southwell, *The History of Golden's Schools*, 34; "School News," *Daily Pickings* (Golden, CO), January 9, 1908, 3; "School News," *Daily Pickings* (Golden, CO), October 21, 1907, 4; "Semi-Professional Baseball for 1910," *Statesman* (Golden, CO), April 16, 1910, 5; "Boys' Industrial School Band Will Play at City Park at 2:30 Sunday Afternoon," *Jefferson County Republican* (Golden, CO), May 6, 1926, 1; The school newspaper, *Daily Pickings* (Golden, CO), published the names of each boy who received a family visitor on a weekly basis. From 1906 through 1910, Andrew's name was never listed as having any visitors.

34. "School News," *Daily Pickings* (Golden, CO), January 8, 1908, 3; "School News," *Daily Pickings* (Golden, CO), January 27, 1908, 3; "School News," *Daily Pickings* (Golden, CO), February 10, 1908, 4; "School News," *Daily Pickings* (Golden, CO), May 8, 1907, 3; "School News," *Daily Pickings* (Golden, CO), January 14, 1908, 4; Lookout Mountain, Demerit Book [RESTRICTED], 1898–1905, pages 272 and 298, box 19358 C, book 1, State Industrial School for Boys Collection, Colorado State Archive, Denver, CO; "School News," *Daily Pickings* (Golden, CO), January 11, 1908, 4; "School News," *Daily Pickings* (Golden, CO), February 8, 1908, 4; "School News," *Daily Pickings* (Golden, CO), March 5, 1908, 3; *Tenth Biennial Report of the State Board of Charities and Corrections of Colorado*; "Looking for Deserter," *Herald Democrat* (Denver, CO), February 2, 1910, 5; "Local Paragraphs," *Colorado Transcript* (Denver, CO), February 24, 1910, 8; "Marshal Straub Captures Runaway," *Gilpin (CO) Observer*, April 27, 1916, 1; "Boys Try to Free Industrial Lads," *Idaho Springs (CO) Siftings-News*, September 30, 1921, 1.

35. "Settlement Work," *Jewish Outlook* (Denver, CO), March 1906, 7; "School News," *Daily Pickings* (Golden, CO), February 1, 1908, 3; Lookout Mountain, Demerit Book [RESTRICTED], 1898–1905, pages 272 and 298, State Industrial School for Boys Collection, box 19358 C, book 1, Colorado State Archive, Denver, CO; "School News," *Daily Pickings* (Golden, CO), May 4, 1907, 4; "School News," *Daily Pickings* (Golden, CO), June 3, 1908, 3; "Colored Boy Leads School in Scholarship and Deportment and Industry," *Statesman* (Golden, CO), January 6, 1912, 1.

36. The Receiving and Discharge Register from Andrew's years at State Industrial School has not survived. However, the register from 1914 through 1924 does still exist and provides a window into the process. Incidentally, the register is the same version that was used in Kansas' industrial school. Receiving and Discharge Register/Record, 1914–1924, page 10, box 19417 B, Industrial School for Boys Collection, Colorado State Archive, Denver, CO; Receiving and Discharge Register/Record, 1914–1924, pages 11, 15, and 26, box 19417 B, Industrial School for Boys Collection, Colorado State Archive, Denver, CO; "School News," *Daily Pickings* (Golden, CO), December 20, 1907, 4; One of Andrew Monroe's report cards has survived on micro-form. See Intimate Card File, no. 2279, 1901–1910, box 240, folder 2180, State Industrial School Collection, Colorado State Archive, Denver, CO.

37. "Average Weather in Laramie," WeatherSpark, accessed July 13, 2021, https://weatherspark.com/m/3574/1/Average-Weather-in-January-in-Laramie-Wyoming-United-States; Michael Ward, "Occasional Survey: Frostbite," *British Medical Journal* 1, no. 5897

(1974): 67–70; Tina M. Mäkinen et al., "Occurrence of Frostbite in the General Population - Work-Related and Individual Factors," *Scandinavian Journal of Work, Environment & Health* 35, no. 5 (September 2009): 384–93; "Frostbite," in *Funk & Wagnalls New World Encyclopedia* (Chicago: World Book, 2018); David W. Page, *Body Trauma: A Writer's Guide to Wounds and Injuries* (Lake Forest, CA: Behler Publications, 2006); Record of Examinations, 1906, Industrial School.

38. Record of Examinations, 1906, Industrial School; "Andrew Monroe [pseud.] in Jail Again: Arrested for Beating His Wife After Being Pardoned by Governor of Colorado," *Daily Gate City* (Keokuk, IA), June 18, 1913, 1.

39. "Youth Who Made Good to Get Pardon," *Daily Journal* (Des Moines, IA), November 29, 1912, 1; "19 Year Old Father in Law's Clutches: Rosco Sheldon, Who Escaped Two Years Ago from Denver Institute," *Dubuque (IA) Telegraph-Herald*, November 24, 1912, 1; "Industrial School Boy as Jean Valjean," *Colorado Transcript* (Denver, CO), November 28, 1912, 1; "Industrial School Fugitive Given Discharge," *Telluride (CO) Journal*, December 5, 1912, 7.

40. "'Model Youth' Is Arrested for Wife Beating," *Daily Journal* (Des Moines, IA), June 18, 1913, 1; "Industrial School Boy as Jean Valjean," 1; "Will Not Have to Go Back," *Montrose (CO) Daily Press)*, November 25, 1912, 1; "Said He Was Proud of Him," *Montrose (CO) Daily Press*, November 30, 1912, 1.

41. "Andrew Monroe [pseud.] Says It's No Use to Try; He Cannot Live Down the Past His Wife Accuses," *Des Moines (IA) News*, June 18, 1913, 1; "Monroe [pseud.] Held on Wife's Complaint," *Des Moines (IA) News)*, June 14, 1913, 3; "'Model Youth' Is Arrested for Wife Beating," 1.

42. "Local Paragraphs," *Colorado Transcript* (Denver, CO), January 21, 1915, 3; "Untitled," *Walsenburg (CO) World*, January 21, 1915, 7; "Mere Mention," *Nebraska State Journal* (Lincoln, NE), September 26, 1916, 8; "One to Seven Years for Stealing Auto," *Lincoln (NE) Daily News*, October 3, 1916, 1; World War I Draft Registration Cards, 1917–1918, digital image, Ancestry.com, accessed May 12, 2021, Andrew Monroe [pseud.], World War I Draft Registration Card, 1917, no. 14 (right side numbering), Precinct Lancaster, Nebraska; "Hamilton Held for Murder," *Des Moines (IA) News*, September 18, 1918, 7.

43. The letter can be found wedged in between two pages in the Record of Examinations book in the Colorado State Archives. One of the pages is dedicated to Andrew Monroe [pseud.]. See Letter from Rita Oler to State Industrial School, October 19, 1939, State Industrial School, Record of Examinations [RESTRICTED], 1906, box 18485 C, book 3, State Industrial School for Boys Collection, Colorado State Archive, Denver, CO; Record of Examinations, 1906, Industrial School.

44. World War II Draft Registration Card, 1942, digital image, Ancestry.com, accessed May 12, 2021, serial number 1993, Local Board No. 4, Jefferson County, Sub Court House, Port Arthur, Texas; "Andrew Monroe [pseud.]," *Greeley (CO) Daily Tribune*, January 12, 1971, 7; 407 11th Avenue, Greeley, CO, photographed by Wade Morris, June 7, 2021; "Andrew Monroe [pseud.]," *Greeley (CO) Daily Tribune*, January 12, 1971, 7.

45. Internment Order: Andrew Monroe [pseud.], January 14, 1971, Macy-Allmatt Funeral Home Records, Sunset Memorial Gardens, Greeley, CO; Sterling Ross Monroe [pseud.] gravesite, photographed by Wade Morris, June 7, 2021, Sunset Memorial Gardens, Greeley, CO.

46. Stanley Kubrick, director, 1971, *A Clockwork Orange*, Polaris Productions, Warner Bros. Distribution; Record of Examinations, 1906, Industrial School.

47. The actor who played Alex, Malcolm McDowell, said that he assumed through the filming process that they were making a comedy. See "McDowell on 40th Anniversary of *A Clockwork Orange*," May 23, 2011, BBC Breakfast News.

48. Lookout Mountain Youth Center Administrative Building, photographed by Wade Morris, June 10, 2021, Golden, CO; Lookout Mountain Youth Center Soccer Field, photographed by Wade Morris, June 10, 2021, Golden, CO.

49. Jennifer Brown, "A Youth Corrections Center Plagued by Escapes, Drugs, and a Riot Is Headed for a Physical—and Cultural—Reorganization," *Colorado Sun* (Denver, CO), January 31, 2020; Rob Low, "Video Shows Riot at Lookout Mountain Youth Services Center: Problem Solvers Investigation," *Fox31 News*, March 29, 2019; Janet Oravetz, "'Violent Offender' Escapes Lookout Mountain Youth Services Center," *NBC 9 News*, June 25, 2019; Dara Bitter and Rob Low, "Shots Fired After 18-Year-Old Tries to Escape Lookout Mountain Youth Services Facility," *Fox31 News*, May 19, 2021; Jennifer Brown, "Colorado Youth Corrections System Sees Biggest Spike in Violent Offenders in a Decade," *Colorado Sun* (Denver, CO), January 8, 2021.

50. In a March 1978 lecture, Foucault mentioned that "there is not much sense" in calling "a delinquent a dissident." The delinquent, Foucault explained, is one who is guilty of "not conducting oneself properly." Foucault concluded that delinquents, mad people, and patients who engaged in "counter-conduct" should not be called "dissidents" because they were not worthy of the process of "sanctification or hero worship" associated with the term. See Foucault, *Security, Territory, Population: Lectures at the Collège de France, 1977–1978*, ed. Michael Senellart, trans. Graham Burchell (New York: Palgrave Macmillan, 2007), 201–2.

Chapter 5 · Mobility, Anxiety, and Merit

1. Daniel Schorr, *Staying Tuned: A Life in Journalism* (New York: Pocket Books, 2001), 2–3. Like the dynamic in chapter 4, from the 1910s through the 1930s, report cards became a form of external communication beyond the school community. Chapter 4 focused on the juvenile corrections system as the recipient of the communication. Chapter 5 focuses report cards communicating information for college admissions. Once again, Ethan Hutt and Jack Schneider deserve credit for noticing this broader development in the history of grades in the United States. "Unlike ordered rankings, which only communicated a student's relative standing within his or her class," Hutt and Schneider wrote, "grades also promised to serve as an external communication device to admissions boards, employers, and others." Schneider and Hutt, "Making the Grade: A History of the A–F Marking Scheme," *Journal of Curriculum Studies* 46, no. 2 (March 4, 2014): 209.

2. Schorr, *Staying Tuned*, xiii.

3. Daniel Schorr's niece wrote that Daniel's father was actually from Wyhanotsch, Russia, a nearby village. Daniel seemed to be unaware of this fact. In interviews and in his memoir, Daniel made no mention of Wyhanotsch, instead focusing on Telechan as the source of his ancestral roots. See Jessica Schorr Saxe, email message to Lisbeth Schorr, October 23, 2021.

Telechan Memorial Book, 1963, pages 66, 117, and 138, box 2, folder 2, MSS85407, Daniel Schorr Papers, Library of Congress, Manuscripts Division, Washington, DC (hereafter cited as *Telechan Memorial Book*, 1963, relevant page). See also Yohanan Petrovsky-Shtern, who described the preindustrial "golden age" of shtetls before the disruption of railroads and new trade routes. Yohanan Petrovsky-Shtern, *The Golden Age Shtetl: A New History of Jewish Life in East Europe* (Princeton, NJ: Princeton University Press, 2014); "Jewish Sources: Telechany," 1992, box 2, folder 2, MSS85407, Daniel Schorr Papers, Library of Congress, Manuscripts Division, Washington, DC; Nat Godiner, "May Their Memory Be Blessed: The Memoirs of Nat Godiner," trans. Diana Cohen, n.d., box 2, folder 8, MSS85407, Daniel Schorr Papers, Library of Congress, Manuscripts Division, Washington, DC; Telechan Memorial Committee, *Telechan*, 1986, box 2, folder 2, MSS85407, Daniel Schorr Papers, Library of Congress, Manuscripts Division, Washington, DC (hereafter cited as Godiner, "May Their Memory Be Blessed"; note: the pamphlet does not have page numbers).

4. The Pale of Settlement stretched from the Black Sea to the Baltic Sea, comprising about 386,000 square miles. By the late nineteenth century, 94 percent of the Jewish population within Russia lived in the massive area, or about 4.9 million people. This population

accounted for about 12 percent of the total population in the region. See Irving Howe, *World of Our Fathers* (New York: Harcourt Brace Jovanovich, 1976), 5.

Shlomo Lambroza, "The Tsarist Government and the Pogroms of 1903–06," *Modern Judaism* 7, no. 3 (1987): 287; Mark S. Simpson, "The 'Svyaschonnaya Druzhina' and Jewish Persecution in Tsarist Russia," *New Zealand Slavonic Journal* 1978, no. 2 (1978): 20; Shlomo Lambroza and John D. Klier, "The Pogroms of 1903–1906," in *Pogroms: Anti-Jewish Violence in Modern Russian History* (Cambridge: Cambridge University Press, 1992), 28; Monty Noam Penkower, "The Kishinev Pogrom of 1903: A Turning Point in Jewish History," *Modern Judaism* 24, no. 3 (October 2004): 202; Penkower, "The Kishinev Pogrom of 1903," 200–201.

5. See Ben Cionn Pinchuk, "Jewish Discourse and the Shtetl," *Jewish History* 15, no. 2 (2001): 177; see Lambroza and Klier, "The Pogroms of 1903–1906," 220–21; *Telekhan Memorial Book*, 1963, 75; Godiner, "May Their Memory Be Blessed," no page numbers listed; *Telekhan Memorial Book*, 1963, 83.

Telechan no longer exists. In 1941, the German army destroyed the village and murdered almost all its Jewish inhabitants. See Yitzhak Arad, *The Holocaust in the Soviet Union*, trans. Ora Cummings (Jerusalem, Israel: Martyrs' and Heroes' Remembrance Authority, 2009), 133, 163, 267–69, 480; Martin Gilbert, *The Holocaust: A History of the Jews of Europe During the Second World War* (New York: Henry Holt, 1985), 419–24; William Gurstelle, "A Family Member Braves a Return to the Old Family *Shtetl* in Belarus," September 12, 209, *Star Tribune* (Minneapolis, MN).

6. Daniel Schorr's uncle remembered four heders in the town. Godiner, "May Their Memory Be Blessed," no page numbers listed; Saul Stampfer, *Families, Rabbis, and Education: Traditional Jewish Society in Nineteenth-Century Eastern Europe* (Portland, OR: The Littman Library of Jewish Civilization, 2010), 149–56; Steven J. Zipperstein, *Imagining Russian Jewry: Memory, History, Identity* (Seattle: University of Washington Press, 1999), 42; Zipperstein, *Imagining Russian Jewry*, 45.

7. Brian Horowitz, *Russian Idea, Jewish Presence: Essays on Russian-Jewish Intellectual Life* (Brighton, MA: Academic Studies Press, 2013), 92. See also David W. Edwards' history of the Russian government's attempt to control Jewish heders in the mid-nineteenth century. David W. Edwards, "Nicholas I and Jewish Education," *History of Education Quarterly* 22, no. 1 (Spring 1982): 45–53; Benjamin Nathans, *Beyond the Pale: The Jewish Encounter with Late Imperial Russia* (Berkeley: University of California Press, 2002), 73; Zipperstein, *Imagining Russian Jewry*, 47–48; Stampfer, *Families, Rabbis, and Education*, 156; Nathans, *Beyond the Pale*, 73; Stampfer, *Families, Rabbis, and Education*, 147.

8. The Tchornemoretzes may have also departed from Libau, Russia. See Jessica Schorr Saxe, email message to Lisbeth Schorr, October 23, 2021.

Howe, *World of Our Fathers*, 28; Lloyd P. Gartner, "Jewish Migrants En Route from Europe to North America: Traditions and Realities," *Jewish History* 1, no. 2 (49–66): 51, 54; Gartner, "Jewish Migrants En Route from Europe to North America," xix, 50, 59.

9. Daniel Schorr believes that the name change occurred when a customs agent on Ellis Island misunderstood the pronunciation of Tchornemoretz. Daniel Schorr's nephew, Kenneth Schorr, believes that the Tchornemoretzes changed their name on the ship manifest. See Schorr, *Staying Tuned*, 2; Kenneth Schorr, email message to Lisbeth Schorr, October 23, 2021.

Deborah Dash Moore, *Jewish New York: The Remarkable Story of a City and a People* (New York: New York University Press, 2017), 193; Jeffrey S. Gurock, *Jews in Gotham: New York Jews in a Changing City, 1920–2010* (New York: New York University Press, 2012), 14–15; Thomas Kessner, "Jobs, Ghettos and the Urban Economy, 1880–1935," *American Jewish History* 71, no. 2 (December 1981): 224–25; Howe, *World of Our Fathers*, 47–48, 148.

10. Daniel Schorr, interviewed by Benis M. Frank, February 7, 1978, box 3, folder 1, MSS85407, Daniel Schorr Papers, Library of Congress, Manuscripts Division, Washington,

DC (hereafter cited as Schorr interviewed by Frank, 1978, Library of Congress); Schorr, *Staying Tuned*, 2; Moore, *Jewish New York*, 14–15; Gurock, *Jews in Gotham*, 14–15; Selma C. Berrol, "Education and Economic Mobility: The Jewish Experience in New York City, 1880–1920," *American Jewish History* 65, no. 3 (March 1976): 260.

11. Roger L. Geiger, *To Advance Knowledge: The Growth of American Research Universities, 1900–1940* (New York: Routledge, 1986), 13; Charles Dorn, *For the Common Good: A New History of Higher Education* (Ithaca, NY: Cornell University Press, 2017), 122; Ezekiel Kimball, "College Admission in a Contested Marketplace: The Twentieth Century and a New Logic for Access," *Journal of College Admission* (Winter 2011): 21–23.

12. David F. Labaree, *A Perfect Mess: The Unlikely Ascendancy of American Higher Education* (Chicago: University of Chicago Press, 2017), 105–6; John S. Brubacher and Willis Rudy, *Higher Education in Transition: A History of American Colleges and Universities, 1636–1968* (New York: Harper & Row, 1958), 262; Arthur E. Traxler and Agatha Townsend, *Improving Transition from School to College: How Can School and College Best Cooperate?* (New York: Harper & Brothers, 1953), 129.

13. John R. Thelin, *A History of American Higher Education* (Baltimore: Johns Hopkins University Press, 2004), 197; Donald G. Barker, "The History of Entrance Examinations," *Improving College and University Teaching* 15, no. 4 (Autumn 1967): 251; Laurence R. Veysey, *The Emergence of the American University* (Chicago: University of Chicago Press, 1965), 236–37; Andrew V. Beale, "The Evolution of College Admission Requirements," *Journal of College Admission*, Winter 2012, 21; Chara Haeussler Bohan, "Early Vanguards of Progressive Education: The Committee of Ten, the Committee of Seven and Social Education," in *Social Education in the Twentieth Century: Curriculum and Context for Citizenship*, ed. Christine Woyshner, Joseph Watras, and Margaret Smith Crocco (New York: Peter Lang, 2004), 1–19. See also David B. Tyack, *The One Best System: A History of American Urban Education* (Cambridge, MA: Harvard University Press, 1974), 131–37; Brubacher and Rudy, *Higher Education in Transition*, 251; Harry Charles McKown, *The Trend of College Entrance Requirements, 1913–1922* (Washington, DC: Government Printing Office, 1925), 106–7.

14. Publicly funded state universities tended to be less discerning in their admissions policies, the result of decades of pressure from "populist politicians" who called for the dropping of all requirements for entrance into schools like Ohio State, the University of Texas, and the University of Illinois. See McKown, *The Trend of College Entrance Requirements*, 12–22; Frank H. Bowles, *How to Get into College* (New York: E. P. Dutton, 1958), 88–89. See also Stephen Jay Gould, *The Mismeasure of Man* (New York: Penguin Books, 1981), 151 and 157; Nicholas Lemann, *The Big Test: The Secret History of the American Meritocracy* (New York: Farrar, Straus and Giroux, 1999), 32–41.

15. Donald G. Barker, "The History of Entrance Examinations," *Improving College and University Teaching* 15, no. 4 (Autumn 1967): 251; Frederick Rudolph, *The American College and University: A History* (New York: Vintage Books, 1962), 262. Thelin, *A History of American Higher Education*, 196. At the time, elite universities like Harvard, Princeton, and Yale sent nearly half of their incoming freshmen to preparatory departments before final admissions. See Brubacher and Rudy, *Higher Education in Transition*, 247. Clarence D. Kingsley, *College Entrance Requirements* (Washington, DC: Government Printing Office, 1913), 104–5; see Lemann, *The Big Test*; Rebecca Zwick, *Fair Game?: The Use of Standardized Tests in Higher Education* (New York: Routledge Falmer, 2002); Andrew V. Beale, "The More Things Change, the More They Stay the Same: Response to 'The Evolution of College Admission Requirements,'" *Journal of College Admission* (Winter 2012), 23; Habib Amin Kurani, *Selecting the College Student in America: A Study of Theory and Practice* (New York: Bureau of Publications, Teachers College, Columbia University, 1931), 15–17; Associated Press, "Educators Weigh College Entrance," *Evening Star* (Washington, DC), July 18, 1933, A-3.

16. Harold A. Ferguson, "Trends in College Admission Requirements," *School and Society* 48, no. 1239 (September 1938): 408–9; *Gynosure* yearbook (Fargo, ND: Fargo High School, 1927), 155; *West Panther* yearbook (Salt Lake City, UT: West High School, 1933), 145; "The Bunk," *Collinwood Spotlight* (Cleveland, OH), October 31, 1927, 2; Untitled, *Ocaleean Ensign* (Ocala, FL), February 28, 1918, 2; "What Shall You Remember About East, Seniors? Here's What Some Will," *Blue and Gold* (Cleveland, OH), June 6, 1935, 1.

17. Diary of Rosemary Vineys, March 17, 1924, June 2, 1924, and October 2, 1924, MSS 582, Arthur W. Kumm Memorial Book Fund for Books on California and the West, Stanford University, Special Collections, Stanford, CA; Dorothy M. Washburn Diaries, February 2, 1920, April 6, 1920, April 7, 1920, and May 1, 1920, box 1, folder 4, Dorothy M. Washburn Collection, McLean County Historical Society, Bloomington, IL; James O'Donnell Diary, 1932, box WH-90, folder 1, 2009ms132.0818, Wade Hall Collection of American Letters, University of Kentucky Special Collections, Lexington, KY; Lee Anna Embrey Student Diaries, May 11, 1927, and October 30, 1928, item 0151, MSS 0097, University of Delaware Special Collections, Newark, DE.

18. "Listening In," *Dunbar Observer* (Washington, DC), December 13, 1930, 1, Dunbar High School Collection, Charles Sumner School Museum and DC Public School Archive, Washington, DC; *Bumblebee* yearbook (Port Arthur, TX, 1933), 48; "The Windmill," *High Life* (Greensboro, NC), May 29, 1931, 1; Report Cards, 1923–1924, box WH-78, folder 12, 2009ms132.0724, Morford Roddick Papers, Wade Hall Collection of American Letters, University of Kentucky Special Collections, Lexington, KY; Letter from Mother to Katherine Pattillo, November 8, 1931, box 1, folder 6, MS 2893, Pattillo Family Papers, University of Georgia Libraries, Hargrett Rare Book & Manuscript Library, Athens, GA; Letter from Mary Emma to Katherine Pattillo, May 7, 1932, MS 2893, Pattillo Family Papers, University of Georgia Libraries, Hargrett Rare Book & Manuscript Library, Athens, GA; Letter from Mary Emma to Katherine Pattillo, May 17, 1932, MS 2893, Pattillo Family Papers, University of Georgia Libraries, Hargrett Rare Book & Manuscript Library, Athens, GA; Letter from Doris to Betty Hinkle, September 22, 1925, box 1, folder 8, Betty Hinkle Dunn Collection, McLean County Historical Society, Bloomington, IL (hereafter cited as Doris to Betty, relevant date, Dunn Collection); Doris to Betty, October 13, 1925, Dunn Collection; Doris to Betty, October 27, 1925, Dunn Collection; Doris to Betty, November 8, 1925, Dunn Collection; Doris to Betty, March 2, 1926, Dunn Collection; Letter from Doris to Betty Hinkle, March 20, 1926, Dunn Collection; Vivian Crawford Memory Book, May 14, 1920, box 1, 2009ms132.0441, Wade Hall Collection of American Letters, University of Kentucky Special Collections, Lexington, KY; Clara Louis Schiefer Diary, June 23, 1933, 2009.073, College of William and Mary, Special Collections Research Center, Williamsburg, VA; Dean E. Dreyer Scrapbook, May 27, 1927, and September 3, 1927, box 6, MS 3325, Dean E. Dreyer Papers, University of Georgia, Hargrett Rare Book & Manuscript Library, Athens, GA; *Lomoa* yearbook (Peshastin, WA: Peshastin Dryden High School, 1928), 284; Diary of Norman Freed, January 30, 1935, and February 7, 1935, box 44, folder 1, MSS 57285, College of William and Mary, Special Collections Research Center, Williamsburg, VA; Katherine Driscoll Diaries, January 29, 1926, and June 24, 1926, MSS 99889 29052, Connecticut Historical Society Library, Manuscripts Department, Hartford, CT.

19. Gurock, *Jews in Gotham*, 14, 28–30; Moore, *Jewish New York*, 201; Terry Gross, "'Fresh Air' Remembers Journalist Daniel Schorr," *Fresh Air* (Washington, DC: National Public Radio, July 30, 2010), https://www.npr.org/templates/story/story.php?storyId=128846420; Moore, *Jewish New York*, 203; Morton Silverstein, "An Autobiography: Daniel Schorr," *Television in America* (New York: CUNY TV, March 29, 2001), https://www.youtube.com/watch?v=ysLmQj--DZA; Deborah Dash Moore, *At Home in America: Second Generation New York Jews* (New York: Columbia University Press, 1981), 25; Silverstein, "An Autobiography: Daniel Schorr," March 29, 2001; Beth S. Wenger, *New York Jews and the Great Depression* (New Haven, CT:

Yale University Press, 1996), 10–12, 108–9; Letter from Daniel Schorr to Confidence Gbarayor and Shawn Marks, October 18, 1994, box 14, folder 3, MSS85407, Daniel Schorr Papers, Library of Congress, Manuscripts Division, Washington, DC.

20. Alvin L. Schorr, *Passion and Policy: A Social Workers Career* (Cleveland, OH: David Press, 1997), 13, 19; Schorr, *Staying Tuned*, 2–4; Gross, "'Fresh Air' Remembers Journalist Daniel Schorr," July 30, 2010; Kessner, "Jobs, Ghettos and the Urban Economy, 1880–1935," 224, 234–36.

21. Schorr, *Passion and Policy*, 3 and 23; Wenger, *New York Jews and the Great Depression*, 198.

22. Schorr, *Staying Tuned*, 5; Moore, *Jewish New York*, 198; Moore, *At Home in America*, 90; Schorr interviewed by Frank, 1978, sec. 1, pages 17 and 23, Library of Congress.

23. Lila Corwin Berman, "Jews and the Ambivalence of Middle-Classness," *American Jewish History* 93, no. 4 (December 2007): 411; Patricia Albjerg Graham, *Schooling America: How the Public Schools Meet the Nation's Changing Needs* (Oxford: Oxford University Press, 2005), 11–27; Moore, *At Home in America*, 89; Schorr, *Staying Tuned*, 5.

24. Moore, *At Home in America*, 95–96, 102–3; Jonathan Krasner, "The Limits of Cultural Zionism in America: The Case of Hebrew in the New York City Public Schools, 1930–1960," *American Jewish History* 95, no. 4 (December 2009): 350–57.

25. Berrol, "Education and Economic Mobility," 269–70; Moore, *At Home in America*, 92; Berrol, "Education and Economic Mobility," 271; Certificate, League of Arista, January 1933, box 1, folder 1, MSS85407, Daniel Schorr Papers, Library of Congress, Manuscripts Division, Washington, DC.

26. Schorr interviewed by Frank, 1978, sec. 1, pages 10–11, Library of Congress; Letter from Jewish Education Association, November 2, 1928, box 14, folder 4, MSS85407, Daniel Schorr Papers, Library of Congress, Manuscripts Division, Washington, DC; Hebrew School, Pupil's Monthly Certificate, 1925, box 1, folder 1, MSS85407, Daniel Schorr Papers, Library of Congress, Manuscripts Division, Washington, DC.

27. Howe, *World of Our Fathers*, 261; Bella Abzug, interviewed by Rosalind Mayer, May 20, 1983, sec. 2, page 9, William E. Wiener Oral History Collection, New York Public Library, Library of the American Jewish Committee, New York, NY; Benjamin Miller, "Immigrant Parents and Their Children," *Forward* (New York, NY), September 25, 1922, 3; Ruth Zuckoff, "Mothers Who Go to School with Their Children," *Forward* (New York, NY), January 18, 1925, 3.

28. "What Was the Happiest Moment of Your Life?" *Forward* (New York, NY), October 5, 1926, 5; Rudolph I. Coffee, "Be Thou a Blessing," *Hebrew Standard* (New York, NY), May 18, 1917, 3; "'Friendly America' and Its Helping Hand to Immigrants," *B'nai B'rith Messenger* (Los Angeles, CA), February 29, 1924, 1; "The Sabbath Angel," *Sentinel* (Chicago, IL), September 21, 1933, 23.

29. "What Is the Meanest Invention?" *Forward* (New York, NY), August 13, 1925, 3; "Thorough Logic," *Forward* (New York, NY), December 6, 1925, 3; "East-Sidelights," *Forward* (New York, NY), January 16, 1927, 4.

30. Repentance, n.d., box 14, folder 5, MSS85407, Daniel Schorr Papers, Library of Congress, Manuscripts Division, Washington, DC; Schorr interviewed by Frank, 1978, sec. 1, page 38, Library of Congress.

31. Letter from Dad to Philip Hardy, November 7, 1921, box 4, folder 7, RG2000.AM, Philip Seacrest Hardy Collection, Nebraska State Historical Society, Lincoln, NE; Report of Philip S. Hardy, 1922, box 6, folder 5, RG2000.AM, Philip Seacrest Hardy Collection, Nebraska State Historical Society, Lincoln, NE; Letter from Dad to Philip Hardy, June 2, 1922, box 4, folder 1, RG2000.AM, Philip Seacrest Hardy Collection, Nebraska State Historical Society, Lincoln, NE; Letter from Dad to Philip Hardy, June 12, 1922, box 4, folder 1, RG2000.AM, Philip Seacrest Hardy Collection, Nebraska State Historical Society, Lincoln, NE.

32. Report Card, Milwaukee University School, June 1940, box 25, folder 122, Sh. 295, 300–303, Nunnemacher/Weschler Family Papers, Milwaukee County Historical Society,

Milwaukee, WI; Letter from Robert B. Riondan to E. A. Weschler, January 9, 1940, box 25, folder 122, Sh. 295, 300–303, Nunnemacher/Weschler Family Papers, Milwaukee County Historical Society, Milwaukee, WI; Letter from Rev. Robert C. Hoff to E. A. Weschler, March 12, 1940, box 25, folder 122, Sh. 295, 300–303, Nunnemacher/Weschler Family Papers, Milwaukee County Historical Society, Milwaukee County Historical Society, Milwaukee, WI; Letter from Robert C. Hoff to Mrs. E. A. Weschler, March 14, 1940, box 25, folder 122, Sh. 295, 300–303, Nunnemacher/Weschler Family Papers, Milwaukee County Historical Society, Milwaukee, WI.

33. "K. C. Scholarships," *Catholic Bulletin* (St. Paul, MN), January 21, 1922, 4; "Brentwood Youth Edison Candidate," *Evening Star* (Washington, DC), June 7, 1929, 10; "Scholarships at Yale Given Out," *New Britain (CT) Herald*, November 10, 1926, 3; "Wallace Student Gets J. J. Day Scholarship," *Daily Star-Mirror* (Moscow, ID), July 14, 1922, 4; "Scholarship Saves Mona Kay a Year, Now Valedictorian Can Go to University," *Las Vegas (NV) Age*, July 23, 1929, 8; "95 Per Cent Is 1-Year Average of Miss Vivier," *Brownsville (TX) Herald*, May 21, 1922, 3; "List of U.D.C. Scholarships Received by Local Chapter," *Pensacola (FL) Journal*, March 5, 1922, 14.

34. Her father later became president of the NAACP; however, while Virginia was in high school, he had not yet gained national fame; Virginia Spottswood Diary, 1932, pages 7, 9, 16, and 43, box 16, folder 4, MSS 1057, Walter Augustus Simon and Virginia Spottswood Simon Family Papers, Emory University, Stuart A. Rose Manuscript, Archives, and Rare Book Library, Atlanta, GA; Virginia Spottswood Diary, January 4, 1932, and April 12, 1932, box 16, folder 4, MSS 1057, Walter Augustus Simon and Virginia Spottswood Simon Family Papers, Emory University, Stuart A. Rose Manuscript, Archives, and Rare Book Library, Atlanta, GA (hereafter cited as Spottswood Diary, relevant date, Simon Papers); Spottswood Diary, September 13, 1934, and December 2, 1934, Simon Papers; Spottswood Diary, December 6, 1934, Simon Papers; Letter from D. W. Pierce to Virginia Spottswood, June 23, 1937, OBV1, MSS 1057, Walter Augustus Simon and Virginia Spottswood Simon Family Papers, Emory University, Stuart A. Rose Manuscript, Archives, and Rare Book Library, Atlanta, GA.

35. Letter from Harry Blackmun to Parents, September 24, 1925, box 10, folder 1, MSS84430, Harry A. Blackmun Papers, Library of Congress, Manuscripts Division, Washington, DC; Saint Paul Public School, Monthly Report, January 29, 1917, box 8, folder 2, MSS84430, Harry A. Blackmun Papers, Library of Congress, Manuscripts Division, Washington, DC; Report Cards, Mechanic Arts High School, 1922–1925, box 7, folder 14, MSS84430, Harry A. Blackmun Papers, Library of Congress, Manuscripts Division, Washington, DC; Dailylogue, February 3, 1920, January 14, 1924, June 12, 1922, and June 7, 1920, box 11, folder 8, MSS84430, Harry A. Blackmun Papers, Library of Congress, Manuscripts Division, Washington, DC; Dailylogue, April 28, 1923, box 11, folder 8, MSS84430, Harry A. Blackmun Papers, Library of Congress, Manuscripts Division, Washington, DC; "Mechanics Youth Wins Scholarship Given by Harvard," *St. Paul (MN) Pioneer*, August 15, 1925, 1.

36. Jerome Karabel, *The Chosen: The Hidden History of Admission and Exclusion at Harvard, Yale, and Princeton* (New York: Houghton Mifflin, 2005), 51, 89, 110, 112, 114, and 116; Arthur M. Cohen, *The Shaping of American Higher Education: Emergence and Growth of the Contemporary System* (San Francisco, CA: Jossey-Bass, 1998), 119; Geiger, *To Advance Knowledge*, 135; Frederick M. Binder and David M. Reimers, *All the Nations Under Heaven: An Ethnic and Racial History of New York City* (New York: Columbia University Press, 1995), 166.

37. Jennifer M. Nations, "How Austerity Politics Led to Tuition Charges at the University of California and City University of New York," *History of Education Quarterly* 61, no. 3 (August 2021): 286–87; Benjamin Fine, *Admission to American Colleges: A Study of Current Policy and Practice* (New York: Harper & Brothers, 1946), 176; Sherry Gorelick, *City College and the Jewish Poor: Education in New York, 1880–1924* (New Brunswick, NJ: Rutgers University Press, 1981), 195; Fine, *Admission to American Colleges*, 176; Chris Quintana, "What a '30s Antifascist Protest Says About Rallies Now," *Chronicle of Higher Education* 68, no. 33

(2017): 32–33; Gurock, *Jews in Gotham*, 48; Zev Eleff, "Jewish Immigrants, Liberal Higher Education, and the Quest for a Torah u-Madda Curriculum at Yeshiva College," *Tradition: A Journal of Orthodox Jewish Thought* 44, no. 2 (Summer 2011): 20; Gurock, *Jews in Gotham*, 48; Berrol, "Education and Economic Mobility," 269.

38. "Obituary: Jacob A. Arlow (1912–2004)," *International Journal of Psychoanalysis* 85, no. 6 (2004): 1515–18; Letter from Berlita Cohen Seader to Jacob A. Arlow, n.d., box 12, folder 9, MSS85369, Jacob A. Arlow Papers, Library of Congress, Manuscripts Division, Washington, DC; Letter from Jewish Education Association to Jacob A. Arlow, June 23, 1924, box 12, folder 8, MSS85369, Jacob A. Arlow Papers, Library of Congress, Manuscripts Division, Washington, DC; Independent Order of Birth Sholom, n.d., box 12, folder 9, MSS85369, Jacob A. Arlow Papers, Library of Congress, Manuscripts Division, Washington, DC; Report Cards, Thomas Jefferson High School, June 30, 1925, box 12, folder 8, MSS85369, Jacob A. Arlow Papers, Library of Congress, Manuscripts Division, Washington, DC.

39. Decades later, as Schorr reflected on his early years, he would say that he always felt called to be a journalist, to serve as the dispassionate observer of events. His first work of journalism came at the age of twelve, when he witnessed a woman fall to her death from his apartment building. He "heard the plop" of the woman's body and then lingered at the scene to interview police officers, ultimately selling his story to a local Bronx newspaper for five dollars. From then on, Daniel Schorr was hooked on the life of journalism. By the end of his high school years, he enjoyed the act of reporting and writing so much that he was ready to commit to a career. This commitment caused tensions with his mother, Tillie, who had no frame of reference in her Russian experiences for what, exactly, a reporter did. She had envisioned Daniel attending City College to become a lawyer or doctor. A journalist, Tillie assumed, was something more akin to an entertainer. See Schorr interviewed by Frank, 1978, sec. 1, page 10, Library of Congress.

"Arista Accepts New Members," *Clintonian News* (Bronx, NY), October 28, 1932, 3, DeWitt Clinton High School Archive, Bronx, NY; Mikhail Bakhtin, *Rabelais and His World*, trans. Helene Iswolsky (Bloomington: Indiana University Press, 1984), 3–11; Carole Anne Taylor, "Ideologies of the Funny," *The Centennial Review* 36, no. 2 (Spring 1992): 175; Michael Mulkay, *On Humor: Its Nature and Its Place in Modern Society* (New York: Basil Blackwell, 1988), 4–5.

40. Gerard J. Pelisson and James A. Garvey, III, *The Castle on the Parkway: The Story of New York City's DeWitt Clinton High School and Its Extraordinary Influence on American Life* (Scarsdale, NY: Hutch Press, 2009), 57, 58–61, and 64–68; David Leeming, *James Baldwin: A Biography* (New York: Arcade, 1994), 26–47; Patrice O'Shaughnessy, "Once Upon a Time 'Genius Schools' Were Called New York City Public High Schools," *New York Daily News*, November 2, 2011; Kate Buford, *Burt Lancaster: An American Life* (Cambridge, MA: Da Capo Press, 2000), 55.

41. Daniel L. Schorr, "More Pupils—More Teachers," *Clinton News* (Bronx, NY), May 20, 1932, 1, DeWitt Clinton High School Archive, Bronx, NY; Daniel L. Schorr, "Elmer Gantry," *Clinton News* (Bronx, NY), June 3, 1932, 3, DeWitt Clinton High School Archive, Bronx, NY; Daniel L. Schorr, "Diary of a Senior," *Clinton News* (Bronx, NY), January 13, 1933, 2, DeWitt Clinton High School Archive, Bronx, NY (hereafter Schorr, "Diary of a Senior," 2); Daniel L. Schorr, "An Expensive Game," *Clinton News* (Bronx, NY), April 15, 1932, DeWitt Clinton High School Archive, Bronx, NY; Daniel's joke was as follows: "Teacher, trying to explain the meaning of the word 'magnanimity,' asked what I would call it if he befriended a mule in distress. 'Brotherly love,' I replied." Schorr, "Diary of a Senior," 2; DeWitt Clinton High School, *Clintonian* yearbook (Bronx, NY, 1930), 30.

42. *Glenville High School Annual* (Cleveland, OH: Glenville High School, 1922), 38; *Attucks* yearbook, (Indianapolis, IN, 1933), 32; "Wit and Nit-Wit," *Dunbar Observer* (Washington, DC), December 20, 1928, 1, Dunbar High School Collection, Charles Sumner School

Museum and DC Public School Archive, Washington, DC; see Kerry Soper, "The Pathetic Carnival in the Cubicles: The Office as Meditation on the Misuses and Collapse of Traditional Comedy," *Studies in American Humor* 3, no. 19 (2009): 83–85; Dustin Griffin, *Satire: A Critical Reintroduction* (Lexington: University Press of Kentucky, 1994), 158; Mulkay, *On Humor*, 153.

43. *Grinds* yearbook (Missoula, MT, 1928), 38; "Can You Imagine?" *Junior Pointer* (High Point, NC), March 31, 1938, 1; *Central High School Annual* (Cleveland, OH, 1916), 47; *Central High School Annual* (Cleveland, OH, 1920), 27–28; "Remarks of Some Morris Co-Eds," *Piper* (New York, NY), December 6, 1929.

44. "Did You Ever Have a Case Like This?" *Bitter Root* (Missoula, MT), 1921, 66–67; "The Bunk," *Collinwood Spotlight* (Cleveland, OH), October 31, 1927, 2; "Cold Showers," *Collinwood Spotlight* (Cleveland, OH), January 13, 1928, 2; *The Bronco* yearbook (Denton, TX: Denton High School, 1932), 89.

45. *The Caldron* yearbook (Madison, OH: Madison Memorial High School, 1932), 62; "Can Ya Imagine," *Perry News* (Indianapolis, IN), May 24, 1935, 2; "Was It You?," *Ogden High School Scrapbook*, 1934, OHS_1934-1935_003, Ogden School Library Collection, Weber State University Archive, Ogden, UT; *The Deerfield* yearbook (Highland Park, IL: Deerfield-Shields High School, 1929), 117; *The Lookout Yearbook* (Plymouth, MN: Wayzata High School, 1923), 21; *South High School* yearbook (Columbus, OH: South High School, 1922), 112; Flo Herrschberg, "Footlights and Fools," *John Hay Ledger* (Cleveland, OH), April 10, 1931, 1; Schorr, "Diary of a Senior," 2.

46. "Cut Plug," *Campanile* (Palo Alto, CA), October 24, 1923, 1; *The Kingsfordian* yearbook (Kingsford, MI: Kingsford High School, 1928), 96; *The Tatler* yearbook (Minneapolis, MN: Northrop Collegiate, 1928), 6.

47. Ruby Ransom, "A Student's Prayer," *Industrial High School Record* (Birmingham, AL), May 1933, 3; "Grinds," *The Bitter Root* yearbook (Missoula, MT: 1911), 89; Schorr, "Diary of a Senior," 2.

48. Schorr, *Staying Tuned*, 7–15.

49. *Finding Your Roots with Henry Louis Gates, Jr.*, season 5, episode 7, "No Laughing Matter," aired February 19, 2019, Public Broadcasting Service.

50. During his long career, Schorr rarely, if ever, made any self-deprecating or humorous remarks on the air. Instead, Schorr's seriousness and professionalism won him three Emmys. In 1973, he stoically discovered, on air, that he was number seventeen on Richard Nixon's "enemies list." In 1985, CNN fired him for his refusal to co-anchor a show with a former politician, which Schorr believed would compromise his journalistic integrity. Even the director of the CIA referred to him as "Killer Schorr" and, at the end of his life, colleagues remembered him as abrasive, aggressive, and intimidating. See "CBS—Daniel Schorr Reporting on Nixon's 'Enemies List,'" June 27, 1973, https://www.youtube.com/watch?v=ZUftZXJRoyg. Robert D. Hershey Jr., "Daniel Schorr, Journalist, Dies at 93," *New York Times*, July 23, 2010. Tom Shales, "Schorr Fired by CNN," *Washington Post*, March 9, 1985; Claudia Luther, "Daniel Schorr Dies at 93; Controversial CBS and CNN Broadcaster Became Elder Statesman at NPR," *Los Angeles (CA) Times*, July 24, 2010.

"Alan Greenblatt, Journalism Legend Daniel Schorr Dies at 93," *National Public Radio* (Washington, DC), July 23, 2010; Lisbeth Schorr, email message to the author, October 30, 2021; Jessica Schorr Saxe, email message to Lisbeth Schorr, October 23, 2021; Kenneth Schorr, email message to Lisbeth Schorr, October 23, 2021.

51. Sarah Silverman, *The Bedwetter: Stories of Courage, Redemption, and Pee* (New York: Harper Collins, 2010), 34–38; "Getting with 'The Sarah Silverman Program,'" *Day to Day*, aired February 1, 2007, *National Public Radio*, https://www.npr.org/transcripts/7115666; "Sarah Becomes a Substitute Teacher for a Day," *I Love You, America*, aired November 30, 2017, *A Hulu Original Series*.

52. Bakhtin, *Rabelais and His World*, 3–11; Carole Anne Taylor, "Ideologies of the Funny," *The Centennial Review* 36, no. 2 (Spring 1992): 175; Mulkay, *On Humor*, 4–5.

53. Kerry Soper, "The Pathetic Carnival in the Cubicles: The Office as Meditation on the Misuses and Collapse of Traditional Comedy," *Studies in American Humor* 3, no. 19 (2009): 83–85. Dustin Griffin would probably agree with Soper. Griffin wrote *Satire: A Critical Reintroduction*, analyzing the political objectives of mostly French and British writers like Daniel Defoe, Molière, and Jonathan Swift. Griffin concluded that the great satirists were "not really interested in fundamental rearrangements, only minor adjustments" and that ultimately "satire had little effect on the 'real' world." Griffin, *Satire: A Critical Reintroduction* (Lexington: University Press of Kentucky, 1994), 158.

Even Michael Mulkay, who wrote the often cited *On Humor*, thought that jokes typically gave "symbolic expression to structural 'strains' and 'tensions'" but in the process helped "lessen these strains and thereby to maintain the established structure of social relationships." Mulkay, *On Humor*, 153.

Chapter 6 · The Pursuit of Educational Dignity

1. William J. Reese, *America's Public Schools: From the Common School to "No Child Left Behind"* (Baltimore: Johns Hopkins University Press, 2011), 252–53; David B. Tyack, *The One Best System: A History of American Urban Education* (Cambridge, MA: Harvard University Press, 1974), 270.

2. Terrence E. Deal and Robert R. Nolan, *Alterative Schools: Ideologies, Realities, Guidelines* (Chicago: Nelson-Hall, 1978), 1; Mary Anne Raywid, "The First Decade of Public School Alternatives," *Phi Delta Kappan* 62, no. 8 (April 1981): 553; Deal and Nolan, *Alterative Schools*, 4. See also "Enrollment in Public Elementary and Secondary Schools, by Level and by Grade," *Digest of Education Statistics*, National Center for Education Statistics, 2017, accessed April 26, 2022, https://nces.ed.gov/programs/digest/d17/tables/dt17_203.10.asp; Gerald Brunetti, "Alternative Schools: Can They Survive?," *The Clearing House* 48, no. 5 (January 1974): 267; James Rothenberg, "The Open Classroom Reconsidered," *Elementary School Journal* 90, no. 1 (September 1989): 72.

3. Diane Ravitch, "Re-Reforming Schools: Troubled Teachers," *New York Times*, May 8, 1977, C19; Dennis Miller, "Summerhill Documentary" (Ottawa, Canada: National Film Board, 1966), accessed March 12, 2022, https://www.youtube.com/watch?v=D8ko7DGsf5s&t =27s; Miller, "Summerhill," 1966; Larry Cuban, *How Teachers Taught: Constancy and Change in American Classrooms, 1880--1890* (New York: Teachers College Press, 1993), 151; Goodwin Watson, "Summerhill," in *Summerhill: For and Against*, ed. Harold H. Hart (New York: Hart, 1970), 185–86; see also Daniel Linden Duke, *The Retransformation of the School: The Emergence of Contemporary Alternative Schools in the United States* (Chicago: Nelson-Hall, 1978), 6.

4. Roland S. Barth, *Open Education and the American School* (New York: Agathon, 1972), 89; John C. Holt, *How Children Fail* (New York: Dell, 1964), 43; Charles E. Silberman, *Crisis in the Classroom: The Remaking of American Education* (New York: Random House, 1970), 130; Jonathan Kozol, *Letters to a Young Teacher* (New York: Crown, 2007), 85, 244–46.

5. George Leonard, *Education and Ecstasy* (Berkeley, CA: North Atlantic Books, 1987), ix–xi; Joel Mokyr, "Why 'More Work for Mother'? Knowledge and Household Behavior, 1870–1945," *Journal of Economic History* 60, no. 1 (March 2000): 9; Holt, *How Children Fail*, xiv; Deal and Nolan, *Alterative Schools*, 6; Robert D. Barr, "Whatever Happened to the Free School Movement?" *Phi Delta Kappan* 54, no. 7 (March 1973): 454.

6. Raywid, "The First Decade of Public School Alternatives," 552; Cuban, *How Teachers Taught*, 165; Barr, "Whatever Happened to the Free School Movement?," 456; Gene I. Maeroff, "Liberals Defend Open Classes Against Back-to-Basics Forces," *New York Times*, April 20, 1975, 40; Barbara J. Case, "Lasting Alternatives: A Lesson in Survival," *Phi Delta Kappan* 62,

no. 8 (April 1981): 554; Joan LaLiberte, "Pocatello Tables Fundamental Education—At Least for Now," *Idaho State Journal* (Pocatello, ID), July 16, 1976, 15.

7. "Metropolitan Learning Center Controversy Reflects Administrators' 'Incredible Lack of Understanding' About School's Roots, Rep. Lew Frederick Says," *Oregonian* (Portland, OR), May 9, 2014, 1; Lynn Lilliston, "A Daring Departure in Public Education," *Los Angeles (CA) Times*, October 1, 1972, 11; Anne M. Juhasz, "The Key to Mental Health," *Illinois Journal of Education* 63, no. 1 (1972): 29; Mary Springer, "They Know No No's," *News-Pilot* (San Diego, CA), February 17, 1974, 9; Joseph Featherstone, "Getting Out of Their Way: Environments for Learning," in *Radical School Reform*, ed. Beatrice and Ronald Gross (New York: Simon and Schuster, 1969), 208.

8. Allen Graubard, *Free the Children: Radical Reform and the Free School Movement* (New York: Vintage Books, 1972), 172; Margaret M. Clifford, "Effects of Competition as a Motivational Technique in the Classroom," *American Educational Research Journal* 9, no. 1 (Winter 1972): 123; Alfred C. Lintner and Joseph Ducette, "The Effects of Locus of Control, Academic Failure and Task Dimensions on a Student's Responsiveness to Praise," *American Educational Research Journal* 11, no. 3 (Summer 1974): 23; J. Merrell Hansen, "Personalized Achievement Reporting: Grades That Are Significant," *High School Journal* 60, no. 6 (1977): 257–58; Linda R. Jensen, "Using Creativity in Elementary School Mathematics," *Arithmetic Teacher* 23, no. 3 (March 1976): 210–12; Herbert R. Kohl, *The Open Classroom: A Practical Guide to a New Way of Teaching* (New York: Vintage Books, 1969), 10; "Alternative School Offers Fresh Slant to Learning," *Valley News* (Van Nuys, CA), December 3, 1974, 10; Art Campos, "San Juan Trustees Want Data on Alternative Plan," *Sacramento (CA) Bee*, October 24, 1973, B2.

9. Daniel Linden Duke, "Challenge to Bureaucracy: The Contemporary Alternative School," *Journal of Educational Thought* 10, no. 1 (April 1976): 34; Fred Ferretti, "The Death of a Special High School: The Untimely Death of a Special School," *New York Times*, January 28, 1979, NJ2; Walter E. Schafer and Eunice A. Schafer, "Wanderjahr School: Learning from a Case Study," *California Journal of Teacher Education* 3, no. 2 (Spring 1975): 20; Danny Moran, "Amasa Gilman, 90, an Eccentric Educator and Artist Was Founding Principal of Metropolitan Learning Center," *Oregonian* (Portland, OR), February 1, 2013, 15; Jonathan Kozol, *Free Schools* (Boston: Houghton Mifflin, 1972), 2–6; Lena Williams, "School for Good Judgment; School in Scarsdale Debates Alternatives," *New York Times*, June 22, 1980, WC1.

10. Schafer and Schafer, "Wanderjahr School," 2–8; "Alternative High Schools: Some Pioneer Programs," *Educational Research Service Circular* 4 (1972), 35; Ira D. Guberman, "Great Neck Opens School Within a School," *New York Times*, March 1973, 16; Richard Sagor, "Equity and Excellence in Public Schools: The Role of the Alternative School," *Clearing House* 73, no. 2 (December 1999): 74–75; Kozol, *Free Schools*, 11.

11. Duke, *The Retransformation of the School*, 48; Bill Moore, "A School Playground Sparks Imaginary Play," *Asheville (NC) Citizen-Times*, October 8, 1978, C1; "Alternative School: Reaching for the Forgotten," *Miami (FL) Herald*, April 11, 1976, 7-BR; "Developmental Education: Democratic, Individualized," *Indianapolis (IN) Star*, May 13, 1979, 2; Springer, "They Know No No's," 9.

12. Kirsten Albrecht Riehle, interview by the author, March 21, 2022, transcript; Kirsten Albrecht Riehle, interview by Mark Sheehy, May 27, 2008.

13. Kirsten Albrecht Riehle, interview by the author, March 21, 2022, transcript; Kirsten Albrecht, Diary, April 26, 1974, private collection of Kirsten Albrecht Riehle.

14. Kirsten Albrecht Riehle, interview by Mark Sheehy, May 27, 2008; Kirsten Albrecht Riehle, email message to the author, April 23, 2022.

15. Jose Y. Diaz and Gabriel Pina, *The Economic Impact of Minnesota State University, Mankato* (Saint Paul, MN: Wilder Research Center, 2013), 2; Jim Harberts, *City of Mankato*

Land Use Plan (Mankato, MN: Prepared by City Staff, 1986), 10; Theodore C. Blegen and Russell W. Fridley, *Minnesota: A History of the State* (Minneapolis: University of Minnesota Press, 1975), 562; Jim Harberts, *City of Mankato Land Use Plan*, 9; Dennis Duane Braum, *A Population Profile of the Mankato Metropolitan Area* (Mankato, MN: Mankato State University, 1975), 17–20; *Greater Mankato Area* (Chicago, IL: Windsor Publications, 1968), 6.

16. Kathleen M. Long, "Wilson Campus School, 1968–77," *Phi Delta Kappan* 75, no. 7 (March 1994): 540–42.

17. Catherine Watson, "Pupil His Own Boss at 'Laboratory' School," *Star Tribune* (Minneapolis, MN), March 2, 1969, 1B; Catherine Watson, "Wanted: Nontraditional Teachers for Innovative Schools," *Star Tribune* (Minneapolis, MN), June 4, 1972, 1E; Don E. Glines, *Creating Humane Schools* (Mankato, MN: Campus Publishers, 1971), 8, 20, and 41.

18. Lynn Russ, interview by Mark Sheehy, April 22, 2008, transcript, Wilson Oral History Project, Minnesota State University, Mankato, MN; Richard K. Weil, "Life in Year-Round Experimental School Is Described by One of Its Teachers," *Berkshire Eagle* (Pittsfield, MA), August 19, 1970, 23; Weil, "Life in Year-Round Experimental School Is Described by One of Its Teachers," 2; Long, "Wilson Campus School, 1968–77," 543.

19. Lynn Russ, interview by Mark Sheehy, April 22, 2008; Claire Faust, interview by Mark Sheehy, February 26, 2008, transcript, Wilson Oral History Project, Minnesota State University, Mankato, MN; Joint Steering Committee, A Descriptive Study of the Wilson Campus School Evaluation, 1969–1970, box 1, folder 29, page 7, MSU ARC 307, Wilson Campus School Collection, Minnesota State University Archive, Mankato, MN; David Phelps, "'Learning How to Learn' Basis to Wilson Campus School Program," *Daily Reporter News* (Mankato, MN), July 24, 1971, 1; Gene Broughton, interview by Mark Sheehy, May 1, 2008, transcript, Wilson Oral History Project, Minnesota State University, Mankato, MN; Gene Biewen, interview by Mark Sheehy, June 11, 2008, transcript, Wilson Oral History Project, Minnesota State University, Mankato, MN; Weil, "Life in Year-Round Experimental School Is Described by One of Its Teachers," 23; Long, "Wilson Campus School, 1968–77," 541; Orville Jenson, interview by Mark Sheehy, October 22, 2008, transcript, Wilson Oral History Project, Minnesota State University, Mankato, MN; Steve Stockmar, "Womack Takes School Committee Members to Task," *Daily Courier* (Minneapolis, MN), February 26, 1997, 1B.

20. Lynn Russ, interview by Mark Sheehy, April 22, 2008; Gene Broughton, interview by Mark Sheehy, May 1, 2008; Claire Faust, interview by Mark Sheehy, February 26, 2008; Hubert H. Humphrey to Don E. Glines, July 3, 1970, box 1, folder 25, MSU ARC 307, Wilson Campus School Collection, Minnesota State University Archive, Mankato, MN; Walter F. Mondale to Don E. Glines, February 25, 1970, box 1, folder 25, MSU ARC 307, Wilson Campus School Collection, Minnesota State University Archive, Mankato, MN; "Principals Told About Wilson Campus School," *Wausau (WI) Daily Herald*, January 28, 1972, 17; "Innovator in Education Speaker at a Teacher In-Service Meeting," *Emporia (KS) Gazette*, August 21, 1973, 6; "School Concepts To Be Discussed," *Elk Grove (IL) Herald*, February 22, 1971, 6; "Area Educators to Hear Noted Change 'Apostle,'" *Rapid City (SD) Journal*, April 9, 1970, 25.

21. Wilson Campus School Administration, The Decision Making at Wilson Campus School, box 2, folder 14, MSU ARC 307, Wilson Campus School Collection, Minnesota State University Archive, Mankato, MN; International Association for Learning Alternatives, Mankato Wilson Campus School: Remembered, 2002, box 3, folder 35, page 3, MSU ARC 307, Wilson Campus School Collection, Minnesota State University Archive, Mankato, MN (hereafter cited as International Association for Learning Alternatives, Mankato Wilson Campus School); Report of the Wilson Campus School Load Committee, 1968, box 7, folder 11, MSU ARC 307, Wilson Campus School Collection, Minnesota State University Archive, Mankato, MN; Ken E. Berg, "Alex Is an Everyman," *Mankato (MN) Free Press*, September 22, 1970; Phil

Grosz, "Wilson at a Glance," *High News* (Minneapolis, MN), March 7, 1969, 1; Wilson Campus School, Annual Report, 1971–1972, box 1, folder 22, page 44, MSU ARC 307, Wilson Campus School Collection, Minnesota State University Archive, Mankato, MN.

22. "Nothing Is Too 'Far Out' to Be Tried in the Wilson School," *National Observer* (Washington, DC), July 28, 1969, 2; Mark Schuck, interview by Mark Sheehy, June 12, 2008, transcript, Wilson Oral History Project, Minnesota State University, Mankato, MN; Raymond Lewis Holden, A Study of Growth of Healthy Self-Concepts Among Student at Wilson Campus School, 1970, box 7, folder 28, pages 14–18, MSU ARC 307, Wilson Campus School Collection, Minnesota State University Archive, Mankato, MN; Wilson Campus School, Annual Report, 1971–1972, box 1, folder 22, page 45, MSU ARC 307, Wilson Campus School Collection, Minnesota State University Archive, Mankato, MN.

23. Don E. Glines, *Declaring War Against Schooling: Personalized Learning Now* (New York: Rowman & Littlefield, 2012), 32 and 80; Don E. Glines, *Implementing Different and Better Schools* (Mankato, MN: Campus Publishers, 1969), 122–23.

24. Wilson School Administration, Advisor Guidelines, box 1, folder 1, November 25, 1970, MSU ARC 307, Wilson Campus School Collection, Minnesota State University Archive, Mankato, MN; Wilson Campus School, Progress Report, 1972, box 1, folder 2, MSU ARC 307, Wilson Campus School Collection, Minnesota State University Archive, Mankato, MN; International Association for Learning Alternatives, Mankato Wilson Campus School, 4–6; Wilson School Administration, Procedures for Appraising and Reporting Student Progress, September 1970, box 2, folder 13, MSU ARC 307, Wilson Campus School Collection, Minnesota State University Archive, Mankato, MN.

25. Weil, "Life in Year-Round Experimental School Is Described by One of Its Teachers," 23; Mark Kiecker, interview by Mark Sheehy, May 12, 2008, transcript, Wilson Oral History Project, Minnesota State University, Mankato, MN; Orville Jenson, interview by Mark Sheehy, October 22, 2008; Cathy Colby, interview by Mark Sheehy, March 6, 2008, transcript, Wilson Oral History Project, Minnesota State University, Mankato, MN; Wilson Campus School, Annual Report, 1971–1972, box 1, folder 22, MSU ARC 307, Wilson Campus School Collection, Minnesota State University Archive, Mankato, MN; David E. Sweet, "A Brief Description of the Minnesota State College Laboratory Schools," June 1970, box 18, folder 24, MSU ARC 013, President's Office Collection, Minnesota State University Archive, Mankato, MN; Joan Diane Struck, interview by Mark Sheehy, April 1, 2008, transcript, Wilson Oral History Project, Minnesota State University, Mankato, MN; International Association for Learning Alternatives, Mankato Wilson Campus School, 13.

26. Kirsten Albrecht Riehle, interview by Mark Sheehy, May 27, 2008; Brenda Cartenson Boyer, interview by Mark Sheehy, September 24, 2008, transcript, Wilson Oral History Project, Minnesota State University, Mankato, MN; Cathy Colby, interview by Mark Sheehy, March 6, 2008; Jodi Orchard, interview by Mark Sheehy, February 27, 2008, transcript, Wilson Oral History Project, Minnesota State University, Mankato, MN.

27. Kirsten Albrecht Riehle, email message to the author, April 23, 2022; Watson, "Pupil His Own Boss at 'Laboratory' School," 1B; Kirsten Albrecht, Diary, April 23, 1974, private collection of Kirsten Albrecht Riehle.

28. Jodi Orchard, interview by Mark Sheehy, February 27, 2008; Long, "Wilson Campus School," 542–44; Kirsten Albrecht Riehle, interview by Mark Sheehy, May 27, 2008; International Association for Learning Alternatives, Mankato Wilson Campus School, 5–6; "Death at Wilson," *Wilson Concept* (Mankato, MN), May 1974, box 4, folder 2, MSU ARC 307, Wilson Campus School Collection, Minnesota State University Archive, Mankato, MN; Kirsten Albrecht Riehle, email message to the author, April 23, 2022; Cathy Colby, interview by Mark Sheehy, March 6, 2008; Orville Jenson, interview by Mark Sheehy, October 22, 2008.

29. Kirsten Albrecht Riehle, interview by the author, March 21, 2022, transcript; Kirsten Albrecht, "Time," *Whodunit: A Wilson Production* (Mankato, MN), Spring 1973, box 3, folder 17, MSU ARC 307, Wilson Campus School Collection, Minnesota State University Archive, Mankato, MN; Kirsten Albrecht, "Explosion," *Whodunit: A Wilson Production* (Mankato, MN), Fall 1974, box 3, folder 17, MSU ARC 307, Wilson Campus School Collection, Minnesota State University Archive, Mankato, MN; Kirsten Albrecht Riehle, interview by Mark Sheehy, May 27, 2008.

30. "Variety of Schools Advocated," *Post-Crescent* (Appleton, WI), June 22, 1972, B1; Weil, "Life in Year-Round Experimental School Is Described by One of Its Teachers," 23; Long, "Wilson Campus School," 542; "Let Students Choose Teachers," *Edmonton (AB) Journal*, February 23, 1971, 20; Watson, "Pupil His Own Boss at 'Laboratory' School," 1B; Orville Jenson, interview by Mark Sheehy, October 22, 2008; Raymond Lewis Holden, "A Study of Growth of Healthy Self-Concepts Among Students at Wilson Campus School," 1970, box 7, folder 28, page 18, MSU ARC 307, Wilson Campus School Collection, Minnesota State University Archive, Mankato, MN.

31. Orville Jenson, interview by Mark Sheehy, October 22, 2008; Weil, "Life in Year-Round Experimental School Is Described by One of Its Teachers," 23; Long, "Wilson Campus School," 544, 546; Glines, *Implementing Different and Better Schools*, 158; Brenda Cartenson Boyer, interview by Mark Sheehy, September 24, 2008; Memo to Faculty, Wilson Campus School Administration, April 10, 1974, box 1, folder 31, MSU ARC 307, Wilson Campus School Collection, Minnesota State University Archive, Mankato, MN; Alan N. Hale, A Proposal for Support of a Demonstration Program in Adventure Training as an Alternative Method of Treatment for Troubled Youth, 1973–1974, box 1, folder 31, MSU ARC 307, Wilson Campus School Collection, Minnesota State University Archive, Mankato, MN; Kirsten Albrecht Riehle, interview by the author, April 15, 2022, transcript; Gene Biewen, interview by Mark Sheehy, June 11, 2008.

32. Mark Schuck, interview by Mark Sheehy, June 12, 2008; Glines, *Implementing Different and Better Schools*, 127; Wilson Campus School Administration, Outhouse Evaluation: Wilson Campus School, June 10, 1970, box 2, folder 13, MSU ARC 307, Wilson Campus School Collection, Minnesota State University Archive, Mankato, MN (hereafter cited as Wilson Campus School Administration, Outhouse Evaluation); Wilson Campus School Administration, Outhouse Evaluation; Transfer Study, Wilson Campus School Administration, 1970, box 7, folder 22, MSU ARC 307, Wilson Campus School Collection, Minnesota State University Archive, Mankato, MN; Jan Albrecht, interview by Mark Sheehy, April 10, 2008, transcript, Wilson Campus Oral History Project, University Archives at Minnesota State University.

33. Patti Ries, "Meeting for Parents of New Students," *The Wilson Concept* (Mankato, MN), March 1975, box 8, folder 10, MSU ARC 307, Wilson Campus School Collection, Minnesota State University Archive, Mankato, MN; Don E. Glines to Elbert W. Ockerman, March 7, 1969, box 1, folder 27, MSU ARC 307, Wilson Campus School Collection, Minnesota State University Archive, Mankato, MN; Don E. Glines to Frank A. Logan, February 3, 1969, box 1, folder 27, MSU ARC 307, Wilson Campus School Collection, Minnesota State University Archive, Mankato, MN; Don E. Glines to Winston R. Carroll, March 14, 1969, box 1, folder 27, MSU ARC 307, Wilson Campus School Collection, Minnesota State University Archive, Mankato, MN; Don E. Glines to Owen E. Semmelson, February 3, 1969, box 1, folder 27, MSU ARC 307, Wilson Campus School Collection, Minnesota State University Archive, Mankato, MN; International Association for Learning Alternatives, Mankato Wilson Campus School, 17 and 19.

34. Wilson Campus School Administration, Wilson Involvement, January 29, 1976, box 1, folder 5, MSU ARC 307, Wilson Campus School Collection, Minnesota State University Archive, Mankato, MN; Wilson Campus School, Annual Report, 1971–1972, box 1, folder 22, page 19, MSU ARC 307, Wilson Campus School Collection, Minnesota State University Archive, Mankato, MN; Wilson Campus School, Annual Report, 1972–1973, box 1, folder 22,

page 16, MSU ARC 307, Wilson Campus School Collection, Minnesota State University Archive, Mankato, MN; Wilson Campus School, Annual Report, 1973–1974, box 1, folder 22, page 16, MSU ARC 307, Wilson Campus School Collection, Minnesota State University Archive, Mankato, MN; Jodi Orchard, interview by Mark Sheehy, February 27, 2008; Orville Jenson, interview by Mark Sheehy, October 22, 2008.

35. Wilson Campus School Administration, Memo: Plans for new students grades 7–12, May 30, 1974, box 1, folder 31, MSU ARC 307, Wilson Campus School Collection, Minnesota State University Archive, Mankato, MN; Wilson Campus School Administration, Outhouse Evaluation; Orville Jenson, interview by Mark Sheehy, October 22, 2008; Claire Faust, interview by Mark Sheehy, February 26, 2008; Mark Kiecker, interview by Mark Sheehy, May 12, 2008; Joan Diane Struck, interview by Mark Sheehy, April 1, 2008; Brenda Cartenson Boyer, interview by Mark Sheehy, September 24, 2008; Long, "Wilson Campus School," 541; Cathy Colby, interview by Mark Sheehy, March 6, 2008; Brenda Cartenson Boyer, interview by Mark Sheehy, September 24, 2008.

36. Mark Kiecker, interview by Mark Sheehy, May 12, 2008; Mark Schuck, interview by Mark Sheehy, June 12, 2008; Wilson Campus Student Progress and Evaluation Reports, Summer 1975, box 1, folder 1, SMHC Manuscript Collection 179, Jodi Orchard Papers, Minnesota State University Archive, Mankato, MN; Wilson Campus Student Progress and Evaluation Reports, Spring 1974, box 1, folder 1, SMHC Manuscript Collection 179, Jodi Orchard Papers, Minnesota State University Archive, Mankato, MN.

37. Kirsten Albrecht Riehle, email message to the author, April 23, 2022; Kirsten Albrecht Riehle, interview by the author, April 15, 2022; Kirsten Albrecht Riehle, interview by the author, March 21, 2022, transcript.

38. Maeroff, "Liberals Defend Open Classes Against Back-to-Basics Forces," 40; Terry Ryan, "American Schools Stress Basic Skills," *Sun Herald* (Biloxi, MS), February 28, 1975, A12; Raywid, "The First Decade of Public School Alternatives," 553; Sue Bernstein, "Why It's Time for a 'Traditional School,'" *Ithaca (NY) Journal*, March 31, 1975, 3.

39. Jal Mehta, *The Allure of Order: High Hopes, Dashed Expectations, and the Troubled Quest to Remake American Schooling* (New York: Oxford University Press, 2013), 74; Rothenberg, "The Open Classroom Reconsidered," 70; Reese, *America's Public Schools*, 268, 280.

40. Richard Sagor, "Equity and Excellence in Public Schools: The Role of the Alternative School," *Clearing House* 73, no. 2 (December 1999): 75; Julie Fernandez, "Alternative Schooling: The Concern Is That It Can Become an Alcatraz," *Austin (TX) American-Statesman*, September 18, 1977, H1; Fred Ferretti, "The Death of a Special High School," *New York Times*, January 28, 1979, NJ2; "Editorial: Alternative School," *The Morning Record and Journal* (Meriden, CT), February 23, 1979, 6; Wayne Hammond, "Will Looking Back Improve Future of Education?," *Watertown (SD) Public Opinion*, June 29, 2000, 4.

41. Barr, "Whatever Happened to the Free School Movement?," 457; Moran, "Amasa Gilman, 90, an Eccentric Educator and Artist Was Founding Principal of Metropolitan Learning Center," 15; Carolyn Moilanen, *Portland Public Schools Internal Alternative Schools* (Portland, OR: Evaluation Department, Portland Public Schools, 1983), 14; Cuban, *How Teachers Taught*, 176; John H. Wilson, "Advice and Dissent: Alternative Schools," *The Wichita (KS) Beacon*, April 2, 1977, 3C.

42. Rothenberg, "The Open Classroom Reconsidered," 79; "Developmental Education: Democratic, Individualized," *Indianapolis (IN) Star*, May 13, 1979, 2; Juhasz, "The Key to Mental Health," 29.

43. Case, "Lasting Alternatives," 554; Deal and Nolan, *Alterative Schools*, 6; Barr, "Whatever Happened to the Free School Movement?" 457.

44. Fred M. Hechinger, "About Education: Looking Back at Failure," *New York Times*, May 18, 1982, C7.

45. Liz Albrecht, "Editorial," *Whodunit: A Wilson Production*, Fall 1974, box 3, folder 17, MSU ARC 307, Wilson Campus School Collection, Minnesota State University Archive, Mankato, MN; Charles Waterman and Jack Miller, "An Open School Is Closed," *North Country Anvil* (Winona, MN), June 1977, 18–21; Joseph R. Schulze to Visitors of Wilson, April 21, 1975, box 1, folder 4, MSU ARC 307, Wilson Campus School Collection, Minnesota State University Archive, Mankato, MN.

46. Lynn Closway and Cathie Netgie, "Wilson's Future Is on the Line," *Mankato (MN) Free Press*, March 12, 1976, 15; Douglas R. Moore to Fred Norton, April 22, 1975, box 7, folder 1, MSU ARC 307, Wilson Campus School Collection, Minnesota State University Archive, Mankato, MN. Moore wrote, "Wilson Campus School is as an integral part of our teacher education program and not simply as a community service activity. . . . We are genuinely convinced that Wilson provides an invaluable and unique service to elementary and secondary education in this state."

Student Pamphlet, Save Our School, November 7, 1975, box 1, folder 5, MSU ARC 307, Wilson Campus School Collection, Minnesota State University Archive, Mankato, MN; Kirsten Albrecht Riehle, interview by Mark Sheehy, May 27, 2008; Dave Phelps, "Student Tears Mark Hearing at Wilson," *Mankato (MN) Free Press*, November 8, 1975, 9.

47. Cathie Neitge, "Legislators Bomb Away at MSU, University System," *Mankato (MN) Free Press*, February 20, 1976, 1; "Fate of Campus School Undecided," *Winona (MN) Daily News*, May 25, 1976, 2b; International Association for Learning Alternatives, Mankato Wilson Campus School, 20; Kirsten Albrecht, protest lyrics, 1976, Kirsten's personal collection.

48. Patrick D. Flynn to District 77 School Board, February 24, 1976, box 7, folder 7, MSU ARC 307, Wilson Campus School Collection, Minnesota State University Archive, Mankato, MN.

49. Don Sorensen to Joe Schulze, August 16, 1974, box 7, folder 15, MSU ARC 307, Wilson Campus School Collection, Minnesota State University Archive, Mankato, MN; "Glines, Legislators Trade Verbal Blows," *Mankato (MN) Free Press*, January 14, 1970, 1; Ken E. Berg, "Chet, David and Wilson," *Mankato (MN) Free Press*, September 4, 1969, 10; "The Doughnut Role in Education," *Mankato (MN) Free Press*, October 11, 1968, 1; "Glines, Legislators Trade Verbal Blows," *Mankato (MN) Free Press*, January 14, 1970, 1; Ken E. Berg, "Innovation Entices Kids," *Mankato (MN) Free Press*, June 12, 1969, 11; "Editorial: Options in Our Future?" *Mankato (MN) Free Press*, August 20, 1973, 14; Berg, "Innovation Entices Kids," 11; Wilson Campus School Administration, Outhouse Evaluation; Liz Albrecht, "Editorial," *Whodunit: A Wilson Production*, Fall 1974, box 3, folder 17, MSU ARC 307, Wilson Campus School Collection, Minnesota State University Archive, Mankato, MN.

50. Waterman and Miller, "An Open School Is Closed," 18; Thomas F. Stark to Edward McMahon, February 13, 1976, box 7, folder 1, MSU ARC 307, Wilson Campus School Collection, Minnesota State University Archive, Mankato, MN; "Mankato School to Close: Teachers Receive Notices," *Star Tribune* (Minneapolis, MN), May 29, 1976, 12C.

51. Kirsten Albrecht Riehle, interview by the author, March 21, 2022.

52. Kirsten Albrecht Riehle, interview by Mark Sheehy, May 27, 2008; Kirsten Albrecht Riehle, interview by the author, March 29, 2022.

53. Kirsten Albrecht Riehle, interview by Mark Sheehy, May 27, 2008; Kirsten Albrecht Riehle, interview by the author, April 15, 2022.

54. Kirsten Albrecht Riehle, interview by the author, March 29, 2022.

55. Joel A. Sutter and Elizabeth V. Rice, *Student Performance Standards and Testing Programs: Background Information for Legislators* (St. Paul: Minnesota Senate Counsel and Research, 1984), 5; Sutter and Rice, *Student Performance Standards and Testing Programs*, 7; Jane Schleisman, *An In-Depth Investigation of One School District's Responses to an Externally-Mandated, High-Stakes Testing Program, in Minnesota* (Minneapolis: Annual Meeting of the University Council for Educational Administration, University of Minnesota, 1999), 1–3;

Wade W. Nelson, "The Naked Truth About School Reform in Minnesota," *Phi Delta Kappan* 79, no. 9 (May 1998): 679–80; Kristin Liu, Richard Spicuzza, and Ron Erickson, "Educators' Responses to LEP Students' Participation in the 1997 Basic Standards Testing" (St. Paul: Minnesota Department of Children, Families, and Learning, October 1997), 1.

56. J. Ruth Nelson, *High Stakes Graduation Exams: The Intended and Unintended Consequences of Minnesota's Basic Standards Tests for Students with Disabilities* (Minneapolis, MN: National Center on Educational Outcomes, August 2006), 7–8; Mark Davidson, Ernest C. Davenport, and Nohoon Kwak, *Minnesota Education Yearbook, 2000: The Status of Pre-K–12 Education in Minnesota* (Minneapolis: Office of Educational Accountability, University of Minnesota, 2000), 1–4; Dewey G. Cornell, Jon A. Krosnick, and Lin Chiat Chang, "Student Reactions to Being Wrongly Informed of Failing a High-Stakes Test: The Case of the Minnesota Basic Standards Test," *Educational Policy* 20, no. 5 (November 2006): 718.

57. Kirsten Albrecht Riehle, interview by the author, March 29, 2022; Kirsten Albrecht Riehle, email message to the author, April 23, 2022; Kirsten Albrecht Riehle, interview by the author, April 15, 2022.

58. Kirsten Albrecht Riehle, interview by the author, March 29, 2022, transcript.

59. Kirsten Albrecht Riehle, interview by the author, March 29, 2022, transcript; Kirsten Albrecht Riehle, email message to the author, April 23, 2022; Kirsten Albrecht Riehle, interview by the author, April 15, 2022, transcript.

60. Bill Lofy, *Paul Wellstone: The Life of a Passionate Progressive* (Ann Arbor: University of Michigan Press, 2005), 18–24.

61. "Wellstone Recalled as Friend of Public Education," *Education Week* (New York, NY), November 6, 2002, 17.

62. "The New York State Report Card for the 2004–2005 School Year," New York State Department of Education, accessed June 26, 2022, https://www.p12.nysed.gov/repcrd2005 /home.shtml; "2004–2005 School Report Card," Texas Education Agency, accessed June 26, 2022, https://rptsvr1.tea.texas.gov/; "Illinois State Report Card," Illinois Department of Education, accessed June 26, 2022, https://cdn5-ss9.sharpschool.com; "New Jersey's Sex Ed Report Card," SexEdNJ.org, accessed June 26, 2022, https://www.sexednj.org/the-report .html; "Equity and Inclusion Dashboard," Hermosa Beach City School District, accessed June 26, 2022, https://www.hbcsd.org/apps/pages/index.jsp?uREC_ID=2233107&type =d&pREC_ID=2200467; Matthew Ladner, *Report Card on American Education: Ranking State K–12 Performance, Progress, and Reform* (Arlington, VA: American Legislative Exchange Council, 2015), 9.

63. George Veletsianos, *Learning Online: The Student Experience* (Baltimore: Johns Hopkins University Press, 2020), 122–23; Mark Stevens and Mary F. Rice, "Collaborating to Create Middle Level Blended Learning Environments," in *The Online Classroom: Resources for Effective Middle Level Virtual Education,* ed. Brooke B. Eisenbach and Paula Greathouse (Charlotte, NC: Information Age Publishing, 2019), 83–96; Sigrid Hartong, "The Power of Relation-Making: Insights into the Production and Operation of Digital School Performance Platforms in the US," *Critical Studies in Education* 62, no. 1 (January 1, 2021): 34; Pat Lynch, "Higher Ground Education Raises $30M Series D and Acquires Award-Winning FreshGrade Platform to Accelerate 'Montessori Everywhere' Mission," *BusinessWire,* April 8, 2021.

64. Darrell M. West, *Digital Schools: How Technology Can Transform Education* (Washington, DC: Brookings Institution Press, 2012), 23–25; Parija Kavilanz, "Why Teachers Are Ditching Report Cards," *CNN Business,* September 24, 2015; Ganna Khatser and Maxym Khatser, "Online Learning Through LMSs: Comparative Assessment of Canvas and Moodle," *International Journal of Emerging Technologies in Learning (IJET)* 17, no. 12 (2022): 196; Tyler Sonnenaker, "As Zoom Classes Take Over during the Pandemic, Edtech Companies Provide a Lifeline, but Only for Schools and Parents Willing to Surrender Their Students' Privacy,"

Business Insider, October 13, 2020; "Tenn. Schools Data Get Digital Repackaging: Format Allows Easy Local, State Comparisons," *The Commercial Appeal*, December 15, 2013, B2; Miguel Baptista Nunes and Maggie Mcpherson, eds., *Multi Conference on Computer Science and Information Systems* (New York: International Association for Development of the Information Society, 2014), 26.

65. Veletsianos, *Learning Online*, 122–23; Molly Baker, "To Hover Over Schoolwork, Parents Go Online," *Wall Street Journal*, September 28, 2011, D1.

66. Kirsten Albrecht Riehle, interview by the author, March 29, 2022.

Conclusion · Pulling Weeds and Foucault Fatigue

1. Geoff Shullenberger, "How We Forgot Foucault," *American Affairs*, May 20, 2021; Blake Smith, "The Unwoke Foucault," *Washington Examiner*, March 4, 2021; Justin E. H. Smith, "Covid Is Boring: The Perpetual Hygiene Regime and the Stemification of the Intellectuals," Justin E. H. Smith's Hinternet, September 18, 2021, accessed October 22, 2021, https://justinehsmith.substack.com/p/covid-is-boring; Samuel Clowes Huneke, "'Do Not Ask Me Who I Am': Foucault and Neoliberalism," *Point Magazine*, June 2, 2021; Ross Douthat, "How Michel Foucault Lost the Left and Won the Right," *New York Times*, May 25, 2021; Christopher Caldwell, "Meet the Philosopher Who Is Trying to Explain the Pandemic," *New York Times*, August 21, 2020; Lisa Lerer, "How Republican Vaccine Opposition Got to This Point," *New York Times*, September 12, 2021.

2. "2021 Edelman Trust Barometer," *Edelman*, May 18, 2021, https://www.edelman.com/trust/2021-trust-barometer; "Confidence in Institutions," *Gallup, Inc.*, 2021, accessed October 22, 2021, https://news.gallup.com/poll/1597/confidence-institutions.aspx; Ethan Zuckerman, *Mistrust: Why Losing Faith in Institutions Provides the Tools to Transform Them* (New York: W. W. Norton, 2021), 46; Brittany Murray et al., "Civil Society Goes to School: Parent-Teacher Associations and the Equality of Education Opportunity," *RSF: Russell Sage Foundation Journal of the Social Sciences* 5, no. 3 (March 2019): 41–63; Dana Goldstein and Alicia Parlapiano, "The Kindergarten Exodus," *New York Times*, August 7, 2021.

3. Patrick J. Ryan, "A Case Study in the Cultural Origins of Superpower: Liberal Individualism, American Nationalism, and the Rise of High School Life, A Study of Cleveland's Central and East Technical High Schools," *History of Education Quarterly* 45, no. 1 (Spring 2005): 71–72, 93; Michael Bowbridge and Sean Blenkinsop, "Michel Foucault Goes Outside: Discipline and Control in the Practice of Outdoor Education," *Journal of Experiential Education* 34, no. 2 (2011): 149–63; Holly Link, Sarah Gallo, and Stanton E. F. Wortham, "The Production of Schoolchildren as Enlightened Subjects," *American Educational Research Journal* 54, no. 5 (October 2017): 851–53.

4. Mark Bevir, "Foucault and Critique: Deploying Agency Against Autonomy," *Political Theory* 27, no. 1 (February 1999): 68–77.

Michel Foucault is buried deep in the heart of this book. I am an ambivalent Foucauldian. On the one hand, generations of scholars have rightly criticized Foucault's historical methods and his willingness to generalize without sufficient evidence. For that criticism, see Richard Hamilton's *The Social Misconstruction of Reality: Validity and Verification in the Scholarly Community* (1996), Ronald Butchart's "What's Foucault Got to Do with It? History, Theory, and Becoming Subjected" (2011), Allan Megill's "The Reception of Foucault by Historians" (1987), Mark Bevir's "Foucault and Critique: Deploying Agency against Autonomy" (1999), and Jeffrey Weeks' "Foucault for Historians" (1982).

Foucault's disciples have left their mark on educational analysis: Stephen J. Ball's *Foucault and Education: Disciplines and Knowledge* (1990), Michael Bowbridge and Sean Blenkinsop's "Michel Foucault Goes Outside: Discipline and Control in the Practice of Outdoor Education" (2011), and Lizbet Simmons' *Schools under Surveillance: Cultures of Control in Public Education* (2010). For two biographies of Foucault, see *The Passion of Michel Foucault* (1993) by James Miller and *Michel Foucault* (1991) by Didier Eribon. And, of course, one should read Foucault for oneself: *Aesthetics, Method, and Epistemology* (1984), *Discipline and Punish* (1975), *The History of Sexuality*, Volume I (1976), *"I, Pierre Rivière, Having Slaughtered My Mother, My Sister, and My Brother"* (1973), *Power, Psychiatric Power: Lectures at the Collège de France* (1974), *Security, Territory, Population: Lectures at the Collège de France* (1978).

Chapter 1. Rousing the Attention of Parents

Chapter 1 builds on the work of the great classics in educational history, scholars who captured the main themes of market capitalism, religious fervor, and republican virtue ubiquitous in the antebellum common school era: Carl Kaestle's *Pillars of the Republic: Common Schools and American Society* (1983), Joyce Appleby's *Recollections of the Early Republic* (1997), Joseph Kett's *Rites of Passage: Adolescence in America* (1977), William J. Reese's *America's Public Schools from the Common School to "No Child Left Behind"* (2005), Nancy Beadie's *Education and the Creation of Capital in the Early American Republic* (2010), and David Hogan's "Modes of Discipline: Affective Individualism and Pedagogical Reform in New England" (1990).

For more on the Second Great Awakening's impact on American schooling, see "The Second Great Awakening and the New England Social Order" (1970) by Richard D. Birdsall, "The Invention of the Great Awakening" (1991) by Joseph Conforti, "The Fight against Corporal Punishment in American Schools" (1952) by James P. Jewett, *A Shopkeeper's Millennium: Society and Revivals in Rochester, New York, 1815–1837* (1978) by Paul E. Johnson, "The Burned-over District Reconsidered: A Portent of Evolving Religious Pluralism in the United States" (1984) by Linda K. Pritchard, "Tropes of Temperance, Specters of Naturalism" (2016) by Anna Pochmara, and "The Urban Threshold and the Second Great Awakening: Revivalism in New York State" (2010) by Richard Lee Rogers. For themes of education and republican virtue, see Rita Koganzon's "'Producing a Reconciliation of Disinterestedness and Commerce': The Political Rhetoric of Education in the Early Republic" (2012) and Holly Link, Sarah Gallo, and Stanton E. F. Wortham's "The Production of Schoolchildren as Enlightened Subjects" (2017). There are quite a few historians who have described the importance of parent–teacher animosity during this period: William W. Cutler's *Parents and Schools: The 150-Year Struggle for Control in American Education* (2000), J. M. Opal's "Exciting Emulation: Academies and the Transformation of the Rural North" (2004), and David F. Allmendinger Jr.'s *Paupers and Scholars: The Transformation of Student Life in Nineteenth-Century New England* (1975).

Above all, I have been inspired by educational historians who dig deep into the daily classroom experiences of ordinary teachers and students: *Fit to Teach: Same-Sex Desire, Gender, and School Work in the Twentieth Century* (2005) by Jackie M. Blount, "A Nation of Ink and Paint: Map Drawing and Geographic Pedagogy in the American Ceylon Mission" (2019) by Mark E. Balmforth, *How Teachers Taught: Constancy and Change in American Classrooms* (1993) by Larry Cuban, *Governing the Young: Teacher Behavior in Popular Primary Schools in Nineteenth-Century United States* (1989) by Barbara Finkelstein, "'Chanting Choristers': Simultaneous Recitation in Baltimore's Nineteenth-Century Primary Schools" (1994) by William R. Johnson, "Reconstructing the Life Histories of Spanish Primary School Teachers" (2014) by Kira Mahamud and María José Martínez Ruiz-Funes, and "Losing Patience and Staying Professional: Women Teachers and the Problem of Classroom Discipline in New York City Schools in the 1920s" (1994) by Kate Rousmaniere.

Chapter 2. Unity, Efficiency, and Freed People

To capture the broader context of William Matthews' childhood, I relied on a wide variety of secondary sources on the experiences of freed people after emancipation. The postbellum period was an incredibly complex one, full of hope, violence, tragedy, and resilience. For further reading, please see Carol Anderson's *White Rage: The Unspoken Truth of Our Racial Divide* (2016), Ira Berlin's *Many Thousand Gone: The First Two Centuries of Slavery in North America* (1998), Paul A. Cimbala's *Under the Guardianship of the Nation: The Freedman's Bureau and the Reconstruction of Georgia* (1997), Edmund L. Drago's "How Sherman's March through Georgia Affected the Slaves" (1973), John Hope Franklin's *Reconstruction After the Civil War* (1994), Michael Golay's *A Ruined Land: The End of the Civil War* (1999), William A. Link and James J. Broomall's *Rethinking American Emancipation: Legacies of Slavery and the Quest for Black Freedom* (2015), Leon F. Litwack's *Been in the Storm So Long: The Aftermath of Slavery* (1979), Clarence L. Mohr's *On the Threshold of Freedom: Masters and Slaves in Civil War Georgia* (1986), Susan Eva O'Donovan's *Becoming Free in the Cotton South* (2007), Michael Perman's *Emancipation and Reconstruction* (2003), Joe M. Richardson's *Christian Reconstruction: The American Missionary Association and Southern Blacks* (1986), and Andrew Ward's *The Slaves' War: The Civil War in the Words of Former Slaves* (2008).

There have now been decades of excellent scholarship on schooling for freed people and nineteenth-century African American education more generally. The obvious classics are Horace Mann Bond's *The Education of the Negro in the American Social Order* (1970), W. E. B. Du Bois's *Souls of Black Folk* (1903), and Carter G. Woodson's *The Mis-Education of the Negro* (1933). James D. Anderson wrote the definitive history of African American education in the wake of the Civil War with *The Education of Blacks in the South* (1988). My personal favorite for capturing the complexities and contradictions of schools for freed people is the work of Ronald E. Butchart, particularly *Northern Schools, Southern Blacks, and Reconstruction* (1980) and *Schooling the Freed People* (2010). Titus Brown's *Faithful, Firm, and True* (2006) is a comprehensive history of Lewis High School, which is where chapter 3's protagonist attended. I also drew upon the following works of history: *A Class of Their Own: Black Teachers in the Segregated South* (2007) by Adam Fairclough, "African American Teachers in the South, 1890–1940: Powerlessness and the Ironies of Expectations and Protest" (1995) by Michael Fultz, "*New Perspectives on Black Educational History* (1978) by Vincent P. Franklin and James D. Anderson, *Educational Reconstruction: African American Schools in the Urban South* (2016) by Hilary Green, *Soldiers of Light and Love: Northern Teachers and Georgia Blacks* (1980) by Jacqueline Jones, "'A Good and Delicious Country': Free Children of Color and How They Learned to Imagine the Atlantic World in Nineteenth-Century Louisiana" (2000) by Mary Niall Mitchell, *Reading, 'Riting, and Reconstruction: The Education of Freedmen in the South* (1976) by Robert C. Morris, "Half a Loaf: The Shift from White to Black Teachers in the Negro Schools of the Urban South" (1974) by Howard N. Rabinowitz, *From Cotton Field to Schoolhouse: African American Education in Mississippi* (2009) by Christopher M. Span, *The Lost Education of Horace Tate: Uncovering the Hidden Heroes Who Fought for Justice in Schools* (2018) by Vanessa Siddle Walker, *The White Architects of Black Education* (2001) by William H. Watkins, and *Self-Taught: African American Education in Slavery and Freedom* (2005) by Heather Andrea Williams.

Chapter 2 also deals with the growth of public schools in the 1870s and 1880s, and with that growth the increasing corporatization of school governance. For more, see Raymond E. Callahan's *Education and the Cult of Efficiency: A Study of the Social Forces That Have Shaped the Administration of the Public Schools* (1962), Benjamin Justice's *The War That Wasn't: Religious Conflict and Compromise in the Common Schools of New York State* (2009), Michael B. Katz's *The Irony of Early School Reform: Educational Innovation in Mid-Nineteenth Century Massachusetts* (1968), David F. Labaree's *The Making of an American High School: The Credentials Market and the Central High School of Philadelphia* (1988), Joel Perlman and Robert A. Margo's *Women's Work?: American Schoolteachers* (2001), Kate Rousmaniere's *The Principal's Office: A Social History of the American School Principal* (2013), Patrick J. Ryan's "A Case Study in the Cultural Origins of Superpower: Modern Youth, American Nationalism, and the Rise of the High School Life" (2005), Kyle P. Steele's *Making a Mass Institution: Indianapolis and the American High School* (2020), Daniel Calhoun's *The Intelligence of a People* (1974), David B. Tyack and Elizabeth Hansot's *Managers of Virtue: Public School Leadership in America* (1986), and William Reese's *Power and the Promise of School Reform: Grassroots Movements During the Progressive Era* (1986).

Chapter 3. Overworn Mothers and Unfed Minds

In chapter 3, I tried to integrate the history of nineteenth-century motherhood with Martha McKay's story in Indianapolis. For more, see Rima Apple's *Perfect Motherhood: Science and Childrearing in America* (2006), Nancy F. Cott's *The Bonds of Womanhood* (1979), Ruth Schwartz Cowan's *More Work for Mother: The Ironies of Household Technology from the Open Hearth to the Microwave* (1983), Linda K. Kerber's "Separate Spheres, Female Worlds, Woman's Place: The Rhetoric of Women's History" (1983), Molly Ladd-Taylor's *Mother-Work: Women, Child Welfare, and the State* (1994), Rebecca Jo Plant's *Mom: The Transformation of Motherhood in Modern America* (2010), Theresa Richardson's *The Century of the Child: The Mental Hygiene Movement and Social Policy in the United States and Canada* (1989), Cynthia Eagle Russett's *Sexual Science: The Victorian Construction of Womanhood* (1989), Alice Boardman Smuts' *Science in the Service of Children* (2006), Peter N. Stearns' *Anxious Parents: A History of Modern Childrearing in America* (2003), Nancy M. Theriot's *Mothers and Daughters in Nineteenth-Century America: The Biosocial Construction of Femininity* (1996), and Jodi Vandenberg-Daves' *Modern Motherhood: An American History* (2014).

The third chapter also links the growth of the women's club movement with the increasingly vocal defense among mothers of female teachers. For context on women's clubs in the nineteenth and early twentieth centuries, I consulted "Social Life and Social Services in Indianapolis: Networks

During the Gilded Age and Progressive Era" (2017) by Katherine Badertscher, *"Everybody's Paid But the Teacher": The Teaching Profession and the Women's Movement* (2002) by Patricia A. Carter, *The Grounding of Modern Feminism* (1987) by Nancy F. Cott, *The Sound of Our Own Voices: Women's Study Clubs* (1989) by Theodora Penny Martin, *G. Stanley Hall: The Psychologist as Prophet* (1972) by Dorothy Ross, *Woman's Proper Place: A History of Changing Ideals and Practices, 1870 to the Present* (1978) by Sheila M. Rothman, *Natural Allies: Women's Associations in American History* (1992) by Anne Firor Scott, "The Female World of Love and Ritual: Relations between Women in Nineteenth-Century America" (1975) by Carroll Smith-Rosenberg, *The National PTA, Race, and Civic Engagement* (2009) by Christine Woyshner, and "G. Stanley Hall, Child Study, and the American Public" (2016) by Jacy L. Young.

Finally, the chapter also touches on the growth of the testing movement and the evolution of grading practices in American primary and secondary schools. Three works of scholarship were particularly important: *Testing Wars in the Public Schools: A Forgotten History* (2013) by William Reese, *Merit: The History of a Founding Ideal from the American Revolution to the 21st Century* (2013) by Joseph Kett, and "Making the Grade: A History of the A–F Marking Scheme" (2014) by Jack Schneider and Ethan Hutt. For more on this topic, see Chara Haeussler Bohan's "Early Vanguards of Progressive Education: The Committee of Ten, the Committee of Seven, and Social Education" (2003), David A. Gamson's *The Importance of Being Urban: Designing the Progressive School District* (2019), Brian Gill and Steven Schlossman's "'A Sin against Childhood': Progressive Education and the Crusade to Abolish Homework" (1996), Patricia Albjerg Graham's *Schooling America: How the Public Schools Meet the Nation's Changing Needs* (2005), Nicholas Lemann's *The Big Test: The Secret History of the American Meritocracy* (1999), Joseph L. Tropea's "Bureaucratic Order and Special Children: Urban Schools, 1890s–1940s" (1987), David Tyack's *The One Best System: A History of American Urban Education* (1974), David Tyack and Larry Cuban's *Tinkering Toward Utopia: A Century of Public School Reform* (1995), Rebecca Zwick's *Fair Game? The Use of Standardized Tests in Higher Education* (2002), David Hogan's "'To Better Our Condition': Educational Credentialing and 'The Silent Compulsion of Economic Relations' in the United States, 1830 to the Present" (1996), Susan M. Brookhart's "A Century of Grading Research: Meaning and Value in the Most Common Educational Measure" (2016), Thomas R. Guskey and Susan M. Brookhart's *What We Know About Grading: What Works, What Doesn't, and What's Next* (2019), Kate Rousmaniere's *City Teacher: Teaching and School Reform in Historical Perspective* (1997), Julius D'Agostino's "Concern for the Future, Ghosts from the Past for American High Schools: The Carnegie Unit Revisited" (1984), Sidney L. Besvinick's "The Expendable Carnegie Unit" (1966), and Paul E. Peterson's *The Politics of School Reform* (1985).

Chapter 4. The Eye of the Juvenile Court

To learn more about Colorado at the turn of the twentieth century, I relied upon Thomas G. Andrews' *Killing for Coal: America's Deadliest Labor War* (2008), Rena K. Fowler's "Settling Down and Proving Up on an Eastern Colorado Homestead: The Correspondence of Estelle Siglin and Home Evans" (2016), Andrew Guilford's *The Woolly West: Colorado's History of Sheepscapes* (2018), Richard Hogan's *Class and Community in Frontier Colorado* (1990), Jim Nelson's *Glenwood Springs: The History of a Rocky Mountain Resort* (1999), William Philpott's *Vacationland: Tourism and Environment in the Colorado High Country* (2013), Melanie Shellenbarger's *High Country Summers: The Early Second Homes of Colorado* (2012), and Duane A. Smith's *The Trail of Silver and Gold: Mining in Colorado* (2009).

The 1890s and early 1900s witnessed the rise of the "child saver" progressives, among them Ben Lindsey. Several biographies of Lindsey were indispensable: D'Ann Campbell's "Judge Ben Lindsey and the Juvenile Court Movement" (1976), Paul Colomy and Martin Kretzmann's "Projects and Institution Building: Judge Ben B. Lindsey and the Juvenile Court Movement" (1995), and Charles Larsen's *The Good Fight: The Life and Times of Ben B. Lindsey* (1972). In order to understand the broader evolution of childhood in this era and efforts by progressives to reform urban life, I consulted Sherri Broder's *Tramps, Unfit Mothers, and Neglected Children: Negotiating the Family in Nineteenth-Century Philadelphia* (2002), Linda Gordon's *Heroes of Their Own Lives: The Politics and History of Family Violence, Boston* (1998), Julia Grant's *The Boy Problem: Educating Boys in Urban America* (2014), Joseph M. Hawes' *Children in Urban Society: Juvenile Delinquency in Nineteenth-Century America* (1971), Joseph E. Illick's *American Childhoods* (2002), Steven Mintz's *Huck's Raft: A History of American Childhood* (2004), Anthony M. Platt's *Child Savers: The Invention of Delinquency* (1969), Andrew J. Polsky's *The Rise of the Therapeutic State* (1991), Steven Schlossman and Stephanie Wallach's "The Crime of Precocious Sexuality: Female Juvenile Delinquency in the Progressive Era" (1978), Tracy L. Steffes' *School, Society, and State: A New Education to Govern Modern America* (2012), Geoff K. Ward's *The Black Child-Savers: Racial Democracy and Juvenile Justice* (2012), Emma Watkins and Barry Godfrey's *Criminal Children: Researching Juvenile Offenders* (2018), Ethan L. Hutt's "Formalism Over Function: Compulsion, Courts, and the Rise of Educational Formalism in America" (2012), Ken McGrew's *Education's Prisoners: Schooling, the Political Economy, and the Prison Industrial Complex* (2007), and Christopher J. Menihan's "Criminal Mind or Inculpable Adolescence? A Glimpse at the History, Failures, and Required Changes of the American Juvenile Correction System" (2014).

For the growth of juvenile courts in the early twentieth century, I consulted "The 'Unchildlike Child': Making and Marking the Child/Adult Divide in the Juvenile Court" (2011) by Elizabeth Brown, *The Condemnation of Blackness: Race, Crime, and the Making of Modern Urban America* (2010) by Khalil Gibrain Muhammad, *Caught: Montreal's Modern Girls and the Law* (2006) and *Youth Squad: Policing Children in the Twentieth Century* (2019) by Tamara Myers, Carl Suddler's *Presumed Criminal: Black Youth and the Justice System in Postwar New York* (2019), and David S. Tanenhaus' *Juvenile Justice in the Making* (2004). In the past few decades, historians have produced some incredibly rich and detailed accounts of reform schools. I highly recommend the following for more on the experience of children in the early years of juvenile corrections: Tera Eva Agyepong's *The Criminalization of Black Children: Race, Gender, and Delinquency in Chicago's Juvenile Justice System* (2018), William S. Bush's *Who Gets a Childhood? Race and Juvenile Justice in Twentieth-Century Texas* (2010), Miroslava García-Chávez's *States of Delinquency: Race and Science in the Making of California's Juvenile Justice System* (2012), Lorna F. Hurl and David J. Tucker's "The Michigan County Agents and the Development of Juvenile Probation" (1997), Anne Meis Knupfer's "'To Become Good, Self-Supporting Women': The State Industrial School for Delinquent Girls at Geneva, Illinois" (2000), Paul D. Nelson's "Early Days of the State Reform School" (2012), Randall G. Shelden's "A History of the Shelby County Industrial and Training School" (1992), and Karin L. Zipf's *Bad Girls at Samarcand: Sexuality and Sterilization in a Southern Juvenile Reformatory* (2016).

Chapter 5. Mobility, Anxiety, and Merit

The fifth chapter attempted to trace the educational experiences of one Russian Jewish family, from their roots living in the Pale of Settlement to the Bronx. For life in Tsarist Russia, I relied on the following: David W. Edwards' "Nicholas I and Jewish Education" (1982), Lloyd P. Gartner's "Jewish Migrants En Route from Europe to North America" (1986), Brian Horowitz's *Russian Idea, Jewish Presence* (2013), Shlomo Lambroza's "The Tsarist Government and the Pogroms of 1903–06" (1987) and *Pogroms: Anti-Jewish Violence in Modern Russian History* (1992), Monty Noam Penkower's "The Kishinev Pogrom of 1903: A Turning Point in Jewish History" (2004), Yohanan Petrovsky-Shtern's *The Golden Age Shtetl: A New History of Jewish Life in East Europe* (2014), Ben Cionn Pinchuk's "Jewish Discourse and the Shtetl" (2001), Mark S. Simpson's "The 'Svyaschonnaya Druzhina' and Jewish Persecution in Tsarist Russia" (1978), and Steven J. Zipperstein's *Imagining Russian Jewry: Memory, History, Identity* (1999).

For the experience of Jews in the United States at the turn of the twentieth century, especially in New York City, I relied upon "Jews and the Ambivalence of Middle-Classness" (2007) by Lila Corwin Berman, "Education and Economic Mobility: The Jewish Experience in New York City" (1976) by Selma C. Berrol, *All the Nations Under Heaven: An Ethnic and Racial History of New York City* (1995) by Frederick M. Binder and David M. Reimers, "Jewish Immigrants, Liberal Higher Education, and the Quest for a Torah u-Madda Curriculum at Yeshiva College" (2011) by Zev Eleff, *City College and the Jewish Poor: Education in New York, 1880–1924* (1981) by Sherry Gorelick, *Jews in Gotham: New York Jews in a Changing City* (2012) by Jeffrey S. Gurock, *World of Our Fathers* by Irving Howe (1976), "The Limits of Cultural Zionism in America: The Case of Hebrew in the New York City Public Schools" (2009) by Jonathan Krasner, and *Jewish New York: The Remarkable Story of a City and a People* (2017) by Deborah Dash Moore.

Daniel Schorr's story became a lens through which to understand the changes in college admissions during this period, a topic upon which the following histories describe to varying degrees: Donald G. Barker's "The History of Entrance Examinations" (1967), Andrew V. Beale's "The Evolution of College Admission Requirements" (2012), Arthur M. Cohen's *The Shaping of American Higher Education* (1998), Charles Dorn's *For the Common Good: A New History of Higher Education* (2017), Roger L. Geiger's *To Advance Knowledge: The Growth of American Research Universities* (1986), Jerome Karabel's *The Chosen: The Hidden History of Admission and Exclusion at Harvard, Yale, and Princeton* (2005), Ezekiel Kimball's "College Admission in a Contested Marketplace: The 20th Century and a New Logic for Access" (2011), David Labaree's *A Perfect Mess: The Unlikely Ascendancy of American Higher Education* (2017), Jennifer M. Nations' "How Austerity Politics Led to Tuition Charges at the University of California and City University of New York" (2021), John R. Thelin's *A History of American Higher Education* (2004), and Laurence R. Veysey's *The Emergence of the American University* (1965).

The history and theory behind humor as a form of resistance proved relevant to chapter 5, especially when examining student subcultures of satire: Mikhail Bakhtin's *Rabelais and His World* (1984), Dustin Griffin's *Satire: A Critical Reintroduction* (1994), Michael Mulkay's *On Humor: Its Nature and Its Place in Modern Society* (1988), Kerry Soper's "The Pathetic Carnival in the Cubicles: The Office as Meditation on the Misuses and Collapse of Traditional Comedy" (2009), Saul Stampfer's *Families, Rabbis, and Education: Traditional Jewish Society in Nineteenth-Century Eastern Europe* (2010), and Carole Anne Taylor's "Ideologies of the Funny" (1992).

Chapter 6. The Pursuit of Educational Dignity

I believe that the definitive history of the alternative school movement of the 1960s and 1970s has yet to be written. Having said that, there were many contemporaneous sources from the era evaluating the movement's progress. For general summaries, William Reese's *America's Public Schools: From the Common School to "No Child Left Behind"* (2005) and Larry Cuban's *How Teachers Taught: Constancy and Change in American Classrooms* (1993) are a good starting point.

There are quite a few books from the 1960s and 1970s that advocated for the spread of alternative schools: *Alterative Schools: Ideologies, Realities, Guidelines* (1978) by Terrence E. Deal and Robert R. Nolan, "The First Decade of Public School Alternatives" (1981) by Mary Anne Raywid, *Open Education and the American School* (1972) by Roland S. Barth, *Crisis in the Classroom: The Remaking of American Education* (1970) by Charles E. Silberman, *Letters to a Young Teacher* (2007) by Jonathan Kozol, *Education and Ecstasy* (1987) by George Leonard, "Lasting Alternatives: A Lesson in Survival" (1981) by Barbara J. Case, *Free the Children: Radical Reform and the Free School Movement* (1972) by Allen Graubard, and *The Open Classroom: A Practical Guide to a New Way of Teaching* (1969) by Herbert R. Kohl. The work of Daniel Linden Duke was slightly more critical: *The Retransformation of the School: The Emergence of Contemporary Alternative Schools in the United States* (1978) and "Challenge to Bureaucracy: The Contemporary Alternative School" (1976).